BLOND'S CORPORATIONS

by
Neil C. Blond
Paul P. Brountas Jr.
Brian A. Burns
Kevin T. Fingeret
Charles Wertman

Edited by
John Marafino

Also Available in this Series:

Blond's Torts
Blond's Evidence
Blond's Property
Blond's Contracts
Blond's Income Tax
Blond's Family Law
Blond's Corporations
Blond's Criminal Law
Blond's Corporate Tax
Blond's Civil Procedure
Blond's International Law
Blond's Criminal Procedure
Blond's Administrative Law
Blond's Constitutional Law
Blond's Multistate Questions

Copyright © 1991 by Sulzburger & Graham Publishing, Ltd.

All rights reserved - No part of this book may be reproduced by any electronic, mechanical or other means without written permission from the publisher.

ISBN 0-945-819-14-5

printed in the USA

Blond's Corporations	CE	CCM	Ha
Chapter 1 Agency	1-25		
Chapter 2 Partnership	25-90	39-122	17-118
Chapter 3 Formation of Corporations	91-191	123-194	119-159
Chapter 4 Corporate Structure	192-248	195-224	
Chapter 5 Close Corporations	329-470	683-784	421-557
Chapter 6 Financial Matters and Distributions	1294-1464	903-1050	396-421
Chapter 7 Securities Regulation	720-927	333-540	929-1077
Chapter 8 Duty of Loyalty	556-719	268-330	769-834
Chapter 9 Duty of Care and Duty to Act Lawfully	471-555	225-267	683-768
Chapter 10 Proxy Regulation	249-328	589-682	622-682
Chapter 11 Shareholders' Suits	928-1087	785-902	1135-1171
Chapter 12 Structural Changes	1088-1293	1167-1282	1172-1191

Blond's Corporations	He	JB	SSB	V
Chapter 1 Agency				
Chapter 2 Partnerships		1-69		18-34
Chapter 3 Formation of Corporation	81-175	70-152	9-32 128-167 238-269	35-130
Chapter 4 Corporate Structure	265-383	153-170	270-341	198-208 299-308
Chapter 5 Close Corporations	587-670	334-440	342-446	751-798
Chapter 6 Financial Matters and Distributions	744-830	893-1008	168-237	160-195 637-683
Chapter 7 Securities Regulation	671-696 713-743	543-611	1168-1312	536-636
Chapter 8 Duty of Loyalty	442-541	441-496 497-524	683-808	224-286 307-361 616-636
Chapter 9 Duty of Care and Duty to Act Lawfully	400-441	171-199	592-680	209-223 290-295
Chapter 10 Proxy Regulation	698-712	287-333	502-590	403-454
Chapter 11 Shareholders' Suits	974-1138	618-767	809-939	455-535
Chapter 12 Structural Changes	830-973 1139-1170	1009-1156	940-995 1133-1167	684-750

Table of Contents

1. Agency 21
   Agency 21
   Authority 21

2. Partnerships 26
   What is a Partnership? 26
   Formation 26
   Types of Partnerships 28
   Management, Control, and Operation of Partnerships . 29
   Capitalization 30
   Transferability 31
   Continuity and Dissolution 32
   Liabilities 34
   Taxes 36

3. Formation of Corporations 56
   Attributes of Corporate Form 56
   State of Incorporation 58
   Organizing a Corporation 60
   Corporate Conduct 61
   Activities by Promoters 64
   Defective Incorporation 67
   Disregard of Corporate Entity 69
   Equitable Subordination 72

4. Corporate Structure 103
   Shareholdership 103
   Allocation of Power 104
   Formalities for Board Action 108
   Formalities Required for Shareholder Action 109

5. Close Corporations 119
   Distinctions With the Public Corporation 119
   Shareholder Voting Arrangements 120
   Restrictions on Share Transfers 121
   Intracorporate dDsputes and Deadlocks 123

6. Financial Matters and Distributions 143
   The Balance Sheet and the Income Statement 143
   Corporate Securities 150
   Initial Public Offerings 159
   Legal Capital 161
   Consideration and Valuation 164
   Dividends 166
   Legal Sources of Dividends 167
   Liability for Unlawful Distributions 170

7. Securities Regulation 205
   Introduction 205
   The Disclosure System 205
   Liabilities in Securities Issuances and Trading 211
   Insider Trading 215

8. Duty of Loyalty 248
   Self-Interested Transactions 248
   Compensation 249
   Corporate Opportunity Doctrine 250
   Sale of Control 252
   Other Duties of Controlling Shareholders 252

9. Duty of Care and Duty to Act Lawfully 278
   Duty of Care 278
   Duty to Act Lawfully 280

10. Proxy Regulation 284
    Shareholder Informational Rights 284
    Proxy Rules 286
    Private Actions Under the Proxy Rules 288
    Communications by Shareholders 289

11. Shareholders' Suits 296
    Introduction 296
    Exhaustion of Internal Remedies 299
    Qualifications of Plaintiff Shareholder 303
    Security for Expenses 304
    Settlement of Derivative Suits 305
    Plaintiff's Litigation Expenses 306
    Corporate Counsel 306

Indemnification and Directors & Officers Insurance . . . 307

12. Structural Changes 331
　　　Mergers 331
　　　Shareholder Protection: Appraisal Rights 336
　　　Freezeouts 340
　　　Recapitalizations 341
　　　Tender Offers and Takeovers 342

Abbreviations Used in this Book

D	Defendant
P	Plaintiff
CE	Cary, Eisenberg, Cases and Materials on Corporations (Sixth Edition 1988)
CCM	Choper, Coffee, Morris, Cases and Materials on Corporations (Third Edition 1989)
Ha	Hamilton, Cases and Materials on Corporations Including Partnerships and Limited Partnerships (Fourth Edition 1990)
He	Henn, Teaching Materials on the Laws of Corporations (Second Edition 1986)
JB	Jennings, Buxbaum, Corporations Cases and Materials (Fifth Edition 1979)
SSB	Soloman, Schwartz, and Bauman, Corporations Law and Policy Materials and Problems (Second Edition 1988)
V	Vaghts, Basic Corporation Law (Third Edition 1989)
U.P.A.	Uniform Partnership Act
U.L.P.A.	Uniform Limited Partnership Act
Del.G.C.L.	Delaware General Corporation Law
RMBCA	Revised Model Business Corporation Act
NYBCL	New York Business Corporation Act
'33 Act	Securities Act of 1933
'34 Act	Securities Act of 1934

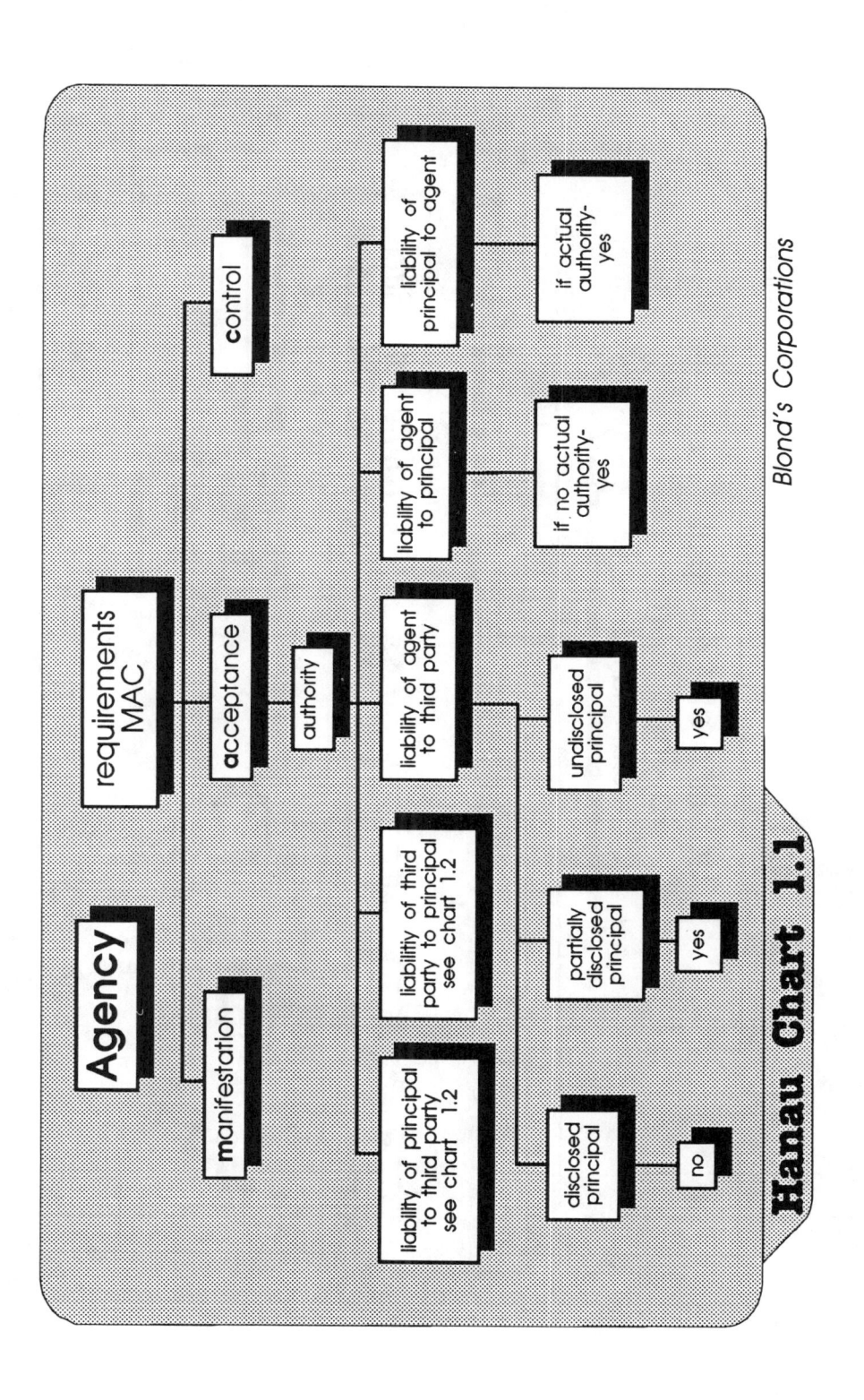

Agency

- **requirements MAC**
  - manifestation
  - acceptance
  - control

authority

- **liability of principal to third party** — see chart 1.2
  - disclosed principal — no
  - partially disclosed principal — yes
  - undisclosed principal — yes

- **liability of third party to principal** — see chart 1.2

- **liability of agent to third party**

- **liability of agent to principal**
  - if no actual authority — yes

- **liability of principal to agent**
  - if actual authority — yes

Blond's Corporations

Hanau Chart 1.1

Hanau Chart 1.2

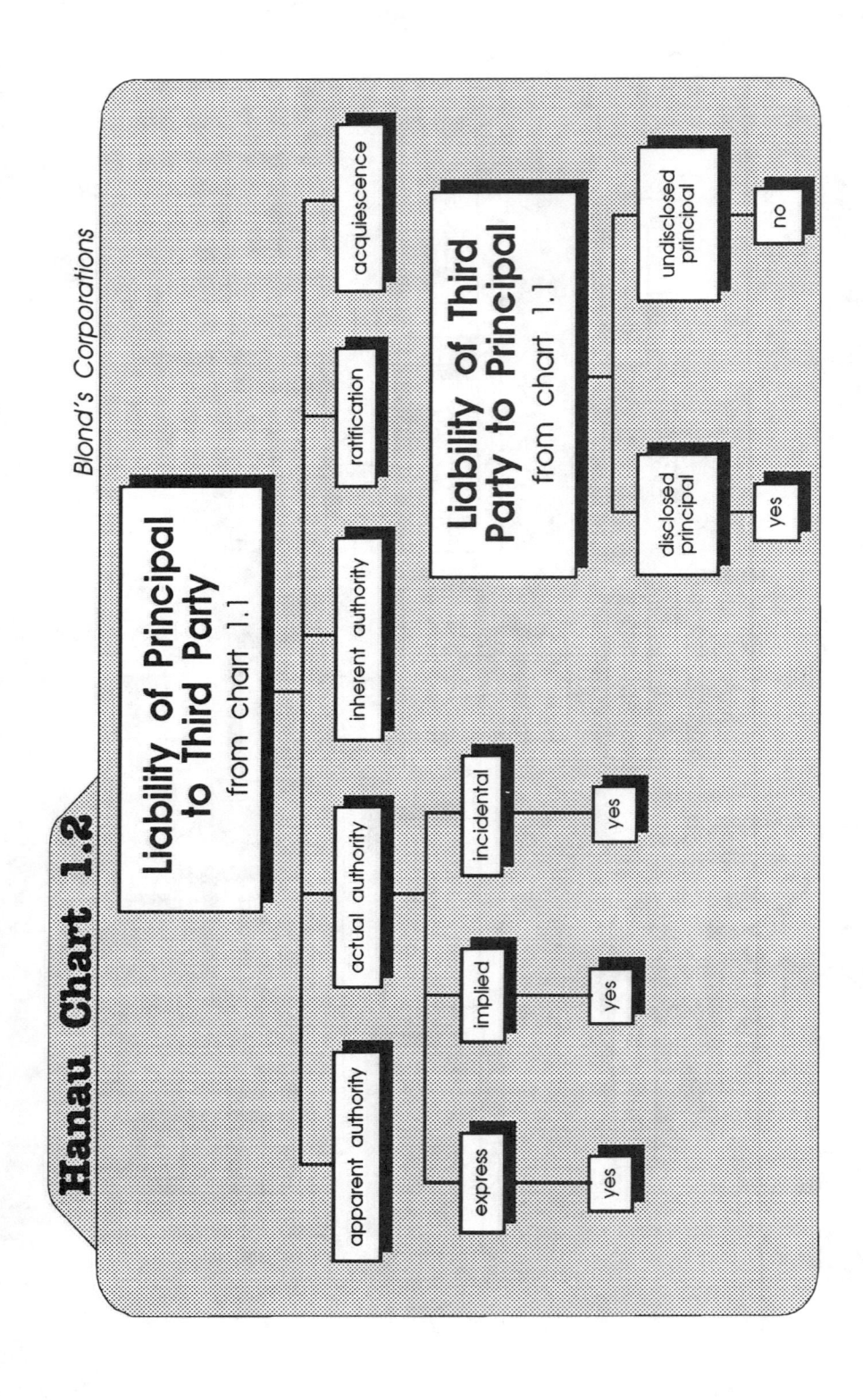

Blond's Corporations

Liability of Principal to Third Party (from chart 1.1)
- apparent authority
  - express → yes
  - implied → yes
  - incidental → yes
- actual authority
- inherent authority
- ratification
- acquiescence

Liability of Third Party to Principal (from chart 1.1)
- disclosed principal → yes
- undisclosed principal → no

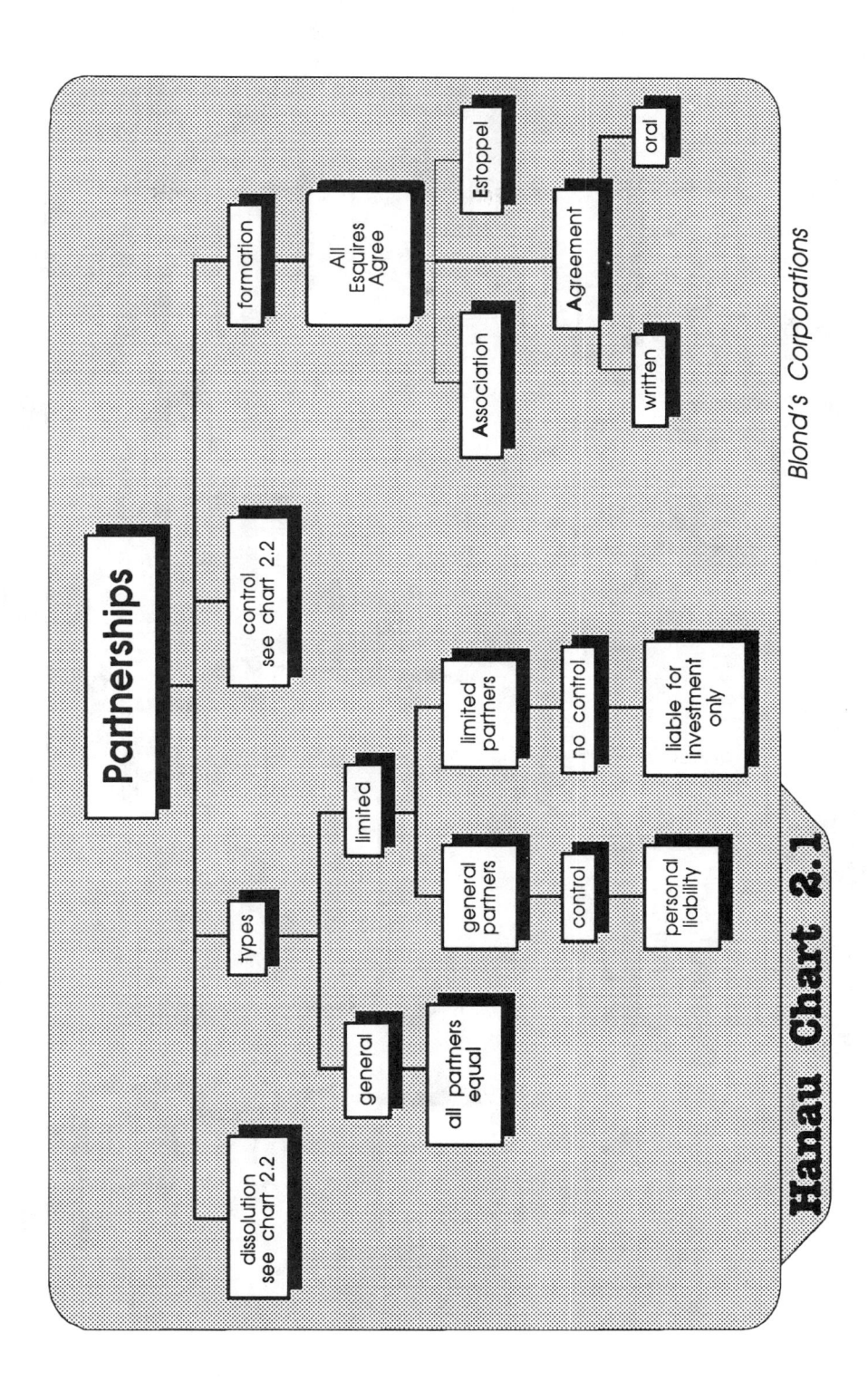

Partnerships

- dissolution see chart 2.2
- types
  - general
    - all partners equal
  - limited
    - general partners
      - control
        - personal liability
    - limited partners
      - no control
        - liable for investment only
- control see chart 2.2
- formation
  - All Esquires Agree
    - Association
    - Estoppel
    - Agreement
      - written
      - oral

Blond's Corporations

Hanau Chart 2.1

Hanau Chart 2.2

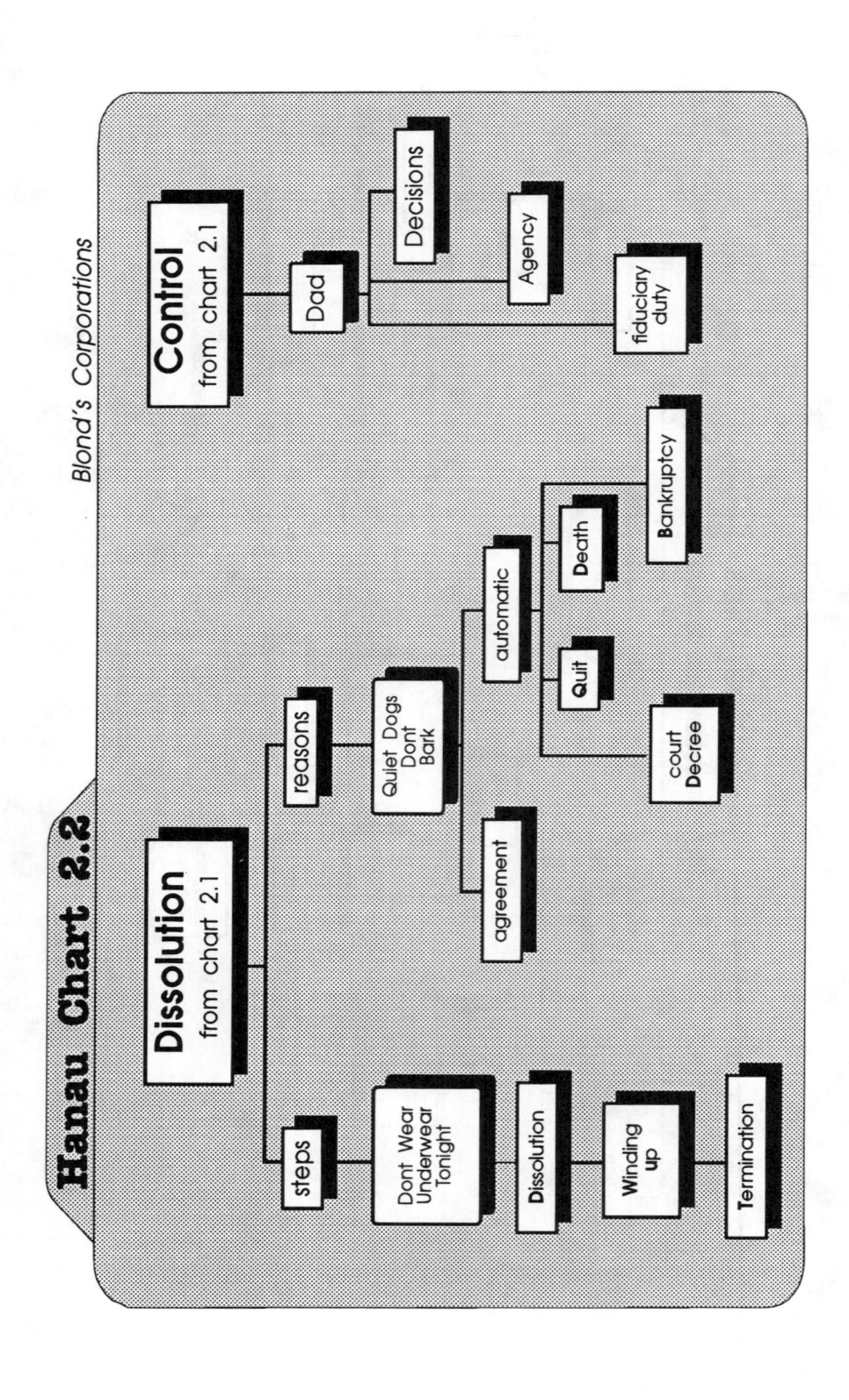

Blond's Corporations

Dissolution (from chart 2.1)
- steps
  - Dont Wear Underwear Tonight
  - Dissolution
  - Winding up
  - Termination
- reasons
  - agreement
  - Quiet Dogs Dont Bark
    - automatic
      - Death
      - Bankruptcy
    - court Decree
    - Quit

Control (from chart 2.1)
- Dad
  - Decisions
  - Agency
  - fiduciary duty

Allocation of Corporate Powers

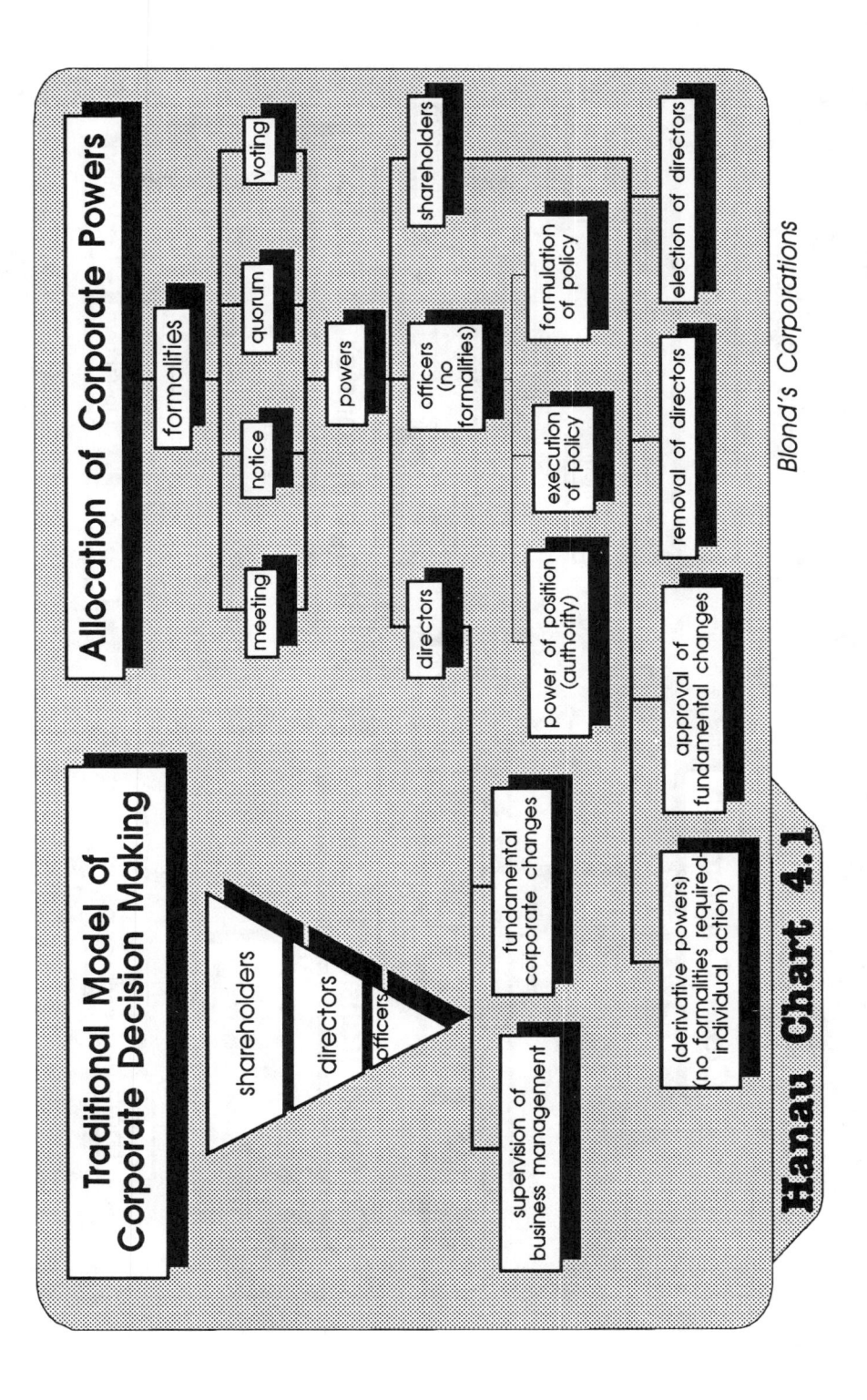

Traditional Model of Corporate Decision Making

- shareholders
- directors
- officers

formalities
- meeting
- notice
- quorum
- voting

powers
- directors
  - fundamental corporate changes
  - supervision of business management
- officers (no formalities)
  - power of position (authority)
  - execution of policy
  - formulation of policy
- shareholders
  - (derivative powers) (no formalities required—individual action)
  - approval of fundamental changes
  - removal of directors
  - election of directors

Blond's Corporations

Hanau Chart 4.1

Hanau Chart 5.1

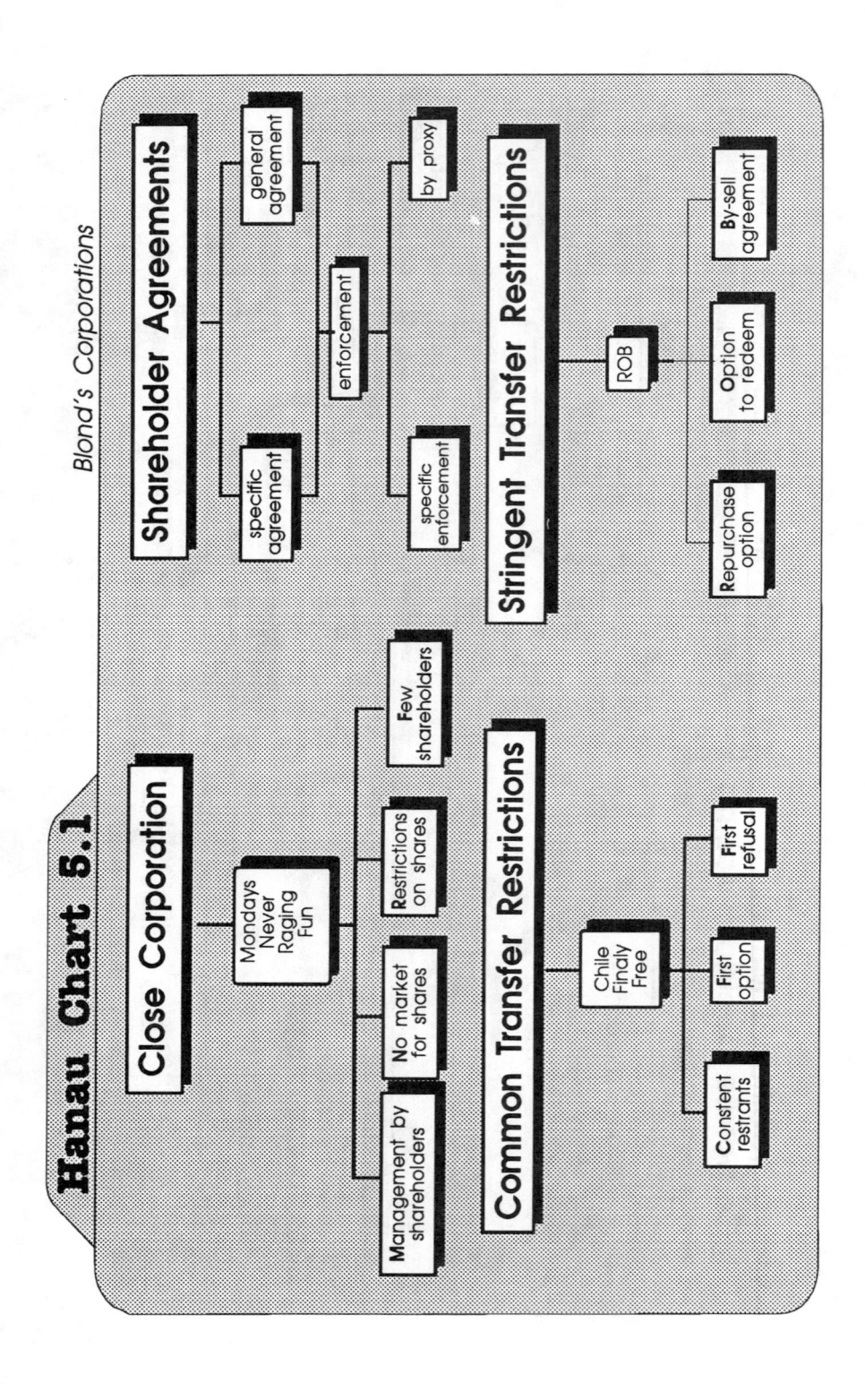

Blond's Corporations

Close Corporation

Mondays Never Raging Fun
- Management by shareholders
- No market for shares
- Restrictions on shares
- Few shareholders

Shareholder Agreements

- specific agreement
- general agreement
- enforcement
  - by proxy
  - specific enforcement

Common Transfer Restrictions

Chile Finally Free
- Constant restraints
- First option
- First refusal

Stringent Transfer Restrictions

ROB
- Repurchase option
- Option to redeem
- By-sell agreement

Valuation

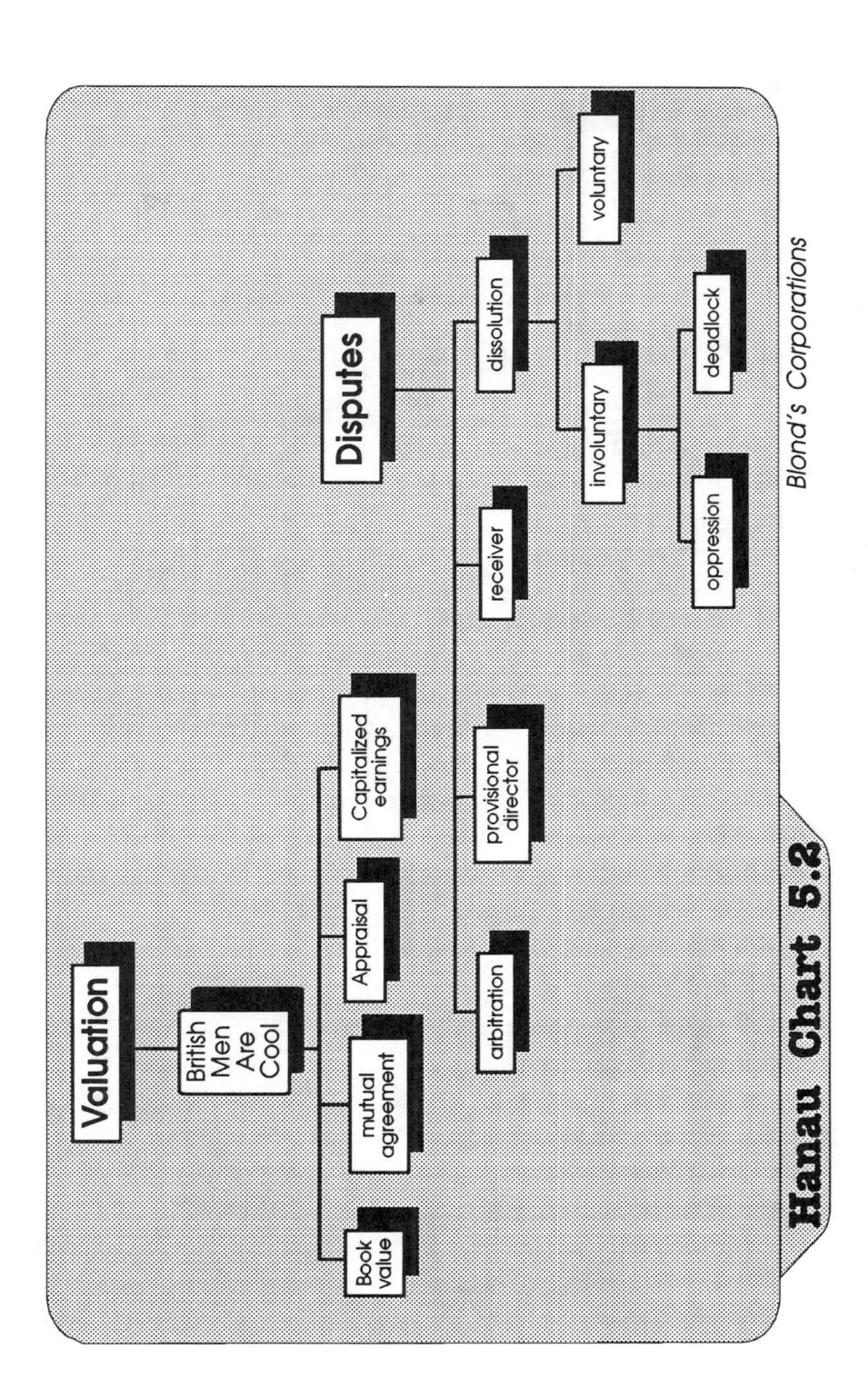

- British Men Are Cool
  - Book value
  - mutual agreement
  - Appraisal
  - Capitalized earnings

Disputes

- arbitration
- provisional director
- receiver
- dissolution
  - voluntary
  - involuntary
    - oppression
    - deadlock

Hanau Chart 5.2 *Blond's Corporations*

Hanau Chart 8.1

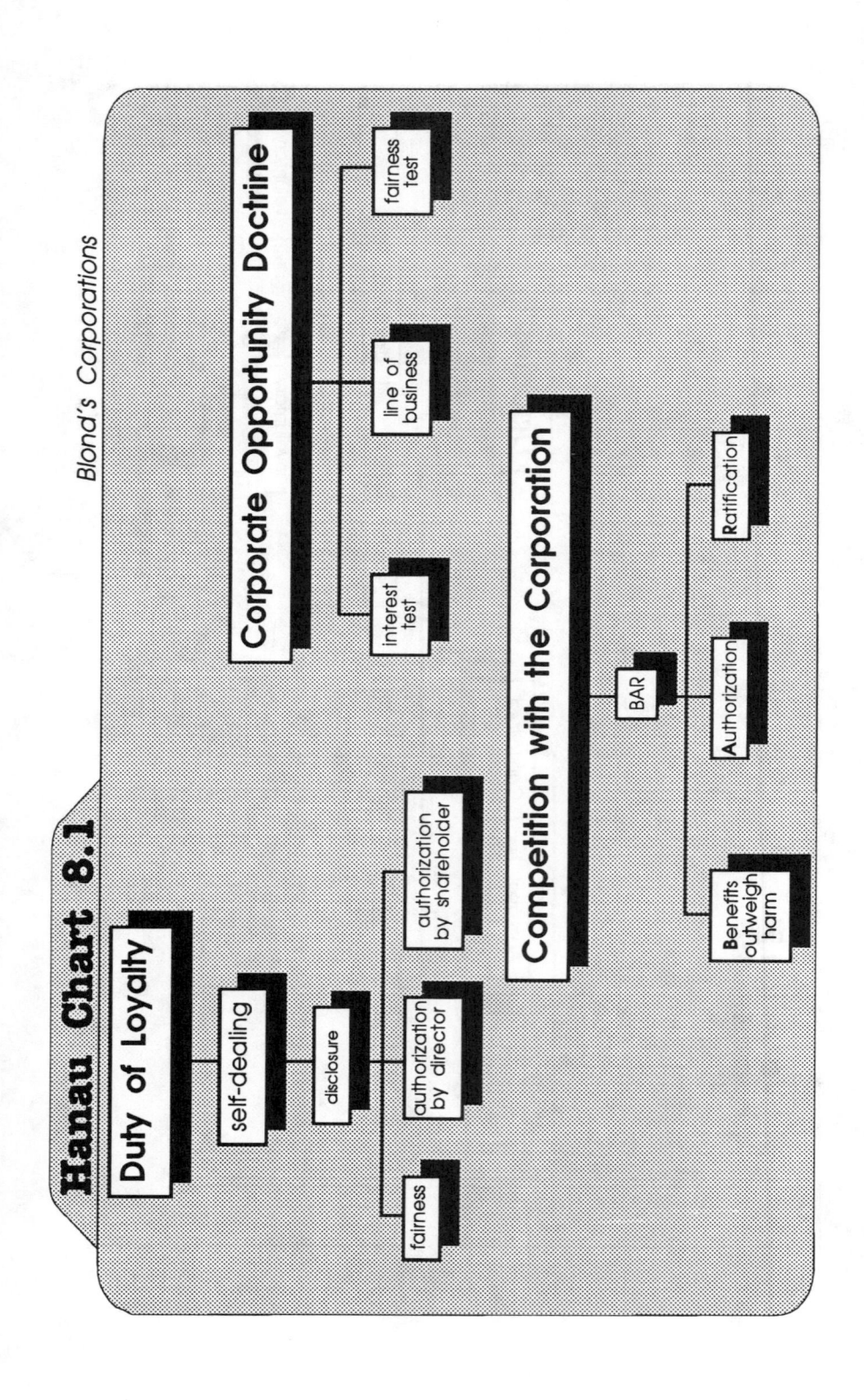

Blond's Corporations

Duty of Loyalty
- self-dealing
  - disclosure
    - authorization by director
      - fairness
    - authorization by shareholder

Corporate Opportunity Doctrine
- interest test
- line of business
- fairness test

Competition with the Corporation
- BAR
  - Benefits outweigh harm
  - Authorization
  - Ratification

Compensation

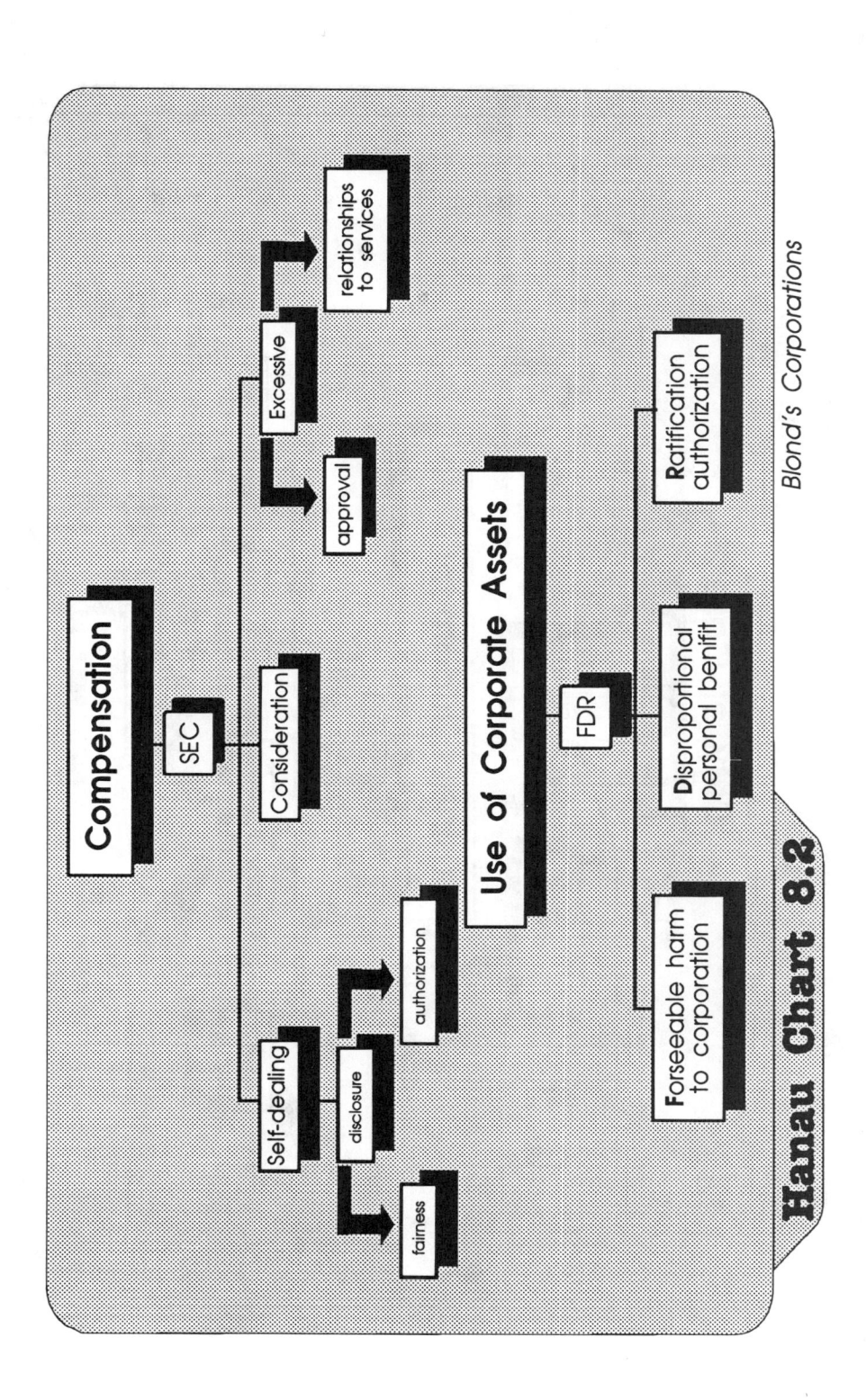

- **SEC**
  - Consideration
  - Excessive
    - relationships to services
    - approval
- Self-dealing
  - disclosure
    - authorization
    - fairness

Use of Corporate Assets

- **FDR**
  - **F**oreseeable harm to corporation
  - **D**isproportional personal benifit
  - **R**atification authorization

Hanau Chart 8.2

Blond's Corporations

Hanau Chart 9.1

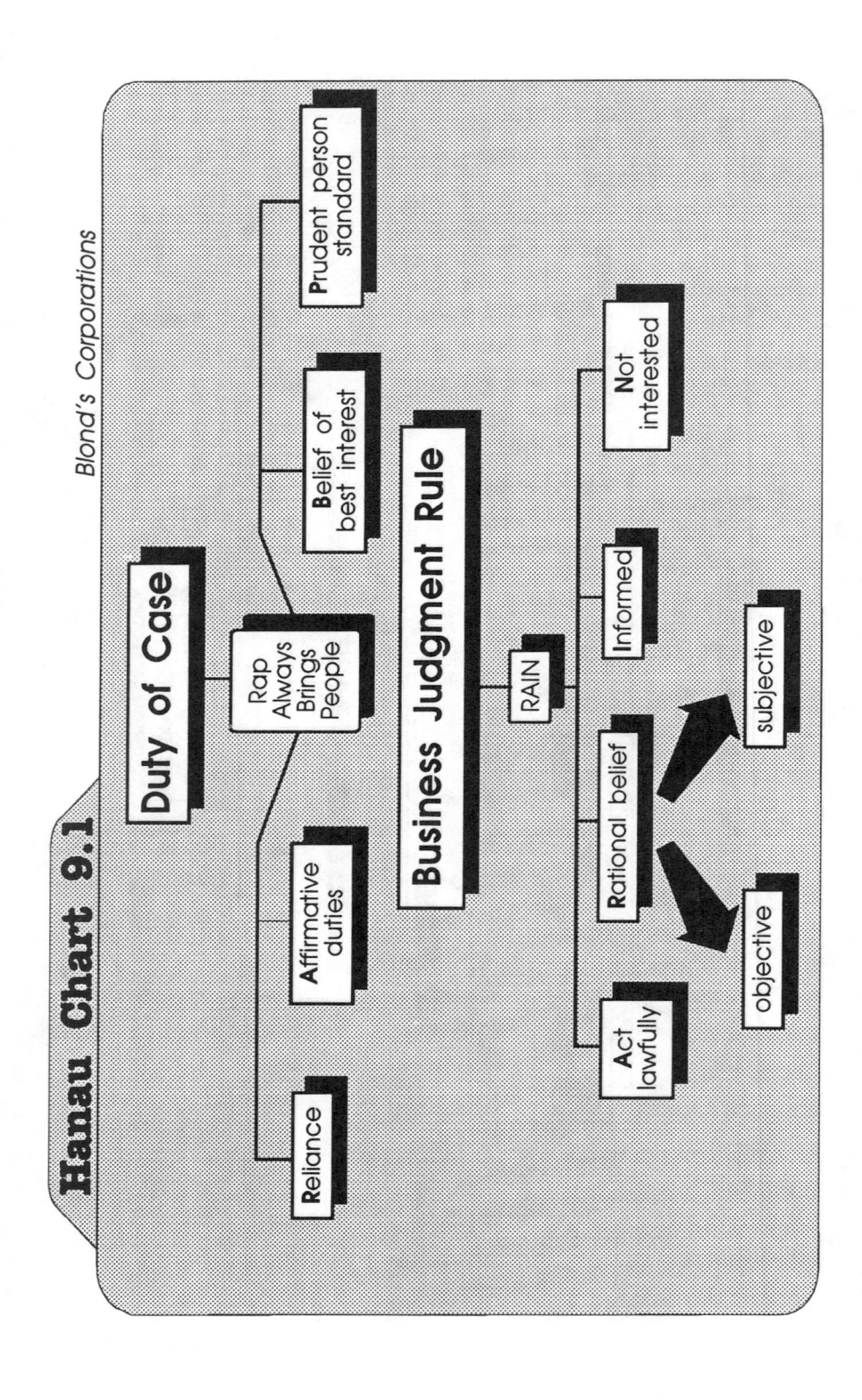

Blond's Corporations

Duty of Case

- Reliance
- Affirmative duties
- Rap Always Brings People
  - Belief of best interest
  - Prudent person standard

Business Judgment Rule

RAIN
- Rational belief
  - subjective
  - objective
- Act lawfully
- Informed
- Not interested

Structural Changes

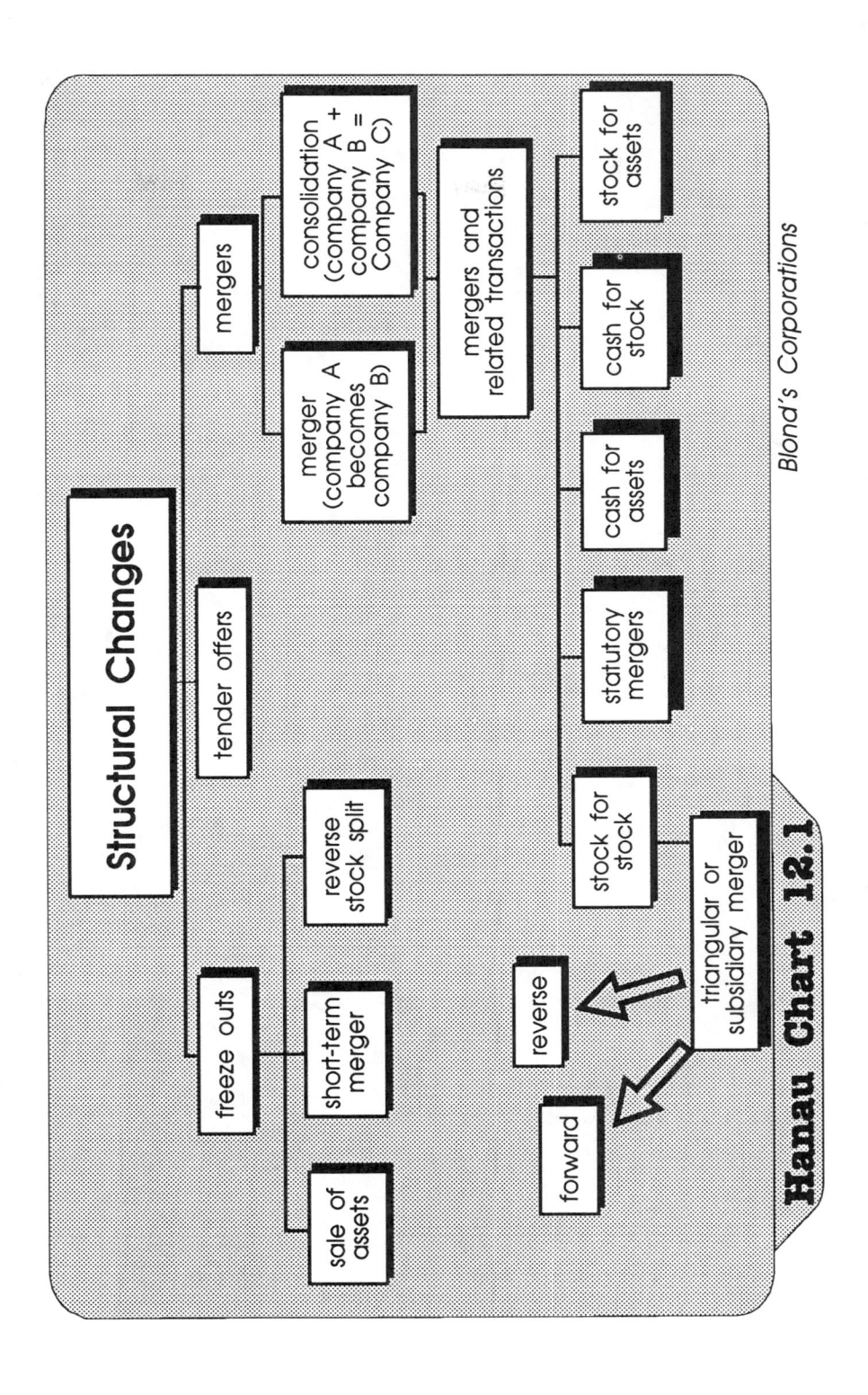

- **freeze outs**
  - sale of assets
  - short-term merger
  - reverse stock split
- **tender offers**
- **mergers**
  - merger (company A becomes company B)
  - consolidation (company A + company B = Company C)
  - mergers and related transactions
    - stock for stock
      - triangular or subsidiary merger
        - forward
        - reverse
    - statutory mergers
    - cash for assets
    - cash for stock
    - stock for assets

Blond's Corporations

Hanau Chart 12.1

5

Chapter 1

AGENCY

I. AGENCY

A. Definition

An agent is a person who agrees to act under the control of another. The person for whom the agent acts is a principal.

B. Requirements for Agency (**MAC**)

1. **M**anifestation
   The principal must **manifest** that the agent will act for him;

2. **A**cceptance
   The agent must **accept** the undertaking; and

3. **C**ontrol
   An understanding that the principal is the party in **control**.

II. AUTHORITY

Liabilities arising out of transactions involving agents, principals, and third parties are addressed by legal rules governing authority.

A. Liability of Principal to Third Party

A principal is liable to a third party for the acts of an agent if the agent has actual, apparent, or inherent authority. The principal is also liable if it in some way indicates that an agent's act was authorized.

22 Agency

1. **Actual Authority**
   An agent has actual authority if a reasonable person in the *agent's position* would believe that the principal had authorized him to so act.

   a. Actual authority may be express or implied from the words used, customs, or relations between the parties.

   b. A common type of actual authority is incidental authority, the authority to do acts reasonably necessary to accomplish an authorized transaction.

2. **Apparent Authority**
   An agent has apparent authority in relation to a third party if the words or conduct of the principal would lead a reasonable person in the *third party's position* to believe the principal had authorized the agent to so act.

3. **Inherent Authority**
   Inherent authority protects third parties dealing with agents by holding principals liable. It does not depend on any kind of authority but derives from the agency relationship itself.

   a. Application
      Inherent authority can subject a principal to tort and contract liability based on activity of the agent.

   b. Restatement § 194
      A principal may be liable for an agent's acts even if the principal's existence is undisclosed to the third party. The theory is that it would be unfair for the principal to gain the benefits of the agent's activity without also taking on the burdens.

4. **Ratification**
   Even if an agent acted without authority, a principal will still be bound if the agent purported to act on the principal's behalf and the principal:

a. manifested intent to treat the conduct as authorized; or

b. engaged in conduct that showed such intent.

5. Acquiescence
The failure of a principal to object to an action undertaken by an agent can be taken as an indication of consent.

B. Liability of Third Party to Principal

1. General Rule — Third Party is Liable
If an agent and a third party enter a contract that makes the third party liable to the agent, the third party will also be liable to the principal.

2. Exception — Third Party is not Liable
The third party will not be liable to the principal if the principal's identity was undisclosed at the time of the transaction and the principal or agent knew that the third party would not deal with the principal.

C. Liability of Agent to Third Party

The liability of an agent to a third party depends in part on whether the principal was disclosed, partially disclosed, or undisclosed.

1. Disclosed Principal

a. General Rule — Agent is not Liable
If the third party knew that the agent was acting on behalf of a principal and knew the principal's identity, and the principal is bound by the agent's act through authority or ratification, the agent is not obligated to the third party.

b. Exception — Agent is Liable
However, if the principal is not bound by the agent's act, the agent is liable to the third party.

24 Agency

2. Partially Disclosed Principal

   a. General Rule — Agent is Liable
   If the third party knows that the agent is acting on behalf of a principal but does not know the principal's identity, the agent is bound to the third party.

   b. Theory
   The third party ought to be able to hold the agent liable since he had no opportunity to investigate the reliability of the principal.

3. Undisclosed Principal

   a. General Rule — Agent is Liable
   If the third party believes that the agent is acting on his own accord at the time of the transaction, the agent is bound to the third party.

   b. Later Disclosure of Identity
   Courts are divided on the liability of the agent if the third party later learns of the principal's identity.

      i. Majority Rule
      The agent is discharged from liability if the third party obtains a judgement against the principal.

      ii. Minority Rule
      Neither agent nor principal is discharged by a judgement against the other.

D. Liability of Agent to Principal

If an agent acts without actual authority and the principal is bound through apparent authority, the agent is liable to the principal for any resulting damages.

E. Liability of Principal to Agent

The principal has a duty to indemnify the agent for payments authorized by the agent on behalf of the principal if the agent has acted within his actual authority.

CASE CLIPS

A. Jensen Farms Co. v. Cargill, Inc. (1983) CE
Facts: Warren defaulted on a contract with P. P sought to recover losses from a creditor (D) of Warren, claiming that D's control and influence over Warren's business created liability as a principal.
Issue: May a creditor be liable as a principal for the obligations of its debtor to other creditors?
Rule: A creditor that exerts control and influence over a debtor's business is liable as a principal for transactions of its agent.

Tarnowski v. Resop (1952) CE
Facts: In making a purchase on behalf of P, D accepted a bribe and passed on false representations made by sellers. P rescinded the contract and sought to recover the amount of the bribe and other losses suffered from D.
Issue: Can a principal recover the value of a bribe accepted by an agent in violation of his duty of loyalty?
Rule: A principal is entitled to recover any profits made by an agent and other resulting damages on the principle that an agent remain loyal to his principal, regardless of whether actual injury is done.

Chapter 2

PARTNERSHIPS

I. WHAT IS A PARTNERSHIP?

There is no consensus on whether a partnership is an entity, separate and apart from the individual partners, like a corporation, or merely an aggregate of its members.

1. The Uniform Partnership Act (U.P.A.), adopted by every state except Louisiana as the law on partnerships, leans toward the aggregate theory, but does not provide a clear answer. It defines partnerships as "an association of two or more persons to carry on as co-owners of a business for profit," § 6(1), and then also treats partnerships as a single entity for other purposes.

2. It becomes a question of legislative intent when determining the status of partnerships in other statutes. U.P.A.'s aggregate definition is relevant, but not dispositive.

3. As entities, partnerships may be prosecuted for violating criminal statutes.

4. For jurisdictional purposes, the citizenship of a partnership is determined by the citizenship of its general partners.

II. FORMATION

A. Partnership Agreement

1. Although it is not required, parties generally enter into a written agreement.

2. With more freedom than in the formation of a corporation, parties can set their own terms on the rights and duties of partners, differing from those stated in U.P.A. § 18.

3. No state involvement is necessary.

   Exceptions:

   i. A fictitious name is used. (One that is not simply the names of the partners.)

   ii. A license to do a particular business is needed.

   iii. Limited Partnerships (see III.B. below) require filing a certificate as provided by state law.

B. Association

   A party can become a partner, irrespective of his intention, when certain characteristics exist in his association with other people.

   1. Sharing of profits is *prima facie* evidence of the existence of a partnership.

   2. Exceptions exist for some partnership characteristics, e.g., the payment of profits shall not permit such an inference when they were received in payment of a debt, as wages, as interest on a loan, etc. U.P.A. § 7(4).

C. Estoppel

   1. Representation to a third party that one who fulfills the definition of a partner is a partner, along with reliance on such representation by the third party, makes one a partner with respect to their dealings with that third party. U.P.A. § 16.

   2. Liability is determined by who has made the representation and the nature of the transaction. U.P.A. § 16(1)(a)&(b).

III. TYPES OF PARTNERSHIPS

A. General Partnerships

All partners are general partners with equal rights, duties, and liabilities. Each partner is personally liable for all the debts of the partnership.

B. Limited Partnerships

1. In a limited partnership there are two kinds of partners:

    a. General partners, similar to partners in a general partnership, control the management and are personally liable for all partnership debts.

    b. Limited Partners do not participate in management and are not liable for debts beyond their initial investment.

2. In order to limit personal liability further, a corporation can exist as the sole general partner in a limited partnership with the limited partners acting as the officers of the corporation. This "wall" has been knocked down by some courts and held up by others with certain requirements, such as:

    a. the corporation also exists for other purposes;

    b. the state clearly allows corporations to be the sole general partner in limited partnerships;

    c. the limited partners act as officers in a corporate, not personal, capacity; and

    d. the contracting parties are aware of the structure of the partnership.

3. Most states have adopted the Uniform Limited Partnership Act (U.L.P.A.) or the newer 1976 Revised Limited Partnership Act (R.U.L.P.A.) to govern limited partnerships.

C. Joint Venture

An association of two or more people to complete a particular "venture" as compared to partners carrying on a business.

IV. MANAGEMENT, CONTROL, AND OPERATION OF PARTNERSHIPS

A. Decisions

1. As to most matters, the vote of the majority controls. U.P.A. § 18(h).

    a. Voice in partnership matters is often determined by capital contribution or interest in earnings.

    b. Actions contrary to the partnership agreement require unanimous approval.

2. Limited Partners surrender right to share in management.

    a. Limited partners who "take control of the business" forfeit limited partner immunity. U.L.P.A. § 7.

    b. The line that a limited partner may not cross in their involvement is not well established.

    c. Under the R.U.L.P.A., limited partners can at least vote for managers and on certain major issues without losing their limited liability. R.U.L.P.A. § 303.

B. Agency

1. All partners act as agents for each other and the partnership.

2. A partner has the authority to bind the partnership to acts within the usual course of business without obtaining written consent of other partners.

3. A partner has the authority to bind the partnership to acts outside the usual course of its business if the other partners have detailed knowledge of its provisions so that it can be said that by their silence there was acquiescence, ratification, or estoppel.

C. Fiduciary Duty

All partners owe their copartners a fiduciary duty of the finest loyalty and, as such, may not separate their interests from each other.

V. CAPITALIZATION

A. There is no requirement that the partners contribute adequate capital, or even, except for limited partners, any capital at all.

B. Partners may lease or loan their assets to the partnership and charge rent or interest thereon instead of contributing property or money.

C. Property that is contributed or acquired by the partnership is held by the partners as co-owners in partnership.

1. Each partner has the right to use partnership property for partnership purposes only.

2. Partnership property may be held in the partnership name or that of a partner.

3. Although considered a tenancy, unlike joint tenancy or tenancy in common, practical considerations concerning partnerships have curtailed the incidents of ownership in copartnership.

   a. Creditors of individual partners cannot attach specific items of partnership property. U.P.A. § 25(2)(c).

b. A partner's conveyance to a third party of his interest in specific partnership property conveys no rights in the partnership.

D. Partners receive an interest in the partnership itself. U.P.A. § 26.

1. This interest is a share in the excess of the partnership assets over liabilities.

2. This interest is considered personal property and is assignable to a limited extent.

E. The shares of the partners in the earnings, losses, and control of the enterprise is not necessarily determined by the amount of capital contributed by them to the partnership. U.P.A. § 18.

1. Section 18 of the Act, Rules Determining Rights and Duties of Partners, sets forth certain presumptions as to these matters.

2. If they wish, the partners can allocate their shares in the earnings, losses, and control differently from that prescribed in the U.P.A..

3. One or more of the partners may be entitled to a salary. This expenditure may be treated as a cost, against the profits or as an advance of the share of the profits the partner is entitled to.

VI. TRANSFERABILITY

A. All partners must consent to the admission of a new partner.

B. A partner may transfer or assign his interests in a partnership to another, allowing the assignee to reap the economic benefits of the assignor's interests, the profits, without becoming a partner.

VII. CONTINUITY AND DISSOLUTION

A. Dissolution Defined: U.P.A. § 29.

   The dissolution of a partnership is the change in the relation of the partners caused by any partner ceasing to be associated in the carrying on, as distinguished from the winding up, of the business.

   1. Dissolution designates the point in time when the partners cease to carry on the business together.

   2. Winding up is the process of settling partnership affairs after dissolution.

   3. Termination is the point in time when the partnership affairs are wound up. U.P.A. § 29, (Official Comment).

   4. The partnership is not terminated upon dissolution, but continues until the winding up of the partnership affairs is completed. U.P.A. § 30.

B. When is a Partnership Dissolved?

   1. By Agreement: U.P.A. § 31(1).

      a. Time of termination may be set by a definite term or a particular undertaking specified in the partnership agreement. U.P.A. § 31(1)(a).

      b. When no time is stated in the agreement, any partner can terminate at will. U.P.A. § 31(1)(b).

      c. All the partners may agree to terminate at will. U.P.A. § 31(1)(c).

      d. Expulsion of any partner from the business bona fide in accordance with such a power conferred by the agreement between the partners will result in dissolution of the partnership. U.P.A. § 31(1)(d).

2. Any partner can, even in violation of the partnership agreement, quit and dissolve the firm. U.P.A. § 31(2).

3. Automatic dissolution occurs by: U.P.A. § 31(3).

   a. The death of any partner;

   b. The bankruptcy of any partner or the partnership; or

   c. A decree of the court under § 32.

C. Avoiding Automatic Dissolution

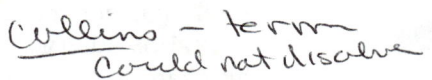

   1. The partnership agreement can stipulate the continuation without winding up or liquidation of the partnership upon the withdrawal of a partner. This agreement will be enforceable if it sets forth a method of paying the withdrawing partner his agreed share and does not jeopardize the rights of creditors.

   2. The partnership agreement can avoid the problems of automatic dissolution by providing for the buying out of a deceased partner's interest and the continuation of the business under a new partnership.

D. Lawful dissolution (or dissolution that is caused in any way except in contravention of the partnership agreement) gives each partner the right to have the business liquidated and his share of the surplus paid in cash.

E. When a partner retires or dies, he or his estate is entitled to the value of his interest in the partnership upon dissolution plus interest or, in lieu of interest, the profits attributable to the use of his right in the dissolved partnership. U.P.A. § 42.

F. A partnership agreement can provide for the expulsion without cause of a member on terms that are not oppressive.

VIII. LIABILITIES

A. All partners in a general partnership are personally liable for all the obligations of the partnership.

   1. Liability is joint for a partnership's contractual obligations. U.P.A. § 15(b).

   2. Liability is joint and several for a partnership's tort liabilities. U.P.A. § 15(a).

   3. Each partner must contribute towards the losses, whether capital or otherwise, sustained by the partnership according to his share in the profits. U.P.A. § 18(a).

   4. Partners are liable for the acts of their copartners that third parties can reasonably believe are within the scope of the partnership business.

B. Limited partners are only personally liable in the amount of their capital contribution. According to U.L.P.A. § 23, limited partners' capital contribution and share of profits are to be returned to him before those of the general partners but after the payment of outside creditors.

C. The partnership must indemnify every partner in respect of payments made and personal liabilities reasonably incurred by him in the ordinary and proper conduct of its business, or for the preservation of its business or property. U.P.A. § 18(b).

D. A partner, who in aid of the partnership makes any payment or advance beyond the amount of capital that he agreed to contribute, shall be paid interest from the date of the payment or advance.

E. Incoming and Outgoing Partners

   1. A new partner is liable for the debts of the existing partnership, except only to the extent of his interest in the partnership property.

2. Outgoing Partners

   a. Outgoing partners are still liable for the debts of the old partnership, except in special circumstances where agreements to the contrary have been reached. See U.P.A. § 36.

   b. Outgoing partners are only liable for the debts of the new partnership to the extent that outsiders, not on notice of his departure, still rely on his credit. U.P.A. § 35.

3. Both incoming and outgoing partners may wish to circumvent these rules, and they may be able to achieve some measure of protection through contractual arrangements.

F. Creditors

1. Problems in reaching individual partner's assets on contract claims have led many states to enact "Joint Debtor Acts" or "Common Name Statutes," which have the effect that a judgment based on service on one partner is collectible from that partner or the partnership, but not from the personal estates of the partners not served. (These problems do no exist for tort claims because tort liability is joint and several.)

2. The Jingle Rule: Partnership Creditors v. Individual Creditors U.P.A. § 40(h).

   a. Partnership creditors have first claim on partnership assets.

   b. Individual creditors have first claim on individual assets.

   c. Any surplus in either category may be applied to the other with the respective creditors rights being equal.

   d. In bankruptcy, this symmetry is abolished since the partnership's bankruptcy trustee has the same rights as to the estates of each bankrupt partner as any other claim. Bankruptcy Code, 11 U.S.C.A. § 723(c).

36 Partnerships

    3. If the business is continued without the liquidation of the partnership affairs, creditors of the first or dissolved partnership are also creditors of the partnership continuing the business. U.P.A. § 41.

IX. TAXES

Partnerships, viewed as an aggregation of individuals for tax purposes, are not separately-taxable entities.

A. Partnerships file an informational tax return, the purpose of which is to determine how much tax the individual partners will pay on the income derived from the operation of the business.

B. Partnerships avoid the double taxation that occurs when corporations and shareholders are taxed.

C. If a corporation's profits are more than $75,000, its tax rate (34%) is higher than a partner's maximum tax rate (28%), that of individuals.

D. A partnership losing money can act as a tax shelter for partners who are actively involved in the management of the partnerships; losses can be used to offset gains from their other activities. (The Tax Reform Act of 1986 has restricted this advantage for partners.)

E. Corporations that wish to be treated as a partnership for tax purposes have the option of being considered a Subchapter S corporation which is not taxed as an entity and can be used as a shelter. The main requirements for this classification are that:

    a. The corporation cannot have more than thirty-five shareholders;

    b. The shareholders themselves must be individuals, estates, or qualified trusts;

c. It can only have one class of stock outstanding (shares that have different voting rights may be considered as belonging to the same class as long as they are otherwise alike); and

d. All the shareholders must consent to be taxed as an S corporation.

Case Clips

Martin v. Peyton (1927) CE, Ha, JB
Facts: Ds were given a share of profits as repayment of a loan to Knauth, Nachod & Kuhne, a partnership in banking and brokerage. In an agreement that expressly stated that it was just a loan and withheld liability from them, Ds were given veto power to prevent misuse of funds, but had no right to initiate or control policy and no agency powers. P, creditor of the partnership, alleged that a partnership had been formed.
Issue: Is a partnership formed when the control and profits given to a party are only meant to protect and pay a off a loan?
Rule: Although statements that no partnership is intended are not conclusive, where a creditor's control of the activity and profits of a partnership is merely the security and repayment of a loan, they will not be deemed partners nor liable to other creditors as such.

Zajac v. Harris (1967) CE
Facts: Harris (P) claimed a partnership existed between him and Zajac (D). P had personally invested in the firm and received a net share of the profits.
Issue: Does personal investment in a firm and receipt of a portion of the firm's profits create a partnership?
Rule: A partnership may vary in an almost infinite variety of ways, but earnings based on profits and personal investment are *prima facie* evidence of its existence.

Summers v. Dooley (1971) CE

Facts: P used personal funds to hire an additional employee for his firm, despite the objection of his partner, D. P sought to recover his expenses from partnership funds.

Issue: Does a partner have the authority to make a business decision in disregard of his partner's objection and then charge the dissenting partner with the costs incurred?

Rule: Since partners have equal rights in the management of a partnership, a majority of partners is required to make business decisions for the partnership provided no other agreement between the partners speaks to the issues.

Owens v. Palos Verdes Monaco (1983) CE

Facts: P sought to stop the sale of land by his partnership. D, buyer, claimed that the partnership was bound to the agreement because the sale had been signed by another partner.

Issue: Is an agreement by one partner sufficient to bind the partnership?

Rule: A partner has authority to bind the partnership to acts within the usual course of its business without obtaining the written consent of the other partners.

Rapoport v. 55 Perry Co. (1975) CE

Facts: P entered into partnership D with another family, Parnes. P attempted to assign a ten percent share of their interest to their adult children. D said they could not without D's consent.

Issue: Absent agreement, can a partner assign a share of his membership to another without the consent of the other partners?

Rule: Under New York's Partnership Law, unless the parties have agreed otherwise, a person cannot become a member of a partnership without consent of all the partners whereas an assignment of a partnership interest may be made without consent, but the assignee is entitled only to receive the profits of the assigning partner.

Meinhard v. Salmon (1928) CE, CCM, Ha

Facts: D was a managing coadventurer with P on a twenty-year lease. Towards the end of the term, D was offered a larger deal, extension of the lease plus other properties, by the lessor. D accepted this new offer without informing P.

Issue: Do coadventurers have a fiduciary duty to inform each other about possible new ventures arising out of their existing relationship?
Rule: Joint adventurers, like copartners, owe each other a fiduciary duty of the finest loyalty, and as such may not separate their interest from each other, communicating any benefit acquired, e.g., not appropriating to their own use a lease renewal.

Dreifuerst v. Dreifuerst (1979) CE
Facts: Brothers P and D formed a partnership consisting of two feed mills. Upon dissolution at the request P, the trial court denied D's request for a sale and instead divided up the assets in-kind.
Issue: In the absence of a written agreement to the contrary, can a partner, upon dissolution and wind-up of the partnership, force a sale of partnership assets?
Rule: Lawful dissolution (or dissolution that is caused in any way except in contravention of the partnership agreement) gives each partner the right to have the business liquidated and his share of the surplus paid in cash.

Page v. Page (1961) CE, CCM, JB
Facts: P sought to dissolve his partnership in a linen supply business with D. D claimed that although not specified, they had an understanding that this partnership was, as their previous one, for a term, not at will.
Issue: Can a partnership be dissolved at will by one partner?
Rule: A partnership may be dissolved "by the express will of any partner when no definite term or particular undertaking is specified." U.P.A. § 31(1)(b).

Drashner v. Sorenson (1954) CE
Facts: P sought to dissolve his real estate, loan, and insurance partnership with D's, the capital investor partners. P demanded a larger share of the income than he was entitled to receive under the partnership agreement, was arrested for reckless driving and served a jail term, demanded that he be allowed to draw money out of the partners' escrow account, and spent a large amount of time during business hours in the Brass Rail Bar and other bars neglecting his duties.

Issue: What constitutes a wrongful dissolution of a partnership?
Rule: A partner causes a dissolution wrongfully by willfully and persistently committing a breach of the partnership agreement, and by so conducting himself in matters relating to the partnership business as to render impracticable the carrying on of the business in the partnership with him.

Holzman v. de Escamilla (1948) CE

Facts: Russell and Andrews were limited partners and de Escamilla the general partner of Hacienda Farms, a limited partnership. Russell and Andrews had the power to withdraw all the money from the partnership accounts without the knowledge or consent of the general partner. In fact, de Escamilla had no power to withdraw funds without one of the limited partners signatures, giving them control over him. Russell and Andrews having the power removed de Escamilla as manager and selected his successor. They were also active in dictating the crops to be planted.
Issue: Can a limited partner be liable as a general partner?
Rule: If, in addition to the exercise of his rights and powers as a limited partner, "he takes part in control of the business," a limited partner shall become liable as general partner. U.L.P.A. § 7.

Frigidaire Sales Corp. v. Union Properties, Inc. (1977) CE, JB

Facts: Mannon and Baxter, limited partners in the limited partnership Commercial Investors, were officers, directors, and shareholders of Union, the sole general partner of Commercial. P sought to recover from Mannon and Baxter as general partners because they exercised the day-to-day control of Commercial.
Issue: Does a limited partner become liable as a general partner when he also participates as an active officer, director, and shareholder of a corporation that is the sole general partner of a limited partnership?
Rule: A limited partner can become liable as a general partner of a limited partnership if "he takes part in the control of the business" under § 7 of the U.L.P.A., but can escape this liability if he does so as an officer, director or shareholder of a corporation that is the sole general partner if control of the partnership is not the sole purpose of the corporation, the state clearly allows corporations to be the sole general partner in limited partnerships, the limited partners act as

officers in a corporate, not personal, capacity, and the contracting parties are aware of this structure. (Distinguished from *Delaney* above.)

Vohland v. Sweet (1982) CCM
Facts: Sweet (P) received a twenty percent share of net profits in a landscaping business, called Vohland's Nursery, he started with Vohland (D). P called his share a "commission" and managed the performance of the business, but not the finances.
Issue: Can a partnership exist without its acknowledgment by the parties involved?
Rule: If parties intend a community of interest in any increment in the value of capital and in the net profit, a partnership exists regardless of how they may later characterize the relationship.

Ogallala Fertilizer Co. v. Salsbery (1971) CCM
Facts: Salsbery owned the farm that she and her husband, Herbert, ran. Herbert purchased fertilizer on credit from Ogallala and subsequently died.
Issue: Is a wife liable as a partner for the transactions made by her husband on behalf of a family business?
Rule: Shared profits, losses, and bank accounts, being usual marital arrangements and consonant with a husband's duty to support his wife, are insufficient to establish a partnership.

Grissum v. Reesman (1974) CCM
Facts: Grissum shared a farming estate with her brother. She did the household work, kept the books, did the banking, paid the bills, fed and sorted the animals, and at times did hard farm labor. She was regarded openly by her brother and other sundry people as a fifty-fifty partner with the profits less living expenses consistently being reinvested. The real property, tax returns, and bank account, however, were all in his name.
Issue: Can a partnership be established by an oral or implied agreement?
Rule: The intention of the parties, the primary criterion in deciding whether a partnership exists, may be established by oral agreement or may be implied from the acts and conduct of the parties, such as

42 Partnership

participation in profits and losses and shared rights in management, or from the circumstances.

Fenwick v. Unemployment Compensation Commission (1945) CCM

Facts: Fenwick signed an agreement with his employee, Arline Chesire, making her a partner in his United Beauty Shoppe. The agreement drawn up by an attorney gave Chesire a weekly salary plus a share of the profits. The agreement did not give Chesire any ownership in the property, control of management, or rights upon dissolution of the agreement. Chesire also did not share in the burden of losses.
Issue: Can one be considered a partner simply by a written agreement labeling her as such without substantially extending her rights and responsibilities beyond that of an employee?
Rule: Partnership status must reflect the intentions of the parties to share the rights in ownership and profits along with the responsibilities of management and losses.

Boyd v. Leasing Associates, Inc. (1974) CCM

Facts: Boyd and Nordstrom, partners in "Nasa Grill," agreed to let Horne take over the restaurant, retain all the profits, and pay all the liabilities. Horne then contracted, in the name of the "Nasa Grill" account, to purchase two trucks.
Issue: When does an agent have the authority to execute a promissory note on behalf of his principal?
Rule: The authority of an agent to bind a principal on a promissory note may be implied when the exercise of such authority is so necessary to the accomplishment of the agency that the intent of the principal to confer it must be presumed in order to make the power of the agent effectual.

Volkman v. DP Associates (1980) CCM

Facts: Volkman contracted for construction advice with McNamee, representing DP Associates, which included his alleged partner Carroll. Carroll stated to Volkman that he was happy to be working with him and McNamee repeatedly seemed to consult Carroll on the deal. Carroll claimed that he was not a partner, that he received no

income, profits, or salary from the Volkman job and, therefore, was not liable to Volkman.
Issue: How is the law of estoppel applicable to partnerships?
Rule: Liability by estoppel may result when one represents himself as a partner by words spoken or written or by conduct, contract, or consent to such representation by another, along with good faith reliance on such representation by the person to whom such representation has been made. (see U.P.A. § 16(a))

Ex rel. Lester (1976) CCM

Facts: Frost ran the law firm of Berman and Frost under a cloud of secrecy whereby partners did not know their true shares, that of their fellow partners, or other financial information beyond what they took home. Upon Berman's retirement, Frost entered into an agreement with him for a retirement plan. The details of this plan were not disclosed until Frost's death two years later. The remaining partners then questioned whether they were bound by Frost's deal with Berman.
Issue: Is a contract that does not carry on the business of a partnership in the usual way and made by a partner as manager and director without the express consent of the other partners binding on the partnership?
Rule: The agreement of a partner acting as agent for the others can be binding on the other partners if they have detailed knowledge of the agreement's provisions, including the parties involved, the conditions, the material representations of the agent or third person when making the contract, and the consideration, so that it can be said that by their silence there was acquiescence, ratification, or estoppel.

Mazzuchelli v. Silverberg (1959) CCM

Facts: P was injured in a car collision arising out, and in the course, of his employment with Summit Wine & Liquor while a passenger in a car driven by D, a partner in Summit. After successfully pressing a compensation claim against Summit under the Workmen's Compensation Act, he brought suit against D as a third person.
Issue: Can a partner, as a third person distinct from the partnership, be held liable to an employee for his own negligence?

Rule: A partner who is negligent, be it in the maintenance of the premises or conduct of the work, would be liable at law, but all of the partners would also be liable by virtue of their mutual agency under the U.P.A.; therefore, each partner may not be pursued individually under Article 2 of the Compensation Act.

Wroblewski v. Brucker (1982) CCM

Facts: P, an Oklahoma citizen, brought an action alleging fraud and collusion by a general partner in the conversion of assets of Exploration Associates, a limited partnership organized under the laws of the State of California. P, one of several limited partners, brought the suit against Joseph K. Morford, II, the sole general partner, in federal court by reason of diversity of citizenship and amount in controversy pursuant to 28 U.S.C. §1332.

Issue: Does a limited partnership have an artificial "citizenship" as an entity, like a corporation, or the multiple citizenship of all or some subgroup of its members?

Rule: For the purposes of determining diversity jurisdiction, a limited partnership is not considered a juridical entity with an artificial citizenship. The citizenship of a limited partnership should be determined by reference to the citizenship of the general partners as real parties in the matter of controversy, without regard to the citizenship of the limited partners, who are not real parties in the matter of controversy because under the U.P.A. they in no sense either (1) hold title to assets of the limited partnership, (2) manage those assets, or (3) control litigation to which the limited partnership is a party.

Klein v. Weiss (1978) CCM

Facts: Fulton and Rinaldi, in order to purchase and develop a tract of land owned by Joint Venture, sought financing from investors by creating a limited partnership. Before filing the partnership agreement, they bought the tract with a loan secured by a mortgage on the land. After they only sold seven units in the partnership, when they expected to sell twenty-five, they rewrote the partnership agreement greatly increasing the amount each limited partner would have to pay to finance the mortgage, without consulting the limited partners.

Issue 1: Do general partners have actual or apparent authority to revise the partnership certificate and agreement absent the express consent of the limited partners?
Rule 1: The principal-agent relationship which exists between parties in an ordinary partnership is not per se present between general and limited partners in a limited partnership. Authority not specifically delegated in the limited partnership agreement to general partners is presumed to be withheld.
Issue 2: Is a certificate of limited partnership filed with unauthorized revisions valid in its original form, thus creating a limited partnership?
Rule 2: The filling of a certificate with unauthorized revisions so fundamental in character that they affected the formation of the partnership itself does not comply with the "good faith" requirement of § 2(2) of the U.L.P.A. and consequently no limited partnership is created.

Delaney v. Fidelity Lease Ltd. (1975) CCM
Facts: D was a limited partnership with its limited partners being the officers, directors, and stockholders of Interlease Corporation, a corporation and sole general partner of the limited partnership. After D breached a lease contract with P, P attempted to recover from the limited partners, seeking to hold them liable as general partners.
Issue: Does a limited partner become liable as a general partner when he also participates as an active officer, director, and shareholder of a corporation which is the sole general partner of the limited partnership?
Rule: A limited partner can become liable as a general partner of the limited partnership if he "takes part in the control of the business" under § 7 of the U.L.P.A.. He does not escape this liability solely because he participated as an officer, director, or stockholder, who ordinarily are protected from personal liability, in the affairs of a corporation that is the sole general partner of the limited partnership.

Cude v. Couch (1979) CCM
Facts: P and D were partners in a laundromat for which they rented space in D's building. D sought to dissolve the partnership, allegedly seeking to quit the laundry business. P and D sold their assets in the business to Platkin at a value artificially depressed by D's refusal to

46 Partnership

permit others to lease the premises. Platkin was actually an agent of D's and D continued the business on his own. P moved to set aside the sale.
Issue: How far does the fiduciary duty of partners extend while the partnership is being liquidated?
Rule: Partners owe each other a fiduciary duty in all matters pertaining to the partnership that continues while the partnership is being liquidated; however, one need not deny his post-partnership best interests if they do not harm his partner.

Marsh v. Gentry (1982) CCM
Facts: P and D were partners in the business of buying and selling race horses. The partnership had two assets, Champagne Woman and Excitable Lady, that D secretly purchased from the partnership in separate transactions. Before and after the deals were completed, P repeatedly questioned D as to the identity of the purchasers. Upon discovering the truth, P sued for an accounting, challenging the sales.
Issue: Can the requirement of full disclosure among partners as to the partnership business be avoided?
Rule: Full disclosure between partners as to partnership business can not be avoided as stated in U.P.A. § 21(1), "Every partner must account to the partnership for any benefit and hold as trustee for it any profit derived by him without the consent of the other partners from any transaction connected with the formation, conduct, or liquidation of the partnership or from any use by him of its profit."

Wilzig v. Sisselman (1982) CCM
Facts: Jerome Sisselman, his wife, Lorraine, and his son, Selig, along with the Goldfingers and the Blumfelds, all owned interests in BCA, a partnership in possession of large tracts of land. Sisselman's four daughter's interest in BCA revolved around a trust that owned a twenty percent share of BCA and that upon Jerome's death passed to his children in equal proportions.
Issue 1: What happens to a partnership when a partner dies?
Rule 1: The death of a partner is cause for dissolution of the partnership without regard to the terms of the partnership agreement. U.P.A. § 31.

Issue 2: If a new partnership is formed after an old one has dissolved, how is it to be managed?
Rule 2: Because partnership law requires unanimous agreement of all partners on all but "ordinary matters," U.P.A. § 18(4), the right of a partner to be heard on fundamental and vital aspects of the partnership enterprise, matters that could substantially affect the investment and liability of a partner, should not be deemed surrendered unless the intention to do so is clearly expressed.

Swann v. Mitchell (1983) CCM

Facts: In 1966, P's now deceased father, business manager of Mitchell Motors from 1940 to 1967, entered into a partnership agreement with the owners to receive a five percent share of the profits. In 1979, twelve years after Swann retired, the partnership was dissolved and replaced by a corporation. Swann was given what was supposed to represent his share of the profits.
Issue: Is the goodwill of a business, the advantage or benefit the business has beyond the mere value of its property and capital, to be included in value of a partnership upon dissolution?
Rule: Goodwill should be recognized as an asset of a business, in the absence of a contract to the contrary, and taken into consideration in any sale or valuation of assets.

Wills v. Wills (1988) CCM

Facts: P sought to garnish the account of Rainbow Lounge, a partnership that D, her ex-husband, owned with Janos.
Issue: Is a partner's interest in the partnership property subject to garnishment?
Rule: Section 25 of the U.P.A. prohibits any attachment or execution of specific partnership property by a judgment creditor of an individual debtor partner. The proper method to "seize" the interests of an individual partner is to apply to the proper court for a charging order in order to charge the individual partner's share of profits and surpluses in the partnership with the unsatisfied amount of the judgment and to foreclose on the partner's "interest" in the partnership. U.P.A. § 28.

In re Comark (1985) CCM

Facts: Newman, creditor of Comark, a limited partnership in bankruptcy, won a judgment against Bell and Owens, the two general partners. The trustee in Comark's bankruptcy responded by bringing suit to enjoin Newman from enforcing the judgment against the property of Bell and Owens to protect the interests of the Comark bankruptcy estate.

Issue: Is the disposition of the general partner's property a property interest arising and related to a partnership case under Chapter 11 of the Federal Bankruptcy Act?

Rule: Since the payment of partnership debt includes the Trustee's ability to recover as against the property interests of the general partners of a debtor partnership, the general partner's assets are considered part of the general fund to which the bankruptcy estate may look to satisfy partnership debts and must be protected from separate individual collection efforts.

Richert v. Handly I (1957) Ha

Facts: P bought the timber and D milled it in a losing joint venture-partnership. In an oral agreement, the parties only agreed to share the profits and losses. The trial court found, disregarding the investment, that the gross revenues should be divided equally without considering the loss of P's investment.

Issue: Absent agreement, how are partnership losses to be borne?

Rule: Not decided. See below.

Richert v. Handly II (1958) Ha

Facts: See facts above. On remand, the trial court found that without prior agreement between them, neither party was entitled to judgment against the other.

Issue: Absent agreement, how are partnership losses to be borne?

Rule: Each partner must contribute towards the losses, whether capital or otherwise, sustained by the partnership according to his share in the profits. U.P.A. § 18(a)

National Biscuit Co. v. Stroud (1959) Ha

Facts: Stroud and Freeman were partners in Stroud's Food Center. Stroud informed P that he would not be responsible for additional bread sold to his Food Center. Acting within the scope of the

partnership's business, Freeman subsequently purchased bread from P. Stroud denied liability for the purchase.
Issue: Does a partner, by advising a future creditor that he will not be responsible for any future debts to them, escape liability for subsequent debts to that creditor incurred by a co-partner?
Rule: The acts of a partner on behalf of the partnership are binding on all co-partners if within the scope of the partnership's business.

Smith v. Dixon (1965) Ha
Facts: E.F. Smith, on behalf of the family partnership E.F. Smith & Sons (D), contracted with Dixon (P) for the sale of family property. D refused to perform and P brought suit.
Issue: Are the acts of one partner binding on the partnership?
Rule: A partnership is bound by the acts of a partner acting within the scope or apparent scope of his authority.

Rouse v. Pollard (1941) Ha
Facts: Fitzsimmons, a partner in a prestigious law firm (D), represented P. Without informing his fellow partners, Fitzsimmons took money from D saying that he was going to invest it in good mortgages. Instead, he converted it to his own use. He was later arrested for defrauding a large number of people and sent to prison. Since Fitzsimmons was insolvent P attempted to recover from the firm.
Issue: Are partners liable for the acts of their co-partners?
Rule: Partners are only liable for those acts of their co-partners that are within the scope of the partnership's business.

Roach v. Mead (1986) Ha
Facts: Mead, a law partner of Berentson (D), took a loan from one of his clients (P), not informing the client properly as to the legal aspects of the loan and misrepresenting the security for the loan. With Mead subsequently debarred and bankrupt, P sued D. D moved for a directed verdict on the grounds that he was not liable for the negligent acts of his partner.
Issue: Are partners liable to third parties for the acts of their copartners that are reasonably believed by the third parties to be within the scope of the business?

50 Partnership

Rule: Partners are liable for the acts of their co-partners that third parties can reasonable believe are within the scope the partnership business.

United States v. A & P Trucking Co. (S.Ct. 1958) Ha
Facts: D, a partnership, was charged with violations of 18 U.S.C.A. § 835, which makes it criminal to knowingly violate Interstate Commerce Commission regulations for the safe transportation in interstate commerce of "explosives and other dangerous articles," and 49 U.S.C.A. § 322(a), the comprehensive misdemeanor provision of the Motor Carrier Act.
Issue: Can a partnership be prosecuted as an entity in violation of a criminal statute?
Rule: (Harlan, J.) Partnerships as entities may be prosecuted for violating criminal statutes.
Concurrence: (dissenting in part) (Douglas, J.) Partnerships may not be prosecuted under criminal statutes that require knowledge unless a partner is culpable.

Collins v. Lewis (1955) Ha
Facts: P and D entered into a partnership known as the L-C Cafeteria where, according to the partnership agreement, P supplied the money and D the management. The partnership was failing because, as the jury found, P was uncooperative and failed to live up to the agreement. P sought to dissolve the partnership.
Issue: May a partner who has not fulfilled his obligations under a partnership agreement dissolve the partnership?
Rule: A partner who has not fully and fairly performed the partnership agreement has no standing in a court of equity to enforce any rights under the agreement and, therefore, can not ask the court to dissolve the partnership.

Cauble v. Handler (1973) Ha
Facts: Cauble and D were partners until Cauble's death. After Cauble's death and dissolution of the partnership, D continued to run the business. P, the administrator of Cauble's estate, sought an accounting of the partnership assets and the estate's rightful share.
Issue 1: How is a partnership valued upon dissolution?

Rule 1: When valuating a dissolved partnership, the market value is used in computing the net worth of a partnership's assets, not the book value.

Issue 2: If one partner continues to operate the business after dissolution, what are the rights of the other partner or his estate?

Rule 2: If one partner continues to operate the business after formal dissolution of the partnership, the other partner or his representative may demand liquidation and his share of the assets or his share of the profits of the continuing enterprise.

Adams v. Jarvis (1964) Ha

Facts: P withdrew from a medical partnership seven years after it was founded. Although under U.P.A. § 29 withdrawal leads to dissolution and eventual termination of the partnership, the partnership agreement stipulated that the partnership would continue upon the withdrawal of one of the partners.

Issue: Does a withdrawal of a partner constitute a dissolution of the partnership under U.P.A. §§ 29, 30 notwithstanding a partnership agreement to the contrary?

Rule: A partnership agreement providing for the continuation of a partnership upon withdrawal of one of the partners, contrary to the U.P.A., is enforceable if it sets forth a method of paying the withdrawing partner his agreed share and does not jeopardize the rights of creditors.

Meehan v. Shaughnessy (1989) Ha

Facts: Meehan and Boyle (D), partners in the law firm Parker Coulter, Daley & White, planned to quit and start their own firm, MBC. Before leaving, they hid their true intentions from their fellow partners and denied them when asked. They also solicited business for their new firm from their existing clients without allowing Parker Coulter the chance to try and keep them.

Issue: Do partners who are withdrawing from a partnership owe their copartners a fiduciary duty?

Rule: At all times, a partner has a fiduciary duty to "render on demand true and full information of all things affecting the partnership to any partner," U.P.A. § 20, and to refrain from acting for purely private gain.

Gelder Medical Group v. Webber (1977) Ha
Facts: D entered into a medical partnership, P, allowing for dismissal without cause and with a covenant not to compete. After being forced out, he began to compete within the restricted area.
Issue: May a partner who has been forced out of a partnership as permitted by the partnership agreement be held to his covenant not to compete within a restricted radius for a set time?
Rule: A partnership agreement providing for the expulsion without cause of a member on terms that are not oppressive, and including a reasonable restrictive covenant, is enforceable.

Smith v. Kelly (1971) Ha
Facts: P was hired by partnership D, an accounting firm. He was not intended to be a partner and took no part in the partnership duties. He was, however, represented as a partner to third parties.
Issue: Can one become a partner in a partnership without the intention of the existing partners to make him one?
Rule: Unless third parties' rights are involved, one can not become a partner in a partnership without the intention of the existing partners to make him one.
Note: The unintended partner can only be considered a partner in regards to liabilities to third parties.

Ellis v. Mihelis (1963) JB
Facts: D was a co-owner of ranching property with his brother. D put the property up for sale without his brother's knowledge and failed to disclose to P, purchaser of the property, his brother's ownership interest at the time of the sale. D's brother refused to sell. P sued D to compel specific performance of the sale of the property.
Issue: Does a partner have agency power to transfer partnership assets without the consent of the other partners?
Rule: Under Uniform Partnership Act § 9(2), a partner must obtain the express written consent of all the other partners in order to transfer partnership assets if the contemplated transaction is not within the usual course of business.

In re Jercyn Dress Shop (1975) JB
Facts: D, a partnership, conducted a general assignment of its assets for the benefit of its creditors, whereupon P, the partnership's

creditors, filed an involuntary bankruptcy petition against both the partnership and each of the partners, individually.
Issue: Is a general assignment by a partnership of its assets for the benefit of its creditors in and of itself an act of bankruptcy by the individual partners as well?
Rule: Under the Bankruptcy Act, a partnership may be adjudged bankrupt without reference to the bankruptcy of partners as individuals.

Gilman Paint & Varnish Co. v. Legum (1951) JB
Facts: P sued to recover the unpaid balance on paint products that P had sold to Tovell Construction Company. D had originally joined Tovell as a limited partner. At the time of the sale of the paint products, there was no indication on public record that D was still a limited partner because the documents renewing the partnership agreement, stating that D was still only a limited partner, were not properly filed.
Issue: If there is nothing on record indicating that a general partner's status in a partnership is that of limited partner, must he then be considered a general partner?
Rule: Under Uniform Limited Partnership Act § 11, a partner who erroneously believes himself to be a limited partner must renounce his interest in the future profits of the business that he had been receiving beyond that received by a limited partner promptly upon ascertaining the error in order to avoid being considered a general partner.

Larson v. Commissioner (1976) JB
Facts: P owned limited partnership interests in two real estate syndications. The sole general partner in each partnership was a corporation, independent of the limited partners, organized for the purpose of promoting and managing such syndications. D determined that the organization was really a corporation for tax purposes.
Issue: When is a partnership with some corporate characteristics deemed a corporation for tax purposes?
Rule: A business is deemed a corporation for tax purposes when more of its characteristics, such as continuity of life, centralized management, limited liability, and transferability of assets, are

corporate rather than noncorporate in nature, with each aspect bearing equal weight.

Goldwater v. Oltman (1980) JB
Facts: P was assignee of a copartnership that had done business for the business trust, Drascena Productions. A promissory note was issued by the president of Drascena to P's assignor. P attempted to recover on the note from D, shareholders in the trust.
Issue: Are members or shareholders of a business trust personally liable to its creditors?
Rule: In a proper business trust the trustees or officers have complete control over its affairs and, therefore, the shareholders are exempt from personal liability.

Steuer v. Phelps (1974) JB
Facts: D and others were members of an unincorporated association, the Assembly Lighthouse Gospel Church, who entrusted one of its members with the group's station wagon. An accident occurred and P attempted to recover from all of the individual members of the group.
Issue: Are the individual members of an unincorporated association liable for the negligent acts of a member entrusted with the associations vehicle?
Rule: If the members of an unincorporated association entrust one of its members with the operation of an automobile, they become responsible, under the doctrine of respondeat superior, for liabilities which result from that member's negligence.

Orser v. George (1967) JB
Facts: Byron Orser was accidently shot by one or two members of a duck hunting club while they were shooting at frogs and mudhens. P, Orser's heirs, attempted to recover from D, another member of the club.
Issue: Are members in an unincorporated association liable for the unlawful acts of other members who were not acting within the course and scope of their activities as club members?

Rule: Mere membership in an unincorporated association does not make all members liable for unlawful acts of other members without their participation, knowledge or approval, e.g., if its not within the course and scope of the club activities.

Chapter 3

FORMATION OF CORPORATIONS

I. ATTRIBUTES OF CORPORATE FORM

A. Limited Liability

  1. Shareholders

     a. Shareholders today are generally not subject to personal liability for the acts of a corporation.

     b. Until the Great Depression, shareholders generally were liable for the par value of stock held.

  2. Managers
     As long as managers are acting on a corporation's behalf and within their scope of authority, they are not personally liable for acts of a corporation.

B. Transferability of Interests

  1. Unlike partnership shares, shares in a corporation are _freely transferable_.

  2. In close corporations, where there is a small number of owner-managers, there are usually agreements to restrict the free transferability of shares.

C. Continuity of Existence

  1. The legal existence of a corporation is perpetual unless a shorter term is prescribed in its articles of incorporation.

2. The continuity of close corporations, despite their corporate form, depends in practice on the continued participation of its owners.

D. Individuality

A corporation, although a creature of law possessing only those powers allowed to it in its articles of incorporation, is empowered to act as an individual. A corporation can bring suit as well as be haled as a defendant. A corollary of this, however, is that shareholders may not bring suit on behalf of a corporation for causes of action such as interference with business. See *Green v. Victor Talking Machine Co.*

E. Centralized Management

1. Under the corporate statutes, corporations are managed by a board of directors.

2. Shareholders have no authority to participate in the management of a public corporation.

3. Shareholders who also act as directors may participate in the management of the corporation and cause it to enter binding agreements without becoming personally liable for the corporation's obligations.

F. Constitutional Issues

Constitutional protections have been held to extend to corporations in connection with:

1. The first amendment right of association;

2. The first amendment right to free speech; and

3. The fourteenth amendment right to due process.

58 Formation of Corporations

G. Costs and Complexities of Incorporation

1. Incorporation Procedures

   a. The process of incorporation can be costly and almost always requires the services of an attorney.

   b. The process of incorporation hinges upon the <u>observance of</u> certain formalities. Failure to comply can expose shareholders to personal liability.

2. Corporate Formalities
   Certain formalities (e.g., shareholders' meetings, board of directors' meetings, minimum capitalization) must also be performed following the successful incorporation of the company <u>to protect</u> shareholders from personal liability.

II. STATE OF INCORPORATION

A. It is a long-held tradition of American corporate law that corporate regulation lies within the province of state, rather than federal, law.

B. Choice of Law Rule

   A corporation's internal affairs are governed by the law of its state of incorporation, even if the corporation has no other contact with that state.

C. Local v. Out-of-State Incorporation

   1. Close Corporations

      Most close corporations choose to incorporate in the state where the principal place of business is located. This route may be less costly:

a. Double Taxation
A corporation must often pay taxes to the state where it is incorporated in addition to the state where its headquarters is located.

b. Legal Advice
Corporate attorneys might not be familiar with the corporate law of other states, requiring consultations with out-of-state counsel.

c. Administrative Concerns
States are free to impose on out-of-state corporations certain regulatory burdens not required of home-state corporations.

2. Publicly Held Corporations
Most public corporations incorporate in a state with a favorable corporate law and tax regime (e.g., Delaware), irrespective of where the corporate headquarters is located.

3. States
Since corporate franchise taxes are a lucrative source of revenue, states with small revenue bases (e.g., Delaware) often tailor their corporate statutes to be attractive to large corporations.

D. Competition among State Incorporation Statutes

1. Proponents of a federal incorporation statute have objected to state incorporation statutes because they are drafted so as to favor the prerogatives of management (e.g., the ability to engage in certain acts without shareholder approval) over the welfare of shareholders.

2. Critics of a federal incorporation statute argue that this ignores the effects of markets on management incentives and point out that a choice of state of incorporation that is not value-maximizing would likely have a detrimental effect on stock prices.

60 Formation of Corporations

   3. The Revised Model Business Corporation Act (RMBCA) represents an attempt to achieve uniformity among the various incorporation statutes and has served as the foundation for the statutes of many states.

E. Delaware's Preeminence as a State of Incorporation

Delaware is the state of incorporation for 158,000 existing corporations and more than half of the Fortune 500 industrials and attracts over 20,000 new incorporations annually. Appearing in 1899 and revised most recently in 1967, the Delaware General Corporation Law (Del.G.C.L.) offers the following advantages:

   1. Because it was drafted by corporation lawyers, the Del.G.C.L. was designed to be attractive to corporations, corporate management, and corporate counsel.

   2. The preeminence of the Del.G.C.L. has generated a large body of case law on corporate matters.

   3. Incorporation in Delaware lends a certain degree of prestige to a corporation.

III. ORGANIZING A CORPORATION

A. Articles of Incorporation

   1. Preparation of articles of incorporation is the first step in the incorporation procedure. Articles of incorporation must be filed with, and approved by, the relevant state official, usually the Secretary of State.

   2. Purpose Clause

      a. Every articles of incorporation must state the purpose for which the corporation is to be formed.

b. Because most state incorporation statutes allow incorporation for any "lawful purpose," most purpose clauses are drafted as broadly as possible.

B. Initial Board of Directors

Under the corporate statutes, potential stockholders cannot purchase stock until the board of directors issues it, usually at the corporation's organizational meeting. There are two mechanisms to accomplish this:

1. The incorporators have the powers of stockholders until the stock is issued and the power of directors until directors are appointed; or

2. The incorporators have the powers of stockholders and directors unless initial directors are named in the corporation's articles of incorporation.

C. Corporate Organization and Attorneys

The way in which a corporation is to be organized is determined by an attorney. This presents an ethical problem, for an attorney faced with the task of organizing a corporation often confronts a divergence in interests among the corporate promoters. The attorney's task is to represent the corporation as a whole while avoiding the role of mediator or advocate for individual promoters.

IV. CORPORATE CONDUCT

A. *Ultra Vires* Doctrine

1. *Ultra Vires* Defined
A corporation's capacity to act is limited by the provisions of its articles of incorporation. Transactions lying outside the scope of these provisions are characterized by courts as *ultra vires* and are unenforceable both by and against the corporation.

62 Formation of Corporations

2. Application

    a. Acts beyond the Purpose of the Corporation
       The *ultra vires* doctrine limits the actions a corporation is permitted to take to those stipulated in the purpose clause of its articles of incorporation.

    b. Acts beyond the Power of the Corporation
       The *ultra vires* doctrine prevents a corporation from exercising powers not specified in its articles of incorporation.

    c. *Ultra vires* traditionally has not been permitted as a defense to tort or criminal liability and has principally been applied to executory contracts, rather than completed transactions.

    d. Where there has been nonperformance or partial performance by one party to an executory contract, *ultra vires* has not traditionally been available to that party as a defense to a suit compelling performance. Where *ultra vires* has been allowed, the nonperforming party has usually been found liable based on some other doctrine (e.g., quasi-contract).

    e. Where there has been unanimous shareholder approval of a transaction, an *ultra vires* defense has usually been barred.

    f. Corporate articles of incorporation are usually drafted broadly to avoid *ultra vires* problems.

3. Common *ultra vires* issues generally involve a corporation's power to:

    a. Guarantee a third party's debts;

    b. Be a general partner;

    c. Make charitable donations; and

    d. Provide pension payments or retirement benefits to outgoing employees.

4. Erosion by Courts of the *Ultra Vires* Doctrine

   a. Courts have not hesitated to imply certain powers not explicitly stated in a corporation's articles of incorporation where they in some way relate to the stipulated corporate purpose. This reflects the widespread view among judges that the *ultra vires* doctrine is flawed.

   b. Both Del.G.C.L. § 124 and RMBCA § 3.04(a) permit the application of the *ultra vires* doctrine in three specific instances, namely, a suit brought by:

      i. A shareholder to enjoin a corporate act;

      ii. The corporation against a corporate officer, director, or agent; and

      iii. The state Attorney General against a corporation.

   c. Both Del.G.C.L. § 124 and RMBCA § 3.04(a) also permit courts to set aside *ultra vires* acts where enforcement would be inequitable.

B. Corporate Conduct: The Modern Approach

Many acts that previously raised legal questions under the *ultra vires* doctrine are now permitted by statute. While the *ultra vires* doctrine looked to the articles of incorporation to determine whether a given corporate act was permissible, courts confronted with this question today focus more on public policy issues, taking into consideration both the role of the corporate entity in society and the nature of the corporate institution itself.

1. Acts Maximizing Profits
   Courts have traditionally deemed acts taken to maximize corporate profits to be permissible corporate conduct, subject to legal and ethical restraints.

2. Acts Not Maximizing Profits
   Courts subject corporate acts that do not directly contribute to corporate profits (e.g., corporate donations to charity) to a variety of different tests, based on a "sound business judgment" standard:

   a. Reasonableness Test
      Expenditures solely motivated by social considerations are subject to a limit of reasonableness. Courts determine reasonableness by examining:

      i. The extent of similar activities by other corporations; or

      ii. The connection between the corporate purpose and the expenditure in question.

   b. Direct Benefit Test
      Expenditures not intended to produce profits must be expected eventually to result in a direct benefit to the corporation. (This test has largely been replaced by the less stringent Corporate Interest Test.)

   c. Corporate Interest Test
      Expenditures not intended to produce profits must reflect the corporation's interests.

V. ACTIVITIES BY PROMOTERS

A. Promoters

   1. Promoters Defined
      A promoter transforms an idea into a profit-making business, bringing all necessary persons together and supervising the various steps required to bring the corporation into existence.

2. Stages of Corporate Promotion

a. Discovery Stage
The promoter generates an entrepreneurial idea.

b. Investigation Stage
The promoter analyzes the resources needed to turn the idea into a business.

c. Assembly Stage
The promoter assembles money, property, and manpower together into an organization. This stage often requires that sales, real-estate, and other contracts be concluded on behalf of the proposed corporation, raising the question of the liability of both the promoter and the corporation.

B. Liability for Pre-Incorporation Contracts

1. RMBCA § 2.04 holds promoters liable for any act made on behalf of a corporation if, at that time, the promoters knew that the corporation had not yet been duly incorporated. This theory is grounded in both agency principles (an agent who acts on behalf of a nonexistent principal is automatically deemed a principal) and the tort doctrine of misrepresentation.

2. Exceptions
Courts have been less rigid in determining promoter liability in the following situations:

a. The promoter honestly and reasonably but erroneously believed the corporation was duly incorporated. Courts will almost always limit promoter liability in this situation. See *Cranson v. International Business Machines Corp.*

b. The promoter has mailed to the relevant state authority the required incorporation documents and has then entered into a contract in the corporate name, following which the documents are rejected. Courts have sometimes limited promoter liability in this situation. See *Cantor v. Sunshine Greenery, Inc.*

c. The other party to the contract has urged the execution of the contract in the corporate name prior to the formation of the corporation. See *Quaker Hill, Inc. v. Parr.*

3. Restatement (2d) of Agency § 326, Comment b. contemplates four alternative liability arrangements for contracts entered into between promoters and third parties. Applicability is determined by courts based on the facts of the particular case.

   a. The contract is a revocable offer that becomes enforceable when the corporation is incorporated and accepts the offer.

   b. The contract is an irrevocable offer for a limited time, consideration for which is the promoter's promise to form the corporation and induce it to accept the offer.

   c. The promoter can expressly agree to liability for the contract up until the time that the corporation is incorporated and ratifies the contract. Courts have held that ratification can be either express or implied through conduct or receipt of contractual benefits. See *McArthur v. Times Printing Co.*

   d. The promoter can expressly agree to joint and several liability with the corporation for performance of the contract.

C. Fiduciary Duty

A promoter has a fiduciary duty to act in good faith for the benefit of the corporation, both during the pre-incorporation stage and after the corporation is formed. This duty usually takes the form of the promoter's duty fully to disclose to the corporation any profit-taking or other personal use of the corporate form during the process of incorporation. See *Frick v. Howard.*

VI. DEFECTIVE INCORPORATION

A. Defective Incorporation Defined

A corporation is defectively incorporated when it has failed to comply with any of the various formal requirements for incorporation or when it has failed to perform certain organizational procedures. Both promoters and shareholders can be exposed to personal liability as a result of defective incorporation, although courts have held that only those shareholders who have significantly participated in the business of the corporation can be held liable.

B. Mandatory v. Directory Provisions

1. Mandatory provisions of incorporation statutes require information for the public record (e.g., articles of incorporation must be submitted to the authorities for approval).

2. Directory provisions contain merely formal requirements (e.g., incorporation documents must be stamped with a company seal).

3. Courts usually deem an entity to be defectively incorporated if it has not complied with all mandatory provisions stipulated in the incorporation statute. Failure to comply with directory provisions is usually not fatal to the incorporation process.

4. What constitutes mandatory and directory provisions is a matter of judicial interpretation.

C. *De Jure* Corporations, *De Facto* Corporations, and Corporation by Estoppel

1. *De Jure* Corporations
   De jure corporations are formed where an entity has complied with all the mandatory provisions of an incorporation statute. A *de jure* corporation's corporate status cannot be attacked by any third party, including the state.

2. *De Facto* Corporations

De facto corporations are usually defined by courts as entities that have fallen short of full compliance with the incorporation statute, but are nonetheless considered corporate entities for purposes of their dealings with third parties and are permitted the limited liability that corporations enjoy. The corporate status of a *de facto* corporation is not, however, immune from attack by the state in a *quo warranto* proceeding (i.e., a suit to prevent usurping of power). The criteria for determining the existence of a *de facto* corporation are:

a. The existence of a law authorizing incorporation;

b. A good-faith, "legally colorable" effort to incorporate under the statute; and

c. Actual use or exercise of corporate powers.

3. Statutory Abrogation of *De Facto* Corporations

Many corporate statutes now stipulate the issuance by the state of the certificate of incorporation as the point at which an entity becomes a duly organized corporation. While this would seem to eliminate the concept of *de facto* corporate existence, some courts sitting in jurisdictions with this provision have ruled that a *de facto* corporation can exist in the absence of the required certificate.

4. Corporation by Estoppel

A corporation by estoppel exists where a third party has dealt solely with the proposed corporation and has relied exclusively on the corporation's assets rather than those of the promoters or individual shareholders and where permitting that party to claim that the corporation does not exist to hold its promoters or shareholders individually liable would produce inequitable results. The third party in this situation would be estopped from denying the existence of the corporation.

5. *De Facto* Status v. Corporation by Estoppel
   While the two doctrines seem similar in both logic and result, there exist significant conceptual differences:

   a. Estoppel can be used in a greater variety of situations. For example, a promoter who has held himself out as a corporation in a transaction with a third party can be estopped from denying corporate status.

   b. Crucial to the estoppel theory is that the third party has dealt with the business as a corporation. This requirement deprives the tort claimant, who is a stranger to the business until the cause of action arises, of the estoppel theory.

   c. Because the estoppel theory does not require that a business make a good-faith attempt to comply with the state incorporation statute, its application is broader than the *de facto* corporation theory.

VII. DISREGARD OF CORPORATE ENTITY

A. Introduction

   The corporate form is treated by courts as a legal entity separate from its shareholders. The limited liability available to shareholders is one of the main attractions of the corporate form. Under the corporate statutes, the personal liability of shareholders is severely circumscribed. Both Delaware General Corporate Law § 102(b)(6) and RMBCA § 6.22 stipulate that stockholders of a corporation will not be held liable for the obligations of the corporation "except as they may be liable by reason of their own conduct or acts."

B. "Piercing the Corporate Veil"

   Corporate veil piercing, or disregard of corporate entity, is an exception to the iron-clad rule of limited liability for corporations. In certain situations, courts will disregard the corporate nature of

70   Formation of Corporations

an entity to hold shareholders liable for the obligations of the corporation, to hold a parent company liable for the obligations of its subsidiary, or, less frequently, to hold corporations liable for the personal obligations of its shareholders.

C. Situations Supporting Disregard of Corporate Entity

1. Instrumentality Rule

    a. Also called the "alter-ego" theory, this rule is applied where shareholders or parent corporations use the corporate form in a fashion where no entity separate from themselves is maintained. Courts traditionally used the following test to determine whether a corporation is a mere instrumentality:

        i. Complete domination of the financial, business, and policy aspects of the corporation by its shareholders or its parent corporation;

        ii. Exercise of such domination to commit fraud or injustice, or to violate the law; and

        iii. Exercise of such domination so as to proximately cause the injury that is the source of the complaint.

    b. While this test is still infrequently applied, many courts today do not require evidence of fraud to pierce the corporate veil. Instead, courts examine whether:

        i. Corporate formalities have been observed (e.g., required meetings have been held, corporate books have been maintained).

        ii. There is a commingling of assets (i.e., whether corporate officers have used corporate funds for personal use).

        iii. The officers of the corporation exercise any actual power over business activities. This is relevant to parent-subsidiary relationships, where the officers of the parent corporation may dictate the internal affairs of its subsidiary, disregarding the subsidiary's executives.

    iv. Board membership of the parent corporation is identical or substantially similar to that of the subsidiary.

  c. Agency Theory
Disregard of corporate entity has also been justified under the similar theory governing the <u>relationship of principal and agent</u>. Under this theory, personal liability for the consequences of corporate acts results when anyone exercises control of the corporation to further personal, rather than corporate, ends, based on the agency principle of authority.

2. Inadequate Capitalization

The question of disregard of corporate entity often arises after a corporation has gone bankrupt and its creditors seek to hold its shareholders liable for outstanding debts.

  a. Theoretical Background
Corporate limited liability is not a free ride; the law stipulates that a corporation must establish a fund from which creditors are to be paid. Up until the middle of the twentieth century, many states required a minimum capitalization amount, but now the law simply supposes both that the fund exists and that the capitalization amount will be sufficient for business requirements. <u>Shareholder liability through disregard of corporate entity is a consequence of doing business in corporate form with inadequate capital.</u>

  b. Determination of whether a corporation is undercapitalized for purposes of piercing the corporate veil is based on whether the capital fund is sufficient to cover any obligations that can reasonably be expected to arise.

VIII. EQUITABLE SUBORDINATION

A. Equitable Subordination Defined

Also called the "Deep Rock" doctrine, equitable subordination is a remedy applied in cases where a corporation has become insolvent and its shareholders seek to claim against the bankrupt corporation at parity with other creditors. Where there has been bad faith on the part of the shareholders, the trustee in bankruptcy may, under the doctrine of equitable subordination, deny or subordinate the claims of the shareholders in the interest of equity. Where there has been no abuse of the corporate form, shareholders are entitled in bankruptcy to assert claims the same as any other creditor.

B. Grounds for Equitable Subordination

1. Breach of Fiduciary Duty
   Where there has been an attempt by the shareholder-creditor to defraud creditors, courts have deemed this a breach of a shareholder's fiduciary duty and have subordinated the shareholder's claim.

2. Disregard of Corporate Entity
   Under circumstances that would have permitted disregard of corporate entity, courts have subordinated the claims of shareholders where:

   a. The bankrupt corporation merely served as a shell for the personal activities of the shareholder-creditor;

   b. The corporation was inadequately capitalized; or

   c. There has been commingling of funds and properties.

3. Mismanagement
   Where the shareholder-creditor has mismanaged the bankrupt corporation in excess of simple negligence, courts have subordinated the shareholder's claim.

C. Where a shareholder has made personal loans to a corporation in excess of the amount necessary for adequate capitalization, the excess amount has been allowed as a shareholder claim on an equal basis with the claims of general unsecured creditors.

CASE CLIPS

Goodman v. Ladd Estate Co. (1967) CE

Facts: One of the directors of Westover Tower, Inc. took out a personal loan, which was endorsed by D based on a guarantee agreement signed by the directors of Westover that protected D from any loss resulting from the loan. The director defaulted on the loan, and D made good on its endorsement. D then sought reimbursement from P, who had purchased all common shares of Westover, and P filed suit to enjoin D from enforcing the guarantee agreement, claiming that the agreement was *ultra vires* the corporation.

Issue: Is a contractual obligation incurred pursuant to a transaction that is *ultra vires* a corporation enforceable?

Rule: Under Delaware General Corporations Law § 124, a contractual obligation incurred pursuant to a transaction that is *ultra vires* a corporation is enforceable unless the result would be inequitable.

Inter-Continental Corp. v. Moody (1966) CE

Facts: P guaranteed a note given by Shively, its president, to D. D knew or should have known that P's guarantee was *ultra vires*. Shively subsequently lost control of P, and D brought suit on the guarantee. P defended on the ground of *ultra vires*.

Issue: Is a contractual obligation incurred pursuant to a transaction that is *ultra vires* a corporation enforceable even where the third party is aware that the corporation lacks the authority to conclude the transaction?

Rule: Under Delaware General Corporations Law § 124, a contractual obligation that is *ultra vires* a corporation is enforceable even where the third party is aware that the corporation lacks the authority to conclude the transaction.

711 Kings Highway Corp. v. F.I.M.'s Marine Repair Serv., Inc. (1966) CE, Ha

Facts: P leased a theater to D. Before the effective date of the lease agreement, P brought suit seeking a declaratory judgment invalidating the lease agreement on the ground that D's operation of a theater would be *ultra vires*.

Issue: Where *ultra vires* is invoked as a cause of action, is its availability limited by the exceptions set forth in New York Business Corporation Law § 203?

Rule: New York Business Corporation Law § 203 limits the availability of *ultra vires* both as a defense and as a cause of action.

Note: New York Business Corporation Law § 203 is similar to Delaware General Corporation Law § 124 and Revised Model Business Corporation Act § 3.04.

A.P. Smith Mfg. Co. v. Barlow (1953) CE, V

Facts: A.P. Smith Mfg. Co. made a charitable donation to Princeton University. A group of individual shareholders challenged the donation, claiming it was *ultra vires* the corporation.

Issue: Are donations by a corporation to charitable institutions *ultra vires* where charitable donations are not expressly authorized in the corporation's articles of incorporation?

Rule: Corporate donations that are within the scope of statutory enactments and are voluntarily made in the reasonable belief that they would aid the public welfare are permissible even where charitable donations are not expressly authorized in a corporation's articles of incorporation.

RKO-Stanley Warner Theatres, Inc. v. Graziano (1976) CE, JB

Facts: P concluded a land sale contract with D, a promoter for a proposed corporation. Paragraph 19 of the contract provided that upon incorporation of the proposed corporation, "all agreements, covenants, and warranties contained herein shall be construed to have been made between Seller and the resultant corporation." P sued to enforce the land sale, and D claimed that Paragraph 19 released him from personal liability.

Issue: Can a promoter be held personally liable for pre-incorporation obligations even after the corporation is incorporated?

Rule: Unless there is a novation or other agreement to release the promoter from liability, a promoter's liability for pre-incorporation obligations continues even after the corporation has been organized.

McArthur v. Times Printing Co. (1892) CE, Ha, He

Facts: P was employed by D's promoters as advertising solicitor under a contract stipulating a one-year term. D was subsequently incorporated, and fired P before the expiration date of the contract. P sued for damages for breach of contract.
Issue: Is a corporation liable for pre-incorporation contractual obligations incurred by its promoters?
Rule: Where the contract at issue is one that the corporation itself could make and one which the usual agents of the company have express or implied authority to make, adoption of the contractual obligations by the corporation may be inferred through its knowledge of, and acquiescence to, the contract, without any requirement of formal action by its board of directors.

Clifton v. Tomb (1947) CE

Facts: Not Provided.
Issue: Not Provided.
Rule: Legal rationales upon which a corporation can be held liable for the contracts of its promoters include ratification, adoption, novation, offer and acceptance, and estoppel.

Cantor v. Sunshine Greenery, Inc. (1979) CE, Ha

Facts: Brunetti (D) entered into a lease agreement with P on behalf of Sunshine Greenery, Inc., a proposed corporation. At the time of the execution of the lease, both P and D believed that Sunshine Greenery had been duly incorporated, when in fact it was not properly incorporated until two days after the execution date. D later breached the lease, and P sought to hold D personally liable for all losses.
Issue: If a party contracts with a *de facto* corporation as a corporation, is he thereafter estopped from denying the corporation's existence to hold its promoters personally liable?

76   Formation of Corporations

Rule: If a party deals with a *de facto* corporation as a corporation, he is thereafter estopped from denying the corporation's existence to hold its promoters personally liable.

Timberline Equipment Co., Inc. v. Davenport (1973) CE, He, JB

Facts: P rented equipment to Aero-Fabb, a defectively incorporated corporation. P sued Bennet (D), an incorporator, director, and stockholder of Aero-Fabb, seeking to hold him personally liable for the unpaid rentals.

Issue: Can a party associated with a defectively incorporated corporation be held personally liable for obligations incurred by the corporation?

Rule: Only those parties who have invested in a defectively organized corporation and who actively participate in the policy and operational decisions of an organization can be held personally liable for obligations incurred by the corporation.

Flanagan v. Jackson Wholesale Bldg. Supply (1984) CE

Facts: D extended credit to Flanagan, the owner of Flanagan Construction Co. Flanagan Construction's corporate status was suspended at the time of the transaction. Flanagan died a year after the transaction, and D sought to collect on the debt from Flanagan's wife (P). P, who had signed Flanagan Construction's certificate of corporation and was one of its original directors, never actively participated in the corporation's business.

Issue: Can a party associated with a defectively incorporated corporation be held personally liable for the obligations incurred by the corporation?

Rule: Only those parties who have invested in the defectively organized corporation and who actively participate in the policy and operational decisions of the organization can be held personally liable for obligations incurred by the corporation.

Walkovsky v. Carlton (1966) CE, CCH, Ha, He, V

Facts: P was struck by a taxi cab owned by Seon Cab Corporation, one of ten taxi cab companies established by D as separate entities to minimize liability insurance costs. P brought a tort action against each cab company and its shareholders, alleging that D operated all of the companies as a single entity. D moved for dismissal of the pleadings for failure to state a cause of action.

Issue: Where a complaint alleges that ownership of assets has been deliberately broken up and intermingled among several corporations, each insufficiently capitalized to ensure adequate recovery in a tort suit, is a cause of action sufficient to support disregard of corporate entity and personal liability of individual shareholders established?

Rule: To support disregard of corporate entity and hold shareholders personally liable, a complaint must allege that the separate corporations were undercapitalized, that their assets have been intermingled, and that the shareholders used the corporations in their personal capacities for purely personal rather than corporate ends.

Zaist v. Olson (1967) CE, CCM

Facts: D established two corporations, The East Haven Homes, Inc. and Martin Olson, Inc., and entered into a contract through East Haven with P for the construction of a shopping mall. D subsequently transferred much of the land for the shopping mall to himself and to Martin Olson, Inc., and concluded additional development agreements with D through East Haven, the benefits of which inured to Martin Olson, Inc. When P was unable to collect the amount due for the development work from East Haven, which was no longer solvent, P sought to hold D and Martin Olson, Inc. liable.

Issue: Can a corporate entity be disregarded where it is utilized by its shareholders as an instrumentality for their own, rather than the corporate, interest?

Rule: Under the instrumentality rule, a corporate entity can be disregarded when the purchasing corporation completely controls the financial, policy, and business affairs of the subsidiary corporation, when this control is used by the purchasing company to commit fraud or injustice, violate statutory duties, or contravene public policy, and when this control is the proximate cause of the injury complained of.

Automotriz Del Golfo De California S.A. De C.V. v. Resnick (1957) CE

Facts: Not Provided.
Issue: Not Provided.

Rule: Disregard of corporate entity is supported where there is unity of interest and ownership that negates the separate personalities of the corporation and individual and where maintaining the corporate fiction will result in inequity.

Minton v. Cavaney (1961) CE, Ha, SSB

Facts: P obtained a tort judgment against Seminole Hot Springs Corporation. Cavaney, D's husband, was Seminole's attorney, and conducted the incorporation of Seminole, served as one of Seminole's three directors, and kept Seminole's records at his office. When P could not enforce its judgment against Seminole, which was undercapitalized, it sought to hold D personally liable as executor of Cavaney's estate under the "alter-ego" doctrine.
Issue: Can a director of a corporation that he knows to be undercapitalized be held personally liable for the obligations of the corporation?
Rule: Undercapitalization of a corporation is an abuse of corporate privilege, resulting in the personal liability of those directors who actively participate in the conduct of its business.

Arnold v. Browne (1972) CE

Facts: Not Provided.
Issue: Not Provided.
Rule: Though undercapitalization, in addition to other factors, may support disregard of corporate entity, undercapitalization alone is not a sufficient ground for disregard of corporate entity.

Gentry v. Credit Plan Corp. of Houston (1975) CE

Facts: Not Provided.
Issue: Not Provided.
Rule: Where the subsidiary corporation is a mere conduit through which the parent conducts its business, the corporate entity may be disregarded to prevent fraud or injustice.

Truckweld Equipment Co., Inc. v. Olson (1980) CE

Facts: Not Provided.
Issue: Not Provided.

Rule: Where a failing corporation has initially been adequately capitalized, a corporate stockholder has no obligation to commit additional private funds.

Costello v. Fazio (1958) CE

Facts: D was a partner in a plumbing supply company and had contributed a considerably larger sum of capital to the partnership than had the other two partners. After the company's business started to fail, D and the other partners decided to incorporate the company, and D withdrew most of the partnership capital from the corporation by converting it into debt evidenced by a promissory note, leaving the corporation with inadequate capital. The corporation subsequently went bankrupt, and D filed creditor's claims with the trustee in bankruptcy (P) for payment of the note. P objected to the claims, arguing that they should be subordinated to the claims of general unsecured creditors.

Issue: Can a bankruptcy court subordinate a claim brought against the bankrupt corporation by one of its shareholders as creditor?

Rule: A bankruptcy court can subordinate a claim brought by a shareholder where the shareholder has exercised control of the corporation for his personal and private benefit, has inadequately capitalized the corporation, and if honoring the claim would do injustice to innocent creditors.

Thompson & Green Machinery Co. v. Music City Lumber Co. (1984) CCM

Facts: Walker (D) was the president of Music City Lumber Co., and purchased, on behalf of Music City, a sawmill from P. Although both P and D dealt with each other as corporations, Music City was not incorporated as of the date of the sale. Music City subsequently declared bankruptcy, and P sought to hold D personally liable for the amount due on the sawmill.

Issue: Can a party who has concluded agreements on behalf of a proposed corporation be held personally liable for resulting obligations?

Rule: In states where there exists a statute that abrogates the doctrine of *de facto* corporation by stipulating the point at which corporate existence begins, a party who has concluded agreements on

80   Formation of Corporations

behalf of a proposed corporation can be held personally liable for resulting obligations.

Don Swann Sales Corporation v. Echols (1981) CCM, He
Facts: P extended credit to Cupid's, Inc., an entity established by D. Although both P and D thought Cupid's, Inc. was a duly organized corporation, it had not been properly registered. P sued to hold D personally liable for the indebtedness, in response to which D raised the defense of corporation by estoppel.
Issue: Is a party entitled to the defense of corporation by estoppel where the facts show that the corporation did not exist at the time the transaction at issue occurred?
Rule: A party is entitled to the defense of corporation by estoppel where the corporation exists under "color of law," but not where no corporation exists at all.

Sulphur Export Corp. v. Carribean Clipper Lines, Inc. (1968) CCM, JB
Facts: A Louisiana state statute required that a corporation be capitalized before it could do business within the state. Carribean Clipper Lines concluded a charter party agreement with P before it had received the statutorily required capital. P sued D, the officers of Carribean Clipper Lines, individually for breach of a charter party.
Issue: Are the officers of a corporation that has failed to comply with statutory capitalization requirements jointly and severally liable with the corporation for the obligations incurred by the corporation?
Rule: Under state statutes requiring a minimum paid-in capital contribution, the officers of a corporation that is not properly capitalized are jointly and severally liable with the corporation for the corporation's obligations only if the officers participated in the transaction of business by the corporation, and did not register in the minutes of a board meeting their dissent to the transaction in question.

Bernardin, Inc. v. Midland Oil Corp. (1975) CCM
Facts: P concluded a manufacturing agreement with Zestee Foods, Incorporated, a wholly owned subsidiary of D. D decided to liquidate Zestee after Zestee's plant burned down. Although the trustee in bankruptcy partially paid the balance due under the manufacturing

agreement, the entire balance remained unpaid. P sued D for the unpaid balance, claiming that Zestee and D were the same corporate entity.
Issue: Can the claims of creditors against the assets of an insolvent subsidiary corporation be imputed to the parent corporation under the instrumentality rule?
Rule: The claims of creditors against the assets of an insolvent subsidiary corporation can be imputed to the parent corporation under the instrumentality rule where it is shown that the parent corporation completely controlled the business, financial, and policy affairs of the subsidiary.

Bartle v. Home Owners Cooperative (1955) CCM, Ha
Facts: D established Westerlea as a wholly owned subsidiary. Westerlea subsequently went bankrupt, and P, the trustee in bankruptcy, sued D to recover $25,639 in capital that D contributed to Westerlea prior to bankruptcy.
Issue: Are the claims of creditors against a bankrupt subsidiary corporation sufficient grounds for disregard of corporate entity?
Rule: Absent a showing of complete control by the parent corporation of its subsidiary for fraudulent or wrongful purposes, claims of creditors against a bankrupt subsidiary corporation are not sufficient grounds for disregard of corporate entity.

Stone v. Eacho (1942) CCM
Facts: The Tip Top Tailors was incorporated in Delaware and operated nine stores, one of which was located in Virginia. Tip Top secured a separate corporate charter for its Virginia store, yet continued to operate it as part of the Delaware corporation, paying all expenses for the operation of the Virginia corporation from its Delaware account. Both companies went bankrupt, and P, receiver for the Delaware corporation, sued for disregard of the Virginia corporation so that the claims of all creditors against both corporations would be treated equally.
Issue: Where both a parent organization and its subsidiary are insolvent, is disregard of corporate entity justified to ensure that creditors share equally in the distribution of the consolidated assets?

Rule: Where both a parent organization and its subsidiary are insolvent, disregard of corporate entity is justified to ensure that creditors share equally in the distribution of the consolidated assets.

Kulka v. Nemirovsky (1936) CCM

Facts: P obtained a tort judgment against D, the principal partner in Samuel Machinery Co. Before P could recover, however, Samuel Machinery Co. was reorganized from a partnership to a corporation. P levied on the premises of the newly formed corporation to secure recovery.
Issue: Is a corporation that succeeds to the assets of a partnership liable for the obligations of the partnership?
Rule: Where a partnership transfers its assets to a corporation composed of substantially the same members as was the partnership, the corporation will bear the liability for the obligations of the partnership.

Tift v. Forage King Industries (1982) CCM

Facts: P was injured by a tractor chopper box manufactured thirteen years previously by Forage King Industries, a sole proprietorship owned by Wiberg. Forage King Industries existed at various times as a sole proprietorship, a partnership, and a corporation before being sold by Wiberg to Tester Corporation seven months prior to P's injury. P sued for tort damages.
Issue: Where a corporation is purchased by a second corporation, can the purchasing corporation be held liable for the obligations of the selling corporation?
Rule: When a corporation is purchased by a second corporation, the purchasing corporation is liable for obligations incurred by the selling corporation when the purchasing corporation is merely a continuation of the selling corporation.

J. F. Anderson Lumber Co. v. Meyers (1973) CCM

Facts: P obtained a judgment against Richard T. Leekley, Inc., a corporation owned by Leekley (D). Before P could recover on the judgment, however, D established a second corporation, Leekley's Inc., transferred all of the assets of Richard T. Leekley, Inc. to Leekley's Inc., and liquidated Richard T. Leekley, Inc. P claimed that

the new corporation was liable for the obligations of the old, since the new corporation was carrying on the same business as the old.
Issue: Where a purchasing corporation carries on the same business as the selling corporation, can the purchasing corporation be held liable for the obligations of the selling corporation?
Rule: Absent a transfer of assets for inadequate consideration, the mere fact that a purchasing corporation is carrying on the same business as the selling corporation is not sufficient to make the purchasing corporation liable for the obligations of the selling corporation.

Pringle v. Hunsicker (1957) CCM
Facts: D, owner of the controlling interest in Amber Duck Products Co., owed P back wages. Following P's departure from Amber Duck Products Co., D incorporated Amber Duck Products Corp., which succeeded to the assets of Amber Duck Products Co., and liquidated Amber Duck Products Co. P sued both D and Amber Duck Products Corp. for the unpaid wages.
Issue: Is a new corporation that succeeds to the assets of a second corporation liable for the obligations of the second corporation?
Rule: A new corporation that succeeds to the assets of a second corporation cannot be held liable for the obligations of the second corporation if the new corporation was created with funds or property contributed by new incorporators having no connection with the previous association, or if there is a change in the persons carrying on the business of the new corporation.

Kridelbaugh v. Aldrehn Theatres Co. (1923) CCM
Facts: The promoters of D employed P, an attorney, to complete a plan for incorporation. Following incorporation, D's officers asked P to obtain a permit authorizing D to sell stock. P, never paid for his services in connection with D's incorporation, sued to recover the unpaid fees.
Issue: Is a corporation liable for pre-incorporation contractual obligations incurred by its promoters?
Rule: A corporation is liable for pre-incorporation contractual obligations incurred by its promoters if subsequent to its creation it

had knowledge of and either expressly or impliedly ratified the contract.

Sherwood & Roberts-Oregon, Inc. v. Alexander (1974) CCM, JB
Facts: P drew up a commitment for a long-term loan to D, a promoter seeking financing for a proposed corporation, and obtained from D a long-term note as a "good faith deposit." The proposed corporation was never organized, and P sued to recover on the note.
Issue: Can a promoter be held personally liable for obligations incurred in pre-incorporation contracts?
Rule: A promoter is personally liable for obligations incurred in a pre-incorporation contract only if the parties to the contract have not agreed to look to an alternative source for payment.

Stanley J. How & Associates, Inc. v. Boss (1963) CCM, Ha, He, SSB
Facts: D, a promoter for a proposed corporation, contracted with P for architectural work. The contract was signed by D as "agent for a ... corporation to be formed who will be the obligor." The proposed corporation was never formed, and P sued to recover the contract price for services rendered.
Issue: Can a party associated with a proposed corporation in concluding a contract be held personally liable for obligations prescribed in the contract?
Rule: A promoter is personally liable for obligations incurred in a pre-incorporation contract only if the parties to the contract have not agreed to look to an alternative source for payment.

Stewart Realty Co. v. Keller (1962) CCM
Facts: D, a promoter of a proposed corporation, concluded a contract with P for the sale of real estate. The proposed corporation was never organized. P sought to hold D personally liable for payments due to it under the contract.
Issue: Can a promoter be held personally liable for contractual obligations incurred on behalf of a proposed corporation?
Rule: A promoter cannot be held personally liable for contractual obligations incurred on behalf of a proposed corporation if the contract was concluded in the name of the proposed corporation, and

the promoter did not expressly state his intention to be personally bound by the contract.

Theodora Holding Corp. v. Henderson (1969) Ha, JB, SSB
Facts: D was the majority stockholder in Alexander Dawson, Inc. Over the objections of P, which held 25% of the issued and outstanding stock of Alexander Dawson, Inc., D caused Alexander Dawson, Inc. to make a charitable contribution of $550,000 of its stock to the Alexander Dawson Foundation, a charitable trust controlled by D. P sued for an accounting of the losses sustained by Alexander Dawson, Inc. and the improper gains received by D.
Issue: Is a corporation that is authorized by statute to make charitable donations free to make any donation it chooses?
Rule: Statutes authorizing corporate donations to charitable or educational institutions permit any corporate gift that is reasonable.

Frick v. Howard (1964) Ha
Facts: Preston was the promoter of Pan American Motel, Inc. Prior to Pan American's incorporation, Preston bought real estate, which he sold to Pan American for a substantial profit. At the time of the sale, Preston was Pan American's principal shareholder and had complete control over the Pan American board of directors. Preston assigned the mortgage on the real estate transaction to Frick, following which Pan American became insolvent. Frick sued the receiver in bankruptcy (D) for foreclosure of the mortgage.
Issue: Can a promoter establish a corporation and use it for his personal financial gain without breaching his fiduciary duty to the corporation?
Rule: A promoter who establishes a corporation and uses it for his personal financial gain commits fraud as a result of his fiduciary duty to the corporation.

Quaker Hill, Inc. v. Parr (1961) Ha
Facts: D, a promoter of Denver Memorial Nursery, Inc., purchased nursery stock from P. At the urging of P, which wanted the transaction completed quickly, the sales contract was signed by D as the president of Denver Memorial. D subsequently formed the contemplated corporation as Mountain View Nurseries, Inc., and continued

to deal with P using the Mountain View name. The nursery stock purchased by D under the Denver Memorial name soon died, and D withheld payment until P replaced the stock under the guarantee provided in the sales contract. P sought to hold D personally liable for the debt.

Issue: If a party knowingly deals with a proposed corporation as a corporation, is he thereafter estopped from denying the corporation's existence to hold its shareholders personally liable?

Rule: If a party knowingly deals with a proposed corporation as a corporation, he is thereafter estopped from denying the corporation's existence to hold its shareholders personally liable.

Robertson v. Levy (1964) Ha

Facts: P and D concluded an agreement under which D was to form a corporation and P was to sell his business to it. D submitted his articles of incorporation to the authorities, after which the sale of P's business was completed and D started operations as a corporation. At the time of the sale, however, the authorities had rejected D's articles of incorporation, and it was only after D began to conduct business and had made a first payment under the sales contract that his articles were approved. The corporation later went bankrupt, and P sought to hold D personally liable for the balance of the sales contract.

Issue: If a party knowingly deals with a proposed corporation as a corporation, is it thereafter estopped from denying the corporation's existence to hold its promoters personally liable?

Rule: If a party knowingly deals with a proposed corporation as a corporation, it may still hold its promoters personally liable for pre-incorporation obligations, since under the relevant statute a promoter incurs obligations in his individual capacity until the issuance of the certificate of incorporation.

Cranson v. International Business Machines Corp. (1964) Ha, SSB, V

Facts: P was the president of Real Estate Service Bureau, which purchased several typewriters from D. Although in incorporating Real Estate Service Bureau D followed all requisite corporate formalities and in all relevant respects Real Estate Service Bureau conducted business as a corporation, an administrative delay in the incorporation process resulted in the corporation not being officially incorporated

until after its transaction with D was completed. D sought to hold P personally liable for the price of the typewriters.
Issue: If a party contracts with a defectively incorporated corporation as a corporation, is he thereafter estopped from denying the corporation's existence to hold its promoters personally liable?
Rule: If a party deals with a defectively incorporated corporation as a corporation, he is thereafter estopped from denying the corporation's existence to hold its promoters personally liable.

Matter of Whatley (1989) Ha
Facts: Whatley organized a corporation (D), obtained from the authorities a corporate certificate, but failed to pay in the required capital, hold required corporate meetings, or prepare required corporate documents. Whatley then individually purchased farm equipment using personal loans from Guaranty Bank & Trust Company (P) and transferred ownership of the equipment to D. D encountered financial difficulties, in response to which it pledged the equipment as security on a loan from the Small Business Administration (P). When D became insolvent, both the bank and the Small Business Administration claimed a creditor's interest in the equipment. The Bank defended its interest by claiming that because Whatley did not comply with corporate formalities, D had no authority to use the equipment as a security interest on the Small Business Administration's loan.
Issue: Can a business entity be granted *de facto* corporate existence despite its failure to comply with certain required corporate formalities?
Rule: A business entity can be granted *de facto* corporate status despite its failure to comply with corporate formalities if there exists a valid incorporation statute, there was a good-faith attempt to comply with the statute, and there was sufficient use of the corporate existence.

DeWitt Truck Brokers, Inc. v. W. Ray Flemming Fruit Co. (1976) Ha
Facts: D operated and served as president of a corporation that sold fruit on commission for growers. The corporation was undercapitalized, failed to adhere to required corporate formalities, and was

dominated by, and operated for, the personal benefit of D. D defaulted on payments to P, which provided D with transportation services, and P sought to hold D personally liable for the debt.
Issue: In the absence of fraud, is disregard of corporate entity supported where the corporation is insufficiently capitalized, and is dominated by and used for the personal benefit of the principal shareholder?
Rule: In the absence of fraud, disregard of corporate entity is supported where the corporation is insufficiently capitalized is dominated by, and used for the personal benefit of, the principal shareholder, and where preserving the corporate form would produce injustice or inequity.

Stark v. Flemming (1960) Ha, He

Facts: P started a corporation and paid herself a salary to qualify for Social Security benefits. The Secretary of the Department of Health, Education and Welfare found that P's corporation was a sham, and denied her claim for benefits.
Issue: Where the motive of the incorporator is suspect, can a corporate entity be disregarded if the incorporator adhered to required corporate formalities?
Rule: A corporate entity cannot be disregarded if it has been organized pursuant to required corporate formalities, irrespective of the motives of the incorporator.

Roccograndi v. Unemployment Compensation Board of Review (1962) Ha, He

Facts: P and two other members of a family corporation filed for unemployment benefits after being laid off. It was customary for the corporation to lay off various family members during business downturns. The Pennsylvania Bureau of Employment Security denied P's claim, ruling that P was self-employed and thus ineligible.
Issue: Where employees have sufficient control of a corporation to lay themselves off, can corporate form be disregarded to deny eligibility for unemployment benefits?
Rule: Corporate entity can be disregarded to determine whether employees claiming unemployment benefits are actually unemployed, or are merely self-employed persons facing a business slowdown.

United States v. Kayser-Roth Corporation (1989) Ha
Facts: D was the owner of Stamina Mills, Inc., a defunct textile corporation. Stamina had dumped toxic chemicals into waters surrounding a residential area, requiring an expensive cleanup effort. The government sought to hold D liable for the cleanup costs, claiming that D's dominance over Stamina's business affairs justified disregard of Stamina's corporate form.
Issue: Does a parent corporation's complete domination of the operations of its subsidiary support disregard of the subsidiary's corporate form?
Rule: Complete domination by a parent corporation of the financial, business, and policy affairs of its subsidiary supports disregard of corporate form.

Pepper v. Litton (S.Ct. 1939) Ha, He
Facts: D was the sole shareholder of a corporation that went bankrupt. Upon bankruptcy, D sought to enforce against the trustee (P) a judgment he obtained against the bankrupt corporation for wage claims.
Issue: Can a bankruptcy court subordinate or disallow a claim brought against the bankrupt corporation by one of its shareholders as creditor?
Rule: (Douglas, J.) A bankruptcy court can subordinate or disallow a claim by a shareholder, even when the claim has been reduced to judgment, if the shareholder bringing the claim has attempted to defraud creditors or if the corporate entity may be disregarded, and if honoring the claim would do injustice to innocent creditors.

Louis K. Liggett Co. v. Lee (S.Ct. 1933) He, JB, SSB
Facts: P, the owner of several chain stores, sued the comptroller of the State of Florida. P challenged the constitutionality of a Florida statute establishing a Chain Store Tax that provided progressively higher rates depending on the number of chain stores owned.
Issue: Not Provided.
Rule: Not Provided.
Dissent: (Brandeis, J.) Industry and commerce had historically been denied the unrestricted right to incorporate due to fear of monopoly. Restrictions on the incorporation of commercial concerns were largely

motivated by a desire to preserve equality of opportunity. Loosening of these restrictions was not motivated by a reduction in these fears, but by the realization that these restrictions were ineffectual.

Mackensworth v. American Trading Transportation (1973) He

Facts: D, a shipping corporation based in New York City, discharged P, one of its employees. P, seeking back wages, brought suit in Eastern District Court based on Pennsylvania's long-arm statute. D moved for dismissal based on lack of personal jurisdiction, claiming that it had no contacts with Pennsylvania. In the year prior to the suit, however, one of D's ships loaded cargo in Pennsylvania.
Issue: Can a foreign corporation that conducts a one-time transaction in a forum and has no intention of future gain be forced to litigate in that jurisdiction by virtue of that jurisdiction's long-arm statute?
Rule: If a foreign corporation conducts an in-state act for pecuniary gain, it will fall within that state's jurisdictional long-arm statute.

Toro Co. v. Ballas Liquidating Co. (1978) He

Facts: P, a manufacturer and distributor headquartered in Minnesota, agreed to distribute D's products in New York, Los Angeles, and San Francisco. D terminated P's distribution arrangements in New York, and P sought to bring an antitrust action in a Minnesota forum. D argued that personal jurisdiction was unconstitutional.
Issue: Is it required that there be a connection between the cause of action and D's business activities within a state to support personal jurisdiction in that state?
Rule: There must be a relationship between the cause of action and D's business contacts within a state to support personal jurisdiction within that state.

Allenberg Cotton Co. v. Pittman (S.Ct. 1974) He, JB

Facts: A Tennessee corporation (P) contracted through a middleman located in Mississippi to buy cotton from a Mississippi farmer (D). D failed to deliver the cotton, and P sued for damages for breach of contract, claiming that under Mississippi law, D did not qualify to do business in Mississippi and, therefore, that it could not enforce its contracts there.

Issue: Does a state statute permitting state courts to find contracts for interstate transactions unenforceable violate the Commerce Clause of the Constitution?
Rule: (Douglas, J.) State statutes limiting the right to sue for breach of contracts made for interstate transactions violate the Commerce Clause of the Constitution.
Dissent: (Rehnquist, J.) States should be permitted to require that corporations qualify to do business within its borders as a condition of using state courts to enforce their contracts.

State ex rel. McCain v. Construction Enterprises, Inc. (1981) He

Facts: The Kansas Secretary of Human Resources sued D, a defectively organized corporation, to recover delinquent unemployment taxes. The state sought a judgment against both the corporation and against its chief officer and operator, personally.
Issue: Can a party associated with a defectively incorporated corporation be held personally liable for obligations incurred by the corporation?
Rule: In states where there exists a statute that abrogates the doctrine of *de facto* corporation by stipulating the point at which corporate existence begins, a party associated with a defectively incorporated corporation can be held personally liable for obligations incurred by the corporation.

Ratner d/b/a The Stereo Corner v. Central Nat'l. Bank of Miami (1982) He

Facts: P, a promoter of The Stereo Corner, entered into a credit card agreement with D. Over a period beginning prior to the incorporation of The Stereo Corner, D received $32,756 in credit card receipts forged by one of The Stereo Corner's employees. When D could not recoup its losses by charge-back to The Stereo Corner, which was no longer solvent, D sought to hold P personally liable for the debt.
Issue: Can a promoter be held personally liable for pre-incorporation obligations even after the corporation is incorporated?
Rule: Unless there is a novation or other agreement to release the promoter from liability, a promoter's liability for pre-incorporation obligations continues even after the corporation has been organized.

92 Formation of Corporations

Tri-State Developers, Inc. v. Moore (1961) He

Facts: P and three others founded Tri-State Developers, Inc. The founders of Tri-State failed to comply with Kentucky's incorporation statute, which required a contribution of at least $1,000 in paid-in capital. D sought to hold P, the three other officers, and Tri-State jointly and severally liable for damages in a breach of contract suit.

Issue: Are the officers of a corporation that has failed to comply with statutory capitalization requirements jointly and severally liable with the corporation for the obligations incurred by the corporation?

Rule: Officers of a corporation that has failed to pay the statutorily required minimum capital contribution are personally liable for obligations incurred by the corporation.

Berger v. Columbia Broadcasting System, Inc. (1972) He

Facts: P, a television producer, concluded a contract with CBS Films, Inc., a wholly owned subsidiary of D, that granted to CBS Films a right of first refusal to license the broadcast of P's show for nine years. CBS Films subsequently breached the contract, and P claimed damages against D, claiming that CBS Films was D's "alter ego."

Issue: Does common ownership, management, and control support disregard of corporate entity?

Rule: Disregard of corporate entity requires the actual and complete domination by a parent company of the finances, policy, and business practices of its subsidiary; demonstration through corporate organizational schemes of the mere potential for such control is insufficient.

Sabine Towing & Transportation Co. v. Merit Ventures, Inc. (1983) He

Facts: P concluded a maritime charter contract with Merit Transportation Company, a subsidiary of D. Merit Transportation Company subsequently went bankrupt, and P sued in admiralty for damages, claiming that Merit Transportation was D's "alter ego."

Issue: Does the possibility of injustice to creditors support disregard of corporate entity?

Rule: When the parent corporation has complete control over the affairs of its subsidiary and its use of the subsidiary, though not fraudulent, adversely affects the subsidiary's profitability, disregard of corporate entity is justified to prevent injustice to creditors.

Edwards Company, Inc. v. Monogram Industries, Inc. (1984) He
Facts: P supplied parts for fire alarms to Entronic Corporation, which was purchased by Monotronics, Inc., a wholly owned subsidiary of D. P was also Entronic's major creditor and had extended Entronic $352,000 in credit prior to learning of its purchase by Monotronics. Entronic declared bankruptcy, and P sought to hold D liable for the debt, claiming that Monotronics had no existence of its own.
Issue: Is disregard of corporate entity supported where there is no evidence showing that the corporate form is being used to commit fraud or injustice?
Rule: There must be evidence showing fraud or injustice to support disregard of corporate entity.

Zubik v. Zubik (1968) He
Facts: D owned barges that he leased under informal arrangements to P, a corporation formed when D transferred his business to his children. D's barges broke loose from their moorings, causing damage to others' property. Multiple judgments in admiralty were entered against both P and D based on the lower court's finding that the way in which P conducted its affairs made it an "alter ego" of D.
Issue: Is mere informality in a corporation's conduct of its internal affairs a sufficient ground for disregard of corporate entity?
Rule: Informality in a corporation's observance of corporate procedure, absent any showing of intermingling of funds, is an insufficient ground for disregard of corporate entity.

Alford v. Frontier Enterprises, Inc. (1979) He
Facts: D was the supplier of fuel to Prime Gasoline and Oil Co., Inc., a company in which P was the principal stockholder and that leased and ran service stations owned by P. D ceased its supply of fuel, following which Prime went bankrupt. P sued for damages, alleging that D's cessation of fuel supply was intended to drive Prime out of business.
Issue: Does a shareholder in a corporation have the right to bring a suit for interference with the business or property of the corporation?
Rule: Where the business or property interfered with is owned or conducted by a corporation, it is only the corporation, and not its shareholders, that has the right of recovery.

Formation of Corporations

United States v. Pisani (1981) He

Facts: D was the president and sole shareholder in Eaton Park Nursing Home, a corporation participating in the Medicare program. Eaton Park was undercapitalized and consistently operated at a loss, financed by personal loans from D. Eaton Park went bankrupt, following which the U.S. Department of Health, Education and Welfare sued D to recover $151,413 in Medicare overpayments.

Issue: Can a shareholder of a bankrupt corporation be held personally liable under the "alter ego" theory for obligations incurred by the corporation?

Rule: A shareholder of a bankrupt corporation who has used the corporation for his own rather than corporate interests, kept the corporation undercapitalized, and failed to observe corporate formalities can be held liable for obligations incurred by the corporation.

Palmer v. Arden-Mayfair, Inc. (1978) JB

Facts: D, a Delaware corporation, was sued by the chairman of its board of directors to obtain a court order requiring D to hold an annual meeting at which it would be declared that certain California statutes governing internal voting and election procedures were void. This action was brought prior to a California court's ruling that the relevant statutes were unconstitutional as they applied to D.

Issue: Do the laws of the state in which a corporation is incorporated govern the corporation's internal affairs?

Rule: Under generally recognized choice of law principles, the law of the state of incorporation will be applied to questions regarding the internal affairs of a corporation.

Asbury Hospital v. Cass County (S.Ct. 1945) JB

Facts: A North Dakota statute required that any foreign or domestic corporation dispose of any farm land not required in the conduct of its business within a ten-year period. Prior to passage of this statute, a Minnesota non-profit corporation (P) acquired farm land in North Dakota in satisfaction of a mortgage debt. P claimed that the North Dakota statute violated the Due Process Clause of the Constitution, since the forced sale under the statute would prevent it from recouping the value of the mortgage debt.

Issue: Does a state statute that requires foreign corporations to dispose of property within the state violate the Due Process Clause of the Constitution?
Rule: (Stone, C.J.) A state may lawfully require foreign corporations holding property within its borders to dispose of it, provided the corporation is given fair opportunity to realize the value of the property.

Sherwood & Roberts-Oregon, Inc. v. Alexander (1974) CCM, JB

Facts: P drew up a commitment for a long-term loan to D, a promoter seeking financing for a proposed corporation, and obtained from D a long-term note as a "good faith deposit." The proposed corporation was never organized, and P sued to recover on the note.
Issue: Can a promoter be held personally liable for obligations incurred in pre-incorporation contracts?
Rule: A promoter is personally liable for obligations incurred in a pre-incorporation contract only if the parties to the contract have not agreed to look to an alternative source for payment.

O'Rorke v. Geary (1903) JB

Facts: P contracted with D to build a bridge. The agreement between the two parties identified D as "Geary for a bridge company to be organized and incorporated." P built the bridge and sued to recover the amount due.
Issue: Can a party acting for a proposed corporation in concluding a contract be held personally liable for the obligations prescribed in the contract?
Rule: A party acting for a proposed corporation can be held personally liable for any contractual obligations he incurs on behalf of the proposed corporation only if the parties to the contract have not agreed to look to an alternative source for payment.

Moe v. Harris (1919) JB

Facts: P rendered services to Yale Mining Co. at the request of D, who claimed to be a director of Yale Mining. After Yale Mining failed to pay for the services rendered, P sued and obtained a judgment. Yale Mining had filed its articles of incorporation, but had

not issued stock, held meetings, or kept books. P, unable to collect on the judgment, consequently sued D.
Issue: Can a party be held personally liable for obligations contracted for on behalf of a *de jure* corporation?
Rule: A party cannot be held personally liable for contracts he concluded on behalf of a *de jure* corporation, regardless of whether or not the corporation has been capitalized.

Kelly v. Bell (1969) JB

Facts: U.S. Steel Corporation was interested in securing the passage of an advantageous tax bill. Toward this end, the directors of U.S. Steel (D) agreed to make certain payments to municipalities opposed to the tax bill. P, a stockholder of U.S. Steel, subsequently sued D, claiming that payments to municipalities constituted economic waste, since they were not legally required. D claimed that the payments were donations for the public welfare.
Issue: Are corporations permitted to use their assets to make donations for the public welfare?
Rule: Under common law principles, corporations can make donations for the public welfare based on a sound business judgment that the donations would advance the interests of the corporation.

Hessler, Inc. v. Farrell (1967) JB

Facts: D, an employee of P, received repeated oral assurances from the president of P that upon retirement he would receive retirement benefits and, relying on these promises, D turned down other job offers. D retired, and the president of P subsequently reneged on his promise. D sued for damages for breach of contract.
Issue 1: Is payment of retirement benefits an illegal gift of corporate assets *ultra vires* the corporation?
Rule 1: Payment of retirement benefits pursuant to repeated promises upon which the recipient has relied does not constitute an illegal gift of corporate assets *ultra vires* the corporation.
Issue 2: Does a corporate officer who has customarily been permitted by the Board of Directors to act on behalf of the corporation in its dealings with third parties have the authority to bind the corporation?
Rule 2: The authority of a corporate officer to act for the corporation is implied from past conduct never challenged by corporate officials.

In re Westec Corp. (1970) JB

Facts: Walker (P) arranged for the purchase by Westec Corp. of another company. In return for P's services, the president of Westec (D) promised to pay P in capital stock. Westec subsequently went bankrupt, and P sued for the value of the stock.
Issue: Does a party doing business with an officer of a corporation have the duty of ascertaining that officer's scope of authority?
Rule: A party doing business with a corporate officer has the duty of ascertaining that officer's scope of authority. Where real authority is lacking, a finding of apparent authority must be based on the standard of the reasonable person using diligence and discretion.

United Paperworkers Int'l. Union v. Penntech Papers, Inc. (1977) JB

Facts: D bought a financially troubled paper company. Following D's purchase, P sought to compel D to arbitrate certain provisions of a collective bargaining agreement between P and the paper company, arguing that the separate corporate entities should be disregarded.
Issue: Is disregard of corporate entity justified in cases where a corporation purchases another corporation and takes an active role in the business of the subsidiary corporation?
Rule: Disregard of corporate entity is justified only when the purchasing corporation completely controls the financial, policy, and business affairs of the subsidiary corporation, when this control is used by the purchasing company to commit fraud or injustice, violate statutory duties, or contravene public policy, and when this control is the proximate cause of the injury complained of.

Wheeling Steel Corp. v. Glander (S.Ct. 1949) SSB, V

Facts: An Ohio statute levied a tax on foreign corporations. P sued, claiming that the tax was discriminatory and violated the fourteenth amendment of the Constitution.
Issue: Are corporations "persons" for purposes of the fourteenth amendment of the Constitution?
Rule: (Jackson, J.) Corporations are "persons" for purposes of the fourteenth amendment of the Constitution.
Dissent: (Douglas, J.) The plain language of the fourteenth amendment reveals its inapplicability to corporations. The Constitu-

tion provides a mechanism for legislatures to extend the fourteenth amendment's protections to corporations; hence, it is not a task for the courts.

First National Bank of Boston v. Bellotti (S.Ct. 1978) SSB, V
Facts: P and five other corporations wished to spend money to publicize their views on a tax referendum pending in Massachusetts. Massachusetts had a statute that prohibited corporations from making expenditures to influence the views of voters, focussing especially on tax issues. P sued to have the statute declared unconstitutional under the first amendment.
Issue: Can a state limit a corporation's first amendment right to free speech on issues not directly affecting the corporation's business?
Rule: (Powell, J.) A state is not free to limit a corporation's first amendment right to free speech on issues not directly affecting the corporation's business unless the state demonstrates a compelling state interest.
Dissent 1: (Burger, J.) It is a legitimate function of the law to limit the activities that a corporation is able to conduct without a shareholder vote.
Dissent 2: (Rehnquist, J.) It is a legitimate function of the law to limit the types of speech in which a corporation is able to engage to that affecting the corporation's business.

Union Pacific Railroad Co. v. Trustees, Inc. (1958) SSB
Facts: D, a shareholder of P, objected to a $5,000 charitable contribution made by P, claiming it was *ultra vires*. Neither P's charter nor state statues authorized corporate charitable contributions. P sued for a declaratory judgment that the donation was valid.
Issue: Is a charitable contribution an act *ultra vires* a corporation where the corporation's articles of incorporation do not expressly authorize charitable contributions?
Rule: A corporate charitable contribution is not an *ultra vires* act, even where it is not expressly authorized, if it is both reasonable and designed to assure a present or foreseeable future benefit to the corporation.

Brunswick Corp. v. Waxman (1979) SSB

Facts: P sold bowling alley equipment to Construction Corp., a corporation that was established by D solely for the purpose of taking title and assuming mortgage obligations. Construction Corp. was insufficiently capitalized and was liquidated after P's bowling alley business began to fail. Its assets transferred to five new corporations that were each undercapitalized. These corporations defaulted on the equipment payments to P, and P sought to hold D personally liable for the debt.

Issue 1: Can a corporate entity be disregarded solely on the basis of insufficient capitalization?

Rule 1: In the absence of fraud on the part of the shareholders, undercapitalization alone cannot support disregard of corporate entity.

Issue 2: If a party knowingly contracts with an undercapitalized corporation, is he thereafter estopped from disregarding the corporation's existence to hold its shareholders personally liable?

Rule 2: If a party knowingly deals with an undercapitalized corporation as a corporation, he is thereafter estopped from disregarding the corporation's existence to hold its shareholders personally liable.

Mangan v. Terminal Transportation System, Inc. (1936) SSB

Facts: P was injured in an accident caused by the negligence of a taxi cab driver. The owner of the taxi cab was an operating company, one of four owned by D, a holding company. D directly or indirectly controlled the financial, personnel, and administrative affairs of the four corporations and appointed the board of directors for each. P sued D, alleging that the operating company was a mere instrumentality of D.

Issue: Does a corporation's complete domination of the operations of an affiliated corporation render the affiliate a mere instrumentality and support disregard of the affiliate's corporate form?

Rule: Complete domination by a corporation of the operations of an affiliated corporation renders the affiliate an instrumentality and supports disregard of corporate entity.

Green v. Victor Talking Machine Co. (1928) V

Facts: P acquired from her deceased husband all the stock of Pearsall Company, which was engaged in the sale of D's products. P sued for damages, alleging that D had attempted to drive her out of business by ceasing its sales to Pearsall, luring Pearsall's employees away, and other interference.

Issue: Does a sole shareholder in a corporation have a right to bring a suit for interference with the business or property of the corporation?

Rule: Where the business or property interfered with is owned or conducted by a corporation, it is only the corporation, and not its shareholders, that has the right of recovery, even where the corporation is owned by a sole shareholder.

Old Dominion Copper Mining & Smelting Co. v. Lewisohn (S.Ct. 1908) V

Facts: D, along with Bigelow, were promoters who established and made themselves the principal shareholders in a corporation (P) for the purpose of selling to it property that they had purchased. The sale resulted in excessive profits for both D and Bigelow, who then directed P to issue to the public shares of common stock to fund P's purchase of the land. When subsequent shareholders learned of the profits from the land sale, which D and Bigelow had kept secret, P sued for rescission of the sale contract or repayment of D's profits.

Issue: Can a promoter establish a corporation and use it for his personal financial gain without breaching his fiduciary duty to the corporation?

Rule: (Holmes, J.) A promoter may establish a corporation and use it for his personal financial gain without breaching his fiduciary duty to the corporation if the shareholders have full knowledge of, and give corporate approval to, the director's actions.

Old Dominion Copper Mining & Smelting Co. v. Bigelow (1909) V

Facts: D, along with Lewisohn, were promoters who established and made themselves the principal shareholders in a corporation (P) for the purpose of selling to it property that they had purchased. The sale resulted in excessive profits for both D and Lewisohn, who then directed P to issue to the public shares of common stock to fund P's purchase of the land. When subsequent shareholders learned of the profits from the land sale, which D and Bigelow had kept secret, P sued for rescission of the sale contract or repayment of D's profits.

Issue: Can a promoter establish a corporation and use it for his personal financial gain without breaching his fiduciary duty to the corporation?
Rule: A promoter who establishes a corporation and uses it for his personal financial gain breaches his fiduciary duty where the financial gain is concealed from shareholders who are originally contemplated as part of the fully established corporation, but who have not yet subscribed for shares.

Association for the Preservation of Freedom of Choice, Inc. v. Shapiro (1961) V

Facts: P, a non-profit organization that advocated the change by peaceful means of New York's anti-discrimination statutes, applied for incorporation under a charter that stated as one of its purposes, "to promote . . . the right of the individual to associate with only those persons with whom he desires to associate."
Issue: Can a state withhold incorporation privileges from an organization that has as its purpose change of the law by peaceful means under § 10 of the Membership Corporations Law, which requires that a proposed corporation have a "lawful purpose"?
Rule: A group the purpose of which is to change the law by peaceful means is lawful under § 10 of the Membership Corporations Law and may not be denied incorporation privileges.
Dissent: Promotion of racial discrimination is not a lawful purpose for purposes of incorporation because it violates public policy as embodied in the pronouncements of the legislature. While freedom of association is a constitutionally protected right, incorporation is a privilege bestowed by the state.

People v. Ford (1920) V

Facts: The Illinois incorporation statute required, among other things, that the applicant for corporate status have the necessary documents stamped with an official seal. D, a promoter, substantially complied with the requirements of the statute, but failed to have the application documents sealed. The Illinois attorney general subsequently sued D for unlawfully exercising privileges reserved for a corporate officer.
Issue: Can a corporation be denied *de jure* status due to its failure to perform every act required by the relevant incorporation statute?

Formation of Corporations

Rule: A corporation can be denied *de jure* status if it fails to comply with a mandatory provision of the relevant incorporation act; if the requirement is merely directory, the corporation cannot be denied *de jure* status.

Dodge v. Ford Motor Co. (1919) V ✲

Facts: In 1916, D anticipated an annual profit of $60,000,000. In the same year, the company announced that it would not pay dividends so that it could pay for the construction of a smelting plant and implement a business plan that called for enhancing the public welfare through the creation of jobs and reductions in car prices. P, a shareholder of D, sued to compel payment of the 1916 annual dividend.

Issue: Can a corporation's board legally conduct the corporation's business affairs in a manner that would benefit third parties at the expense of shareholders' interests?

Rule: A board of directors of a corporation may not legally conduct the business affairs of the corporation for the merely incidental benefit of shareholders and for the primary purpose of benefitting third parties.

Chapter 4

CORPORATE STRUCTURE

I. SHAREHOLDERSHIP

Among publicly held corporations, where ownership is divorced from participation, there are three major categories of shareholder control:

A. Majority Control

A single shareholder or compact group controls a majority of the shares or a block large enough to guarantee a majority of votes in a normal election.

B. Management Control

The largest block of shares owned by a single stockholder or compact group is usually less than 10 percent of the total stock. The position of management is strengthened in two important ways:

1. Lack of Shareholder Stake
   Since shareholders own a small amount of a corporation's stock, most will not want to spend large amounts of time on the corporation's affairs.

2. Proxy Voting
   Voting must be done by proxy, under the control of the corporate management. Because of the high costs of a proxy fight, most dissatisfied shareholders sell rather than fight.

C. Minority Control

The largest block of shares does not maintain majority control but is greater than the 10 percent typical of management control. The minority block may be owned by management or a separate group.

II. ALLOCATION OF POWER

A. Traditional Model of Decision Making

1. Traditional Structure
   The hierarchy is based on an inverted pyramid, with the shareholder as the largest group on top, followed by the directors, and the officers at the bottom.

   a. Shareholders
      The shareholders elect the board and decide on "fundamental" corporate changes.

   b. Directors
      The directors manage the business, make business policy, and select the board's officers.

   c. Officers
      The officers are responsible for executing policy. They act as agents of the board rather than the shareholders.

2. Inadequacies of the Traditional Model of Decision Making

   a. Role of the Board
      The board rarely performs its ostensible role as business manager and policy maker. Its actual role varies in closely held and publicly held corporations:

      i. Close Corporations
         The business is managed by owner-managers without much regard to formal capacities.

ii. Public Corporations
Business management and policy making is carried out by the executives.

b. Reasons For Inadequacies of Board

i. Constraints of Time
Since boards typically meet six to twelve times a year, they do not have nearly enough time to actually manage the affairs of a corporation.

ii. Constraints of Information
With no independent staff, boards must rely on executives for the gathering and evaluating of information.

iii. Constraints of Composition
Boards contain a number of "inside directors," who are company officers and dependent on the executive for both promotion and retention.

B. Power of Board of Directors

The board's power is exercised through resolutions or delegated to executive committees.

1. Supervision of Business Management
Almost all state statutes provide that, subject to limitations in the articles of incorporation, the management of business is to be conducted under the supervision of the board. The power to manage includes responsibility for the election, evaluation, and dismissal of senior executives.

2. Right to Information
Directors have a wide ranging right to inspect corporate records. Some jurisdictions grant an unqualified right to information and others only permit inspection if the director's purpose is not hostile to the corporation.

106   Corporate Structure

3. Fundamental Corporate Changes
   Changes considered major by the board or senior executive must be approved by the board

C. Power of Shareholders

Shareholders maintain very little direct control over the normal affairs of a corporation. Shareholder resolutions dealing with matters other than those listed below have no legal force.

1. Election of Directors
   Depending on the state statute and the articles of incorporation, shareholders elect directors through "straight" or "cumulative" voting. Shareholders have a number of votes equal to their shares and the number of openings available for directors.

   a. Straight Voting
      No share may be voted more than once for any candidate.

   b. Cumulative Voting
      Shareholders may aggregate votes in favor of less candidates than there are positions available.

2. Removal of Directors
   The common law was divided on the ability of shareholders to remove directors, with or without cause, but most statutes now permit directors to be removed by shareholders, without cause, for cause, or only for specified acts such as fraud.

3. Approving Fundamental Changes
   Major corporate changes, such as amendment of the articles of incorporation, merger, dissolution, or alteration of the capital structure, generally require approval of the shareholders, usually on the recommendation of the board of directors.

4. Right to Information
   Under common law and most state statutes, shareholders have the right to inspect corporate records for proper purposes.

5. Derivative Powers
   An important means by which shareholders can hold directors and executives accountable is through a derivative suit, an action brought by a shareholder on behalf of the corporation.

D. Powers of Officers

1. Generally
   Responsibility for executing and, in practice, formulating business policy is vested in officers.

2. Authority of Officers
   The actual and apparent authority of an officer is largely dependent on position of the officer and the nature of his relationship with the third party.

   a. President
      The president has apparent authority to take actions in the ordinary course of business, but not extraordinary actions. The difficulty is distinguishing between "ordinary" and "extraordinary actions," which is often highly dependent on the context of the case. See *Lee v. Jenkins*.

   b. Chairman of the Board
      Because the powers of the position vary so widely, the authority of the chairman of the board is unclear as a general matter.

   c. Vice-Presidents
      The authority of a vice-president is generally limited, although if a vice-president appears to be in a position of power, his acts may be binding on the corporation.

   d. Secretary
      The secretary has the apparent authority to certify records of the corporation, but has virtually no other authority.

108 Corporate Structure

e. Treasurer
The treasurer gains almost no apparent authority from virtue of his position.

III. FORMALITIES FOR BOARD ACTION

A. Requirements

The validity of a board action is governed by statutory rules, in regard to formalities of meetings, notice, quorum, and voting.

1. Meetings
Directors can only act at convened meetings with a quorum present. Board meetings may be conducted through conference telephone call, and most states permit board action to be accomplished without a formal meeting by written consent of all board members.

2. Notice
Directors are given notice of regular board meetings, and notice is required for special board meetings, within a statutorily prescribed period.

3. Quorum
A quorum generally consists of a majority of the full board, although some states permit the certificate of incorporation or bylaws to require a greater number.

4. Voting
A simple majority vote of those present is generally required for action, but the articles or bylaws can set higher requirements.

B. Noncompliance

The consequences of failure to comply with formalities vary for public and close corporations.

1. Public Corporations
   Generally, failure to comply with a formality will render board action ineffective.

2. Close Corporations
   Since formalities are generally not followed in close corporations, the validity of actions lacking formal requirements is less clear.

   a. Unanimous Informal Approval
      Unlike older cases, most modern decisions hold explicit, informal approval by all directors creates a binding obligation on the corporation to a third party.

   b. Unanimous Acquiescence
      If a majority of directors approve of a transaction and the other directors know of the transaction and make no attempt to disapprove it, the obligation is binding.

   c. Majority Acquiescence
      Authority is split on whether an obligation is binding if a majority of directors approve of a transaction explicitly or by acquiescence without the knowledge of the remaining directors.

IV. FORMALITIES REQUIRED FOR SHAREHOLDER ACTION

A. Meeting and Notice

All statutes contemplate that a corporation will hold an annual meeting of shareholders. Notice of time, date and place must be provided to all shareholders. Under the federal proxy rules and some state statutes, notice of the purpose of the meeting must also be provided in instances such as when proposals are presented to amend the articles of incorporation or sell substantially all of a corporation's assets.

B. Quorum

Most state statues require that a quorum equal to a majority of the outstanding shares be present, unless specified otherwise by the certificate of incorporation.

C. Voting

1. Ordinary Matters
   Most statutes require a simple majority of those voting. Almost all statutes permit the certificate of incorporation to require more than a majority.

2. Structural Changes
   Structural changes usually require votes of two-thirds of the voting shares rather than one-half.

3. Election of Directors
   The election of directors requires only a simple majority. The candidates receiving the highest number of votes are elected until the required number of positions are filled.

4. Written Consent
   Shareholders are permitted to vote by written consent instead of attending a formal meeting.

CASE CLIPS

Charlestown Boot and Shoe Co. v. Dunsmore (1880) CE
Facts: Corporate shareholders asserted an action against a corporate director who failed to follow the advice of the man they appointed to close down the corporation.
Issue: Is a corporate director bound to follow the advice of another appointed by the shareholders?
Rule: The only limitations upon the judgement of the director are those imposed by corporate bylaws and direct votes of the shareholders.

Auer v. Dressel (1954) CE, Ha, He, SSB
Facts: Believing the purpose of the meeting was improper, a corporate president refused to comply with the corporation's bylaws that required a special meeting when requested in writing by shareholders.
Issue: Does a president have the right to refuse a stockholder request to call a special meeting required under corporate bylaws?
Rule: A corporate officer does not have the discretion to refuse a stockholder decision within the power granted to them by corporate bylaws.

Campbell v. Loew's Inc. (1957) CE, SSB
Facts: Corporate shareholders removed two directors from office by sending proxies to all shareholders along with reasons for removal of the directors.
Issue: Do shareholders have the power to remove directors from office by conducting a proxy vote while simultaneously providing reasons for their removal?
Rule: The implied shareholder power to remove directors from office for cause requires affording the directors a reasonable opportunity to present their position before the proxy vote is taken.

Lee v. Jenkins Brothers (1959) CE, Ha, SSB, V

Facts: P sought to recover a pension, which he claimed had been promised to him by the president of D corporation to induce him to join the company. The pension was to begin when he reached age sixty, regardless of whether he was still working for the corporation.

Issue: Does a corporate president have authority to bind a corporation to an agreement with an employee outside of the ordinary course of business?

Rule: A president has no apparent authority to bind a corporation to an agreement outside of the ordinary course of business.

Bohannan v. Corporation Commission (1957) CE

Facts: P's attempt to incorporate was rejected by the Corporation Commission because it included a proposal to stagger the election of the nine members of the board of directors.

Issue: Is staggering the election of directors impermissible because it reduces the number of directors who could be elected by minority stockholders?

Rule: While a state's constitution may require a means through which it is possible for minority stockholders to secure representation on the board, it need not guarantee proportional representation of minority stockholders on the board.

Mohr v. State Bank of Stanely (1987) CCM

Facts: A bank (D) permitted Loyd, an officer of a corporation (P), to deposit a corporate check into his personal account. P claimed Loyd had no authority for the act.

Issue: Does a corporate officer have apparent authority to deposit corporate checks into his personal account?

Rule: A corporate officer does not derive authority from his position to deposit corporate checks into a personal bank account.

Yucca Mining & Petroleum Co. v. Howard C. Phillips Co. (1961) CCM

Facts: Without receiving approval from the board of directors, president of a corporation (P) agreed to an oral contract modification. After the modification proved to be disadvantageous to P, it claimed not to be bound by the contract.

Issue: May a corporation be bound to an oral modification made by an officer?
Rule: Although matters outside a corporation's usual course of business generally require approval by the board of directors, a party may not ask for recission of a contract modification made by an officer when results, which it hoped would be beneficial, turn out to be unfavorable.

Lloydona Peters Enterprises v. Dorius (1983) CCM
Facts: By accepting a check, the treasurer of a corporation (P) sold P's interest in a property. P's president initiated litigation on behalf of her corporation to rescind the sale, without obtaining the approval of the board of directors.
Issue: May a corporate president initiate litigation on behalf of her corporation without approval of the board of directors?
Rule: Unless a corporation faces irreparable loss, legal action may not be taken by a president without the approval of the board of directors.

Real Estate Capital Corp. v. Thunder Corp. (1972) CCM
Facts: One corporation (P), in issuing a mortgage to another corporation (D), paid the principal to a third corporation, owned entirely by an 80 per cent shareholder of D without the consent of D's other shareholder. After the loan was not repaid, P sought to foreclose on the property of D.
Issue: May a corporation be bound by an agreement made by an officer and shareholder to convert corporate funds to his own use?
Rule: A corporation is not bound by actions of directors to convert corporate funds to their own use unless the consent of all stockholders is obtained and the rights of creditors are not affected.

Goodman v. Ladd Estate Co. (1967) CCM
Facts: A corporation, organized in part to obtain contracts of mortgage insurance, executed a guaranty agreement to allow one of its directors to acquire funds. The agreement was *ultra vires* and unrelated to any corporate purpose, and a shareholder sought to enjoin enforcement of the agreement.

Corporate Structure

Issue: May an *ultra vires* agreement that permits one of its directors to obtain money unrelated to any corporate purpose be binding on the corporation?
Rule: An *ultra vires* agreement may be binding on a corporation if it is consistent with a purpose for which the corporation was organized.

Baldwin v. Canfield (1879)   Ha, V
Facts: King owned all stock in a corporation whose sole asset was a tract of real property. King pledged part of the stock to P. King later agreed to convey the property deed to D through a written agreement signed by some directors.
Issue: Is a conveyance liquidating a corporation's assets that is approved by some directors outside of a formal meeting binding on the corporation?
Rule: Conveyances approved by some directors that liquidate a corporation's assets are not binding unless they are passed as resolutions within a board meeting.

Schnell v. Chris-Craft Industries, Inc. (1971)   He
Facts: Minority shareholders asserted an action to prevent management from advancing the date of a stockholder's meeting. Moving the date forward was in compliance with state corporation law, but the shareholders claimed it was an attempt to obstruct a proxy contest.
Issue: May directors, in accordance with state corporation law, move the date of a shareholder's meeting forward to obstruct a proxy contest?
Rule: Even if legal, attempts by directors to move forward the date of a shareholder's meeting may not be permitted if inequitable.

Carter v. Portland General Electric Co. (1961)   He
Facts: Corporate officers refused to submit objections from a group of shareholders (P) to the rest of the shareholders before issuing a proxy vote. P alleged a breach of fiduciary duty.
Issue: May a group of shareholders in a corporation not subject to SEC regulations compel officers to submit materials to be considered and voted upon by all shareholders?

Rule: Officers in corporations not subject to SEC rules have no fiduciary duty to submit material from shareholders to be considered and voted upon by all shareholders.

Rosenfeld v. Fairchild Engine & Airplane Corp. (1955) He
Facts: A stockholder sought to compel the return of corporate funds paid to reimburse both sides after a proxy contest. Payment to losing side was authorized by the new board and payment to the prevailing group was ratified by the shareholders.
Issue 1: May a new board, after successfully ousting management in a proxy fight, authorize corporate funds to reimburse the old board for its expenses from the proxy fight?
Rule 1: Since management is entitled to incur reasonable expenses in the waging of a proxy fight over policy, a new board may authorize payments to reimburse the old board for reasonable expenses from a proxy fight.
Issue 2: May shareholders ratify payments to a new board for proxy expenses incurred in gaining control of the corporation?
Rule 2: Shareholders may ratify payments to a new board for the reimbursement of proxy expenses incurred in gaining control of the corporation.

State ex rel. Pillsbury v. Honeywell, Inc. (1971) He, SSB
Facts: A stockholder asserted an action to inspect corporate records with the objective of ending the corporation's involvement in the manufacture of war munitions used in the Vietnam War.
Issue: Does a shareholder have a right to inspect corporate records for social or political reasons?
Rule: A shareholder may inspect corporate records only if his motive is germane to his economic interest as a shareholder.

Dillon v. Scotten, Dillon Co. (1971) He
Facts: Directors sought to overturn the election of board members in which the deciding vote was cast by a board member not legally in office.
Issue: May an election of directors be overturned if dependent on the vote of a director not legally in office?

Rule: Unlike cases where third parties are involved, the election of board members by directors not legally in office may be overturned.

Sterling v. Mayflower Hotel Corp. (1952) He
Facts: Minority stockholders (P) claimed an article in a corporate charter providing that interested directors be counted towards a quorum should be declared invalid because it was in conflict with state common law.
Issue: Is a corporate article in conflict with state common law invalid?
Rule: A corporate article may depart from the common law so long as it is not in conflict with a statute or a public policy settled by the common law.

Matter of Cohen v. Cocoline Products, Inc. (1955) He
Facts: A director asserted an action to inspect corporate records, but during the pendency of his action, he was not reelected to his position.
Issue: After a director is removed from office, does he have an absolute right to inspect corporate records from the time he was in office?
Rule: A director no longer in office does not have an absolute right to inspect corporate records from the time he was in office, but he may be granted a qualified right, at the discretion of a trial court, if he can demonstrate that inspection is necessary to protect his personal responsibility interests and the interests of the stockholders.

Continental Securities Co. v. Belmont (1912) JB
Facts: Shareholders brought an action against their corporation alleging the fraudulent issue of stock and asking for an accounting of the stock and dividends.
Issue: May shareholders confirm and ratify unlawful acts of a board of directors?
Rule: Shareholders have no authority to confirm or ratify unlawful acts of the board of directors unless conferred by statute.

Scientific Holding Co., LTD. v. Plessey (1974) SSB
Facts: A corporate president and chief operating officer expressed doubts about his authority before agreeing to a modification in a

contract that sold all his corporation's assets and business. The president did not inform his corporation of the modification, and several months later the successor to the president's corporation (P) claimed not to be bound to the modification.
Issue: Is a principal bound to an agreement made by an agent beyond the scope of his authority if it was never informed of the agreement?
Rule: A principal that fails to repudiate an agreement made by an agent beyond the scope of his authority is bound to the terms of the agreement even if the principal is never informed of the agreement.

Village of Brown Deer v. Milwaukee (1962) SSB
Facts: President, director, and majority shareholder of a corporation who customarily resolved corporate problems without formal board meetings signed a petition for municipal annexation of land on behalf of the corporation. He did not obtain the written consent of all directors as required under state law for an action by a board of directors.
Issue: Is a corporation bound to an agreement entered into by its president without the written consent of the board as required under state law?
Rule: A corporation is not bound to an agreement made outside of a formal board meeting that does not have written consent of members of the board as required under state law.

Gimbel v. Signal Companies, Inc. (1974) SSB
Facts: Without the consent of shareholders, a board of directors (D), approved a sale of a wholly owned subsidiary constituting 26 percent of the corporation's net sales and 41 percent of its net worth. A shareholder (P) sought to prevent the sale by relying on a state statute that requires shareholder approval for the sale of all or substantially all of a corporation's assets.
Issue: Must directors obtain the consent of shareholders before selling off a wholly owned subsidiary?
Rule: Directors may sell a wholly owned subsidiary without shareholder approval unless the sale is of assets quantitatively vital to the operation of the corporation and substantially affects the existence and purpose of the whole corporation.

Sherman v. Fitch (1867) V

Facts: The president of a corporation executed a mortgage with a sales agent (D). D later received property after the corporation failed to repay the debt.

Issue: Does a president have the authority to execute a mortgage on behalf of his corporation?

Rule: The execution of a mortgage by a president with the knowledge of the directors or their subsequent acquiescence is a binding act on the corporation.

Schwartz v. United Merchants & Manufacturers (1934) V

Facts: P relied on authority of the president and vice-president of D corporation in entering into a contract that would make him exclusive sales agent for two subsidiary corporations. The arrangement was to create a new corporation that would receive a percentage of the profits from the subsidiaries.

Issue: Does a president have authority to enter into contracts on behalf of his corporation that are not in the usual course of business?

Rule: Powers that are usual in a business are presumed to have been granted to a corporate officer, but contracts extending beyond the ordinary course of business require express approval of the directors.

Chapter 5

CLOSE CORPORATIONS

I. DISTINCTIONS WITH THE PUBLIC CORPORATION

A. Definition (Mnemonic: **Mondays Never Raging Fun**)

There is no bright line dividing close and public corporations, but typically close corporations are characterized by:

1. **M**anagement by the Shareholders;

2. **N**o market for Shares;

3. **R**estrictions on the Transferability of Shares; and

4. **F**ew Shareholders.

B. Vulnerability of Minority Shareholders

Because of their inability to sell shares and the rigorous requirements for dissolution of a corporation, minority shareholders in a close corporation are particularly susceptible to exploitation by majority shareholders who, under protection of the business judgement rule, can refuse to declare dividends or drain off earnings through exorbitant salaries.

C. Protection of Minority Shareholders

To insure against exploitation, minority shareholders seek protection through contractual arrangements or by opting to be subject to laws applicable to close corporations.

II. SHAREHOLDER VOTING ARRANGEMENTS

A. Types of Shareholder Voting Agreements

1. Specific Agreement to Vote
   Parties may agree in advance on the exact way they will vote their shares for the term of the agreement.

2. General Agreement to Vote
   Parties may agree to vote their shares as a block without specifying the precise way their votes will be cast until later.

B. Validity of Shareholder Voting Agreements

   Shareholder agreements are generally valid.

C. Enforcement of Shareholder Voting Agreements

   Shareholder agreements can be enforced in two ways:

   1. Specific Enforcement
      Most courts will specifically enforce a shareholder agreement; or

   2. By Proxy
      Courts are even more likely to enforce an arrangement that gives a third party an irrevocable proxy to vote a shareholder's interest.

D. Voting Trusts

   A voting trust transfers legal title of a shareholder's stock to a voting trustee for a specified period. The trustee is granted voting rights, and the shareholders, as "beneficial owners," retain all other stock rights.

   1. Statutes
      Most states have statutes that validate voting trusts meeting certain requirements, such as the maximum length and disclo-

sure. A violation of a statutory requirement may invalidate the voting trust, depending on the seriousness of the violation.

2. Voting Powers of Trustees
Most statutes grant the trustees power to vote on any matter. Courts tend to read the voting power narrowly for proposals that may benefit the trustees or be unfair to the beneficial owners.

E. Classified Stock

Corporations are permitted to issue two or more classes of stock, each of which elects a number of directors. Classified stock is used to insure that minority shareholders will be represented on the board.

F. Agreements Limiting the Board's Discretion

Shareholders often make agreements that attempt to control matters that are determined by the board such as dividends, compensation, and managerial positions.

1. Interference with the Board
Shareholder agreements may be declared invalid if they interfere with the normal statutory provision that a corporation's business is managed by its board.

2. Agreements Generally Upheld
Modern courts generally uphold shareholder agreements that may infringe on the discretion of the board so long as minority shareholders are not injured.

III. RESTRICTIONS ON SHARE TRANSFERS

A. Modern courts tend to enforce agreements that reasonably restrict share transfers. The prevailing test is whether the restraint is sufficiently needed to justify overriding the general policy against restraints on alienation.

B. Common Types of Restrictions

1. First Refusal
   A first refusal prohibits sale of stock to a third party unless the stock is first offered to the corporation on the terms offered to the third party.

2. First Option
   First options prohibit the sale of stock unless the stock is first offered to the corporation at a predetermined price.

3. Consent Restraint
   Consent restraints prohibit the sale of stock without permission from the board of directors or shareholders. In general, consent restraints are not valid in the absence of a statute or authoritative precedent to the contrary.

C. More Stringent Restrictions

Other types of restrictions grant the corporation an option to purchase shares after the occurrence of a contingency even if the shareholder wants to retain the shares.

1. Repurchase Option
   A repurchase option allows a corporation to repurchase stock it has given an employee after the employee is terminated. Repurchase options are generally enforced by courts even when the option price is low in relation to the value of the stock.

2. Option to Redeem
   An option to redeem allows a corporation to cancel its stock in exchange for payment at a designated price.

3. Buy-Sell Agreement
   Under a buy-sell agreement a corporation must purchase a stockholder's shares after death or retirement at a predetermined price.

D. Valuation

In the absence of a market, different means may be employed to determine the value of closely held corporate stock.

1. Book Value
   Book value is equal to a corporation's assets minus its liabilities. Book value may not reflect a stock's real value because it does not take into account a corporation's present goodwill, but courts tend to enforce provisions based on book value even if there is a large disparity between book value and real value.

2. Mutual Agreement
   The parties may agree on a set price for stock that is periodically updated to reflect market value.

3. Appraisal
   The parties may agree to have the price determined by a third party at the time the option is exercised.

4. Capitalized Earnings
   The capitalized earnings method considers the impact of the transferor's withdrawal on future earnings in addition to present stock value.

E. Notice

Under the Uniform Commercial Code, restrictions on the transfer of stock must be conspicuously noted on the certificate so that a reasonable person would notice the restriction.

IV. INTRACORPORATE DISPUTES AND DEADLOCKS

Courts address disputes within close corporations when oppressive actions are taken against minority shareholders or the dispute causes the corporation to be "deadlocked," or paralyzed.

A. Dissolution

One option in intracorporate disputes is for the complaining party to seek to dissolve the corporation.

1. Voluntary Dissolution
All states have statutes that authorize a specific percentage of shareholders to voluntarily dissolve a corporation.

2. Involuntary Dissolution
A minority of shareholders may dissolve a corporation against the will of the majority under applicable statutes, which are enforced at the discretion of the court.

a. Shareholder Oppression
If majority shareholders take actions for their personal benefit that result in minority shareholders suffering a disproportionate loss, the minority may dissolve the corporation. Usually courts will require more than a single "oppressive" act.

b. Shareholder Deadlock
In case of a deadlock, the complaining minority generally must show that dissolution would be beneficial to the corporation's stockholders and not against the public interest. Courts are reluctant to dissolve profitable corporations.

B. Receivers and Provisional Directors

Courts have long had the power to designate a receiver for a corporation in distress. Some statutes allow for an appointment of a provisional director, or "custodian," under a less stringent set of standards.

C. Arbitration

Parties may agree in advance that disputes will be submitted to an arbitrator. Most modern courts find arbitration agreements to be binding.

CASE CLIPS

Donahue v. Rodd Electrotype Co. (1975) CE
Facts: A minority shareholder (P) in a close corporation claimed the board of directors breached their fiduciary duty to her by refusing to purchase her stock at the price paid to another shareholder.
Issue: When purchasing the stock of one shareholder, must a close corporation afford all shareholders the opportunity to sell their stock at the same price?
Rule: The strict fiduciary duty of majority shareholders in a close corporation requires that equal opportunity be provided to all in the purchase of shareholders' stock by the corporation.

Abercrombie v. Davies (1957) CE, CCM
Facts: Shareholders agreed to delegate their voting powers to agents to form a voting block. The stock was placed in an escrow account, although shareholders retained title of their shares.
Issue: Does a pooling agreement among shareholders that does not pass title to voting agents constitute a voting trust?
Rule: The existence of a voting trust does not require that legal title pass from shareholders to voting agents.

Lehrman v. Cohen (1966) CE, CCM, Ha, SSB
Facts: Shareholders amended their corporation's certificate of incorporation to create one share of a new class of stock that entitled the owner to elect one director but did not grant dividend or liquidation rights except repayment at par value.
Issue: Does the issuance of a class of stock with voting rights but no dividend or liquidation rights separate voting rights of owners of the common stock from other attributes of ownership?
Rule: The creation of a new class of stock strictly for voting purposes does not separate the voting rights of the common stock shareholders, each of whom retains complete control over the voting of his stock.

McQuade v. Stoneham (1934) CE, CCM, Ha, JB

Facts: An agreement among corporate directors bound each to use their best efforts to allow the others to remain in their positions as officers. P sought specific performance of the contract after he failed to be reelected as treasurer without support from two parties to the agreement.

Issue: Is a contract that precludes directors from supporting a change of corporate officers, at risk of legal liability, valid?

Rule: A contract that precludes directors from changing corporate officers, at risk of legal liability, is not valid, except by consent of the contracting parties.

Clark v. Dodge (1936) CE, CCM

Facts: A shareholder (P) agreed to share information with his corporation in exchange for a promise that the other shareholder would insure that P continue as director.

Issue: May shareholders make a binding contract to be elected as directors and to remain in the position into the future?

Rule: If two directors are the sole shareholders in a corporation, there is no objection to enforcing an agreement among them to vote for certain people as directors.

Galler v. Galler (1964) CE, Ha, JB, SSB

Facts: P sought to enforce a shareholder agreement in a close corporation that provided for the election of certain individuals to the board of directors and the distribution of mandatory dividends. Both agreements slightly deviated from the standards of the Illinois Business Corporation Act.

Issue: May shareholder agreements that slightly deviate from statutory prescriptions for public corporations be valid in close corporations?

Rule: Shareholder agreements in close corporations may slightly deviate from corporate norms so long as there is no detriment to minority stockholders, creditors, or the public.

Benintendi v. Kenton Hotel (1945) CE, V

Facts: The only two shareholders in corporation adopted bylaws that provided no action be taken by shareholders or directors except by

unanimous vote and that no bylaws be amended except by unanimous vote.
Issue 1: Is a bylaw valid that requires a unanimous vote before shareholders or directors act?
Rule 1: The requirement of unanimity for shareholders or directors to act is a contravention of state corporation law and not valid.
Issue 2: Is a bylaw valid that requires a unanimous vote of shareholders to amend bylaws?
Rule 2: Since the amending of bylaws is of no concern to the state, a bylaw requiring a unanimous vote of shareholders for amendments is valid.

Gearing v. Kelly (1962) CE, Ha
Facts: To prevent a quorum, Meacham did not attend a meeting of the board of directors. P, who supported Meacham's action, claimed the election of new directors at the board meeting should be nullified for lack of a quorum.
Issue: May the elections of directors be overturned for lack of a quorum at the request of a shareholder who actively encouraged a director to not attend the meeting?
Rule: A shareholder may not attack actions of a board of directors that were marred through the actions of a director whom she actively encouraged.

Allen v. Biltmore Tissue Corp. (1957) CE, CCM
Facts: The bylaws of a close corporation (D) provided that, after the death of a shareholder, it would have the option to purchase his stock at the price originally paid.
Issue: Does a provision according a close corporation a first option to purchase the stock of a deceased shareholder at the price originally paid constitute an unreasonable restraint?
Rule: A first purchase option is not an unreasonable restraint on corporation's stock, even if there is a disparity between the option price and the current value of the stock, because it is not an effective prohibition against transfer of the stock itself.

Wilkes v. Springfield Nursing Home, Inc. (1976)
CE, CCM, He, SSB

Facts: A shareholder and director (P) in a close corporation claimed the other directors and shareholders breached a fiduciary duty by eliminating his position as director and officer without legitimate purpose.

Issue: Must majority shareholders in a close corporation show a legitimate purpose for failing to reelect an officer and director?

Rule: Majority shareholders may be found liable for breaching a fiduciary duty to minority shareholders if they can not show a legitimate purpose for failing to reelect a director and officer.

Smith v. Atlantic Properties, Inc. (1981) CE, SSB

Facts: The bylaws of a close corporation with four shareholders contained a provision requiring approval by the shareholders of 80 percent of capital stock for corporate decisions, effectively granting each shareholder veto power over any act. One shareholder used the veto power to refuse distribution of dividends that caused the corporation to suffer loses from penalty taxes.

Issue: May the use of a veto power by a minority shareholder breach the fiduciary duty owed to other shareholders?

Rule: The unreasonable use of veto power by a minority in a close corporation that causes the corporation to incur serious and unjustifiable risks may breach the fiduciary duty owed to other stockholders.

Wollman v. Littman (1970) CE

Facts: Two shareholders each held half of a corporation's stock, were equally represented on its board, and performed independent business functions. One (P) sought to dissolve the corporation, claiming disagreements made effective management impossible. If dissolution were to occur, P appeared to be the only interested party with the financial resources to purchase the corporation's inventory from its receiver, in effect, accomplishing his goal of squeezing D out of the corporation.

Issue: Do irreconcilable differences among evenly divided directors mandate dissolution of a corporation?

Rule: Irreconcilable differences among evenly divided directors of a corporation do not mandate dissolution if the functions of the two disputing interests are distinct or would create a result inequitable to one of the parties.

Ringling Bros.-Barnum & Bailey Combined Shows v. Ringling (1947) CE, CCM, Ha, JB, SSB, V
Facts: Two shareholders entered an agreement to act jointly in the election of corporate directors. P sought to enforce the agreement after the other shareholder refused to agree on a vote for directors or follow the instructions of the arbitrator as mandated in the agreement.
Issue: Are shareholders bound to adhere to agreements with other shareholders to act jointly in corporate elections?
Rule: A group cf shareholders may contract to vote in the future as they determine and may be held liable for failing to adhere to such agreements.

Application of Vogel (1965) CE, JB
Facts: Two 50 percent shareholders, who were the only directors of a corporation, entered an agreement to settle disputes through arbitration. After a subsequent disagreement on extending the lease for property needed for the business, one brought suit to bring the question to arbitration.
Issue: May an agreement between directors to bring disputes to arbitration be binding?
Rule: Unlike cases involving the exercise of business judgement in the management of everyday corporate affairs, agreements to submit disputes to arbitration are binding in cases involving the continued existence of the corporation.

Rafe v. Hindin (1968) CCM
Facts: Two 50 percent shareholders agreed that they would not transfer their stock without the consent of the other shareholder.
Issue: Is an agreement between two 50 percent shareholders that requires the consent of the other shareholder to transfer stock enforceable?
Rule: An agreement arbitrarily restricting the transfer of stock amounts to a destruction of personal property and will not be enforced.

E.K. Buck Retail Stores v. Harkert (1954) CCM
Facts: P agreed to cancel a debt owed to him by D and pay over fifty thousand dollars in cash into a corporation controlled by D in an agreement that made him a 40 percent shareholder in the corporation. As part of the transaction, it was agreed that the number of directors would be reduced from five to four and be maintained at that level.
Issue: Is an agreement by shareholders in a close corporation that limits the number of directors valid?
Rule: Stockholders' control agreements are valid if they are based on sufficient consideration between contracting shareholders and do not contemplate any wrong against creditors or other stockholders.

Clarke Memorial College v. Monaghan Land Co. (1969) CCM
Facts: The formation of a voting trust stated that the trustees would have the power to vote "all shares," at "all meetings," and in "all proceedings." Beneficial owners brought suit after the trustees voted their shares in favor of a resolution authorizing the sale of substantially all of the corporation's assets.
Issue: Do trustees of a voting trust have the right to vote on a resolution authorizing the sale of substantially all of a corporation's assets?
Rule: Since sale of all of a corporation's assets does not entail dissolution as a matter of law, trustees of a voting trust may vote to sell all of a corporation's assets if such a sale is within their powers as defined by the agreement establishing the trust.

Wilson v. McClenny (1964) CCM
Facts: P left his position as president of a company after contracting with promoters to become president of the corporation they sought to form. The corporate bylaws provided that officers were to hold office for one year.
Issue: Is a preincorporation agreement binding as a stockholders agreement after incorporation?
Rule: The state business corporation act, that places limits on the power of the board according to the bylaws and shareholder agreements, permits a pre-incorporation agreement to be binding on a corporation.

Zidell v. Zidell, Inc. (1977) CCM, JB
Facts: A shareholder brought suit to compel another shareholder to transfer to the corporation at cost the shares he had purchased from a third shareholder.
Issue: Must a shareholder, before selling stock, afford a corporation an opportunity to purchase the stock?
Rule: Absent an established corporate policy or express agreement, there is no special corporate interest in the opportunity to purchase its own shares.

Kennerson v. Burbank Amusement Co. (1953) CCM, SSB
Facts: A general manager (P) claimed breach of an employment contract by his corporation. The contract granted P power over all aspects of the corporation's operating and business policies.
Issue: Is a contract valid that grants an employee power to govern the control and management of a corporation?
Rule: Any contract delegating nearly all corporate powers to an agent is void because a board of directors may not pass on its authority to govern the corporation.

Pioneer Specialties, Inc. v. Nelson (1960) CCM
Facts: The bylaws of a corporation provided that the president was to be elected for one year. P was elected president and entered an employment contact for two years. After termination, he sought damages for a breach of his employment contract for the remainder of the two year period.
Issue: May a corporate president receive compensation for the full term of his employment contract after termination if the corporation's bylaws limit the president's period of election to a lesser period?
Rule: A president may not receive compensation for the full term of an employment contract if the period of his election is limited to a term less than the contract's in the corporation's bylaws.

Giuricich v. Emtrol Corp. (1982) CCM
Facts: A 50 percent shareholder brought suit for the appointment of a custodian to break a deadlock within a close corporation that had indefinitely prevented the election of successor directors.

Issue: May a court appoint a custodian when a shareholder deadlock has prevented the election of successor directors?

Rule: Unlike a director deadlock situation, a shareholder deadlock situation does not require a showing of irreparable injury to the corporation and a court may appoint an impartial custodian to resolve a deadlock that permits control of a corporation to remain indefinitely in the hands of a self-perpetuating board of directors.

Strong v. Fromm Laboratories, Inc. (1956) CCM

Facts: A shareholder sought to dissolve a corporation against the will of the other shareholders because of the inability of the directors to fill a vacancy on the board. The corporation's bylaws provided that the board was to conduct no business until any vacancy within the board was filled.

Issue: Must a corporation be involuntarily dissolved at the request of a shareholder when a board of directors is deadlocked so that it has no legal authority to manage the business of the corporation?

Rule: A corporation may be dissolved when a board of directors lacks legal authority to act because of a deadlock among the directors if the state statute for dissolution does not require a showing that liquidation would be beneficial to the shareholders or that irreparable damage would be done to the corporation.

Nelkin v. H.J.R. Realty Corp. (1969) CCM

Facts: Shareholders in a corporation organized to manage a building entered an agreement that allowed them to occupy space in the building at far below its rental value. Two shareholders (P) who no longer benefitted from the low rents sought to dissolve the corporation.

Issue: May a corporation be judicially dissolved when enforcement of a shareholder's agreement benefits the majority shareholders more than the minority?

Rule: A corporation may not be judicially dissolved when majority shareholders are acting in compliance with a shareholder's agreement even if the majority benefits more from the agreement than the minority.

Meiselman v. Meiselman (1983) CCM
Facts: A 30 percent shareholder (P) was fired as an employee after bringing suit against a 70 percent shareholder over a corporate action that excluded P from meaningful participation in the corporation's management. P sought to dissolve the corporation or a "buy-out" of his interests at fair value.
Issue: May a minority shareholder in a close corporation dissolve a corporation or obtain alternative relief after being ousted from employment with the corporation?
Rule: A court may determine that a shareholder in a close corporation is entitled to some form of equitable relief, dissolution of the corporation or otherwise, if the complaining shareholder's reasonable expectations based on the history of the participants involvement have been frustrated for reasons beyond his control. Other forms of relief available include canceling corporate bylaws or resolutions, directing or prohibiting acts of the corporation, and providing for purchase of the complaining shareholder's stock at fair value.

Zion v. Kurtz (1980) Ha, He
Facts: P asserted an action to enforce a shareholder's agreement that barred his corporation from undertaking any business or activities without his consent as a minority shareholder.
Issue: Is a shareholder agreement enforceable that provides that no business or activities of a corporation shall be undertaken without the consent of a minority shareholder?
Rule: A shareholder's agreement that requires no business or activities be undertaken without the consent of a minority shareholder is enforceable between the original shareholders.

Salgo v. Matthews (1974) Ha
Facts: An election inspector during a proxy contest (D) refused to accept votes cast by a party with authorization from a shareholder's court appointed receiver.
Issue: May the receiver of a shareholder authorize a party to take part in a proxy contest on behalf of the shareholder?
Rule: The receiver of a shareholder may authorize another to take part in a proxy contest on behalf of the shareholder.

Close Corporations

Humphrys v. Winous Co. (1956) Ha
Facts: A shareholder asserted an action to enjoin the division of corporate directors into three classes on the grounds that it would divest minority shareholders of control over the corporation.
Issue: Do restrictions on cumulative voting rights ensure representation of minority shareholders on the board of directors?
Rule: The state statute guarantees the right of minority shareholders to vote cumulatively, but does not ensure that there will minority representation on the board.

Brown v. McLanahan (1945) Ha
Facts: A shareholder (P) sought to rescind a corporate amendment, approved by the board of directors, that vested voting rights in debenture holders, claiming that it would decrease the voting power of the shareholders.
Issue: May a board of directors amend a corporate charter in a way that decreases the voting power of the shareholders?
Rule: A board of directors violates its fiduciary duty to shareholders by taking action that impairs the voting power of the shareholders.

Ling and Co. v. Trinity Sav. and Loan Ass'n (1972) Ha
Facts: P sought to foreclose on a certificate for a number of shares pledged to secure a loan, and D objected that stock could not be transferred because conditions restricting its transfer were unfulfilled.
Issue: May a corporation impose conditions that restrict the transferability of its stock?
Rule: A corporation may impose restrictions on the disposition of its stock if the restrictions do not unreasonably restrain transferability and are expressly set forth in the articles of incorporation and referred to on each certificate.

Mickshaw v. Coca Cola Bottling Co. (1950) Ha
Facts: A corporate director made an oral agreement to increase the pay of an employee (P) consistent with a newspaper announcement. One of two other directors was aware of the proposal and did not object to it.
Issue: Is a corporation bound to an oral agreement made by a director?

Rule: A corporation is bound to an agreement made by a director if a majority of the board was aware of the agreement and did not object to it.

Hurley v. Ornsteen (1942) Ha
Facts: Two of three directors of a corporation agreed to forgive an individual debt owed to the corporation. A trustee in bankruptcy sought to rescind their agreement.
Issue: Do directors have authority to forgive a debt owed to their corporation?
Rule: Directors, acting independently of the entire board, have no authority to bind a corporation to agreements outside of a narrow circle of functions pertaining to their offices unless the corporation has repeatedly acquiesced and taken responsibility for similar acts.

Black v. Harrison Home Co. (1909) Ha
Facts: After the president of a corporation (D) entered into a contract without authorization from the secretary as required under corporate bylaws, the corporation claimed not to be bound by the agreement.
Issue: May a president bind a corporation to a contract without authorization from the bylaws or a resolution of the board of directors?
Rule: A president may not bind a corporation to a contract without authorization of the bylaws or a resolution of the board of directors.

In re Drive-In Development Corp. (1966) Ha
Facts: Corporate officers executed a guaranty of payment to another corporation and the secretary provided a certified copy of the authorizing resolution of the board of directors. The corporation claimed not to be bound by the guaranty because the resolution was not recorded in the corporate minutes.
Issue: Does a certified copy of a resolution of a board of directors bind a corporation to an obligation?
Rule: A certified copy of a resolution of a board of directors purporting to grant authority creates a binding obligation on the corporation, whether or not the resolution is in fact adopted.

In re Radom & Neidorff, Inc. (1954) Ha, JB

Facts: A 50 percent shareholder (P) sought the dissolution of a successful corporation under state law because of a dislike and distrust of the other 50 percent shareholder.

Issue: May a 50 percent shareholder dissolve a corporation because of difficulties in operating with the other 50 percent shareholder?

Rule: A corporation may not be dissolved at the request of a 50 percent shareholder unless the court believes that competing interests are so discordant as to prevent efficient management.

Davis v. Sheerin (1988) Ha

Facts: A majority stockholder (D) claimed that a forced buy-out of a minority shareholder's stock was an inappropriate remedy after he was found guilty of attempting to deprive the other shareholder of his stock.

Issue: May a majority shareholder found guilty of oppressive conduct towards a minority shareholder be forced to buy out the minority stock at a fair price?

Rule: A buy-out is an appropriate form of relief after oppressive conduct towards a minority shareholder if less harsh measures are inadequate to protect the rights of the parties.

Kruger v. Gerth (1965) Ha

Facts: Minority shareholders brought an action to dissolve a close corporation, claiming that they received less than a fair return because of bonuses received by a director.

Issue: May minority shareholders dissolve a close corporation because bonuses to directors reduce their return beyond an acceptable level?

Rule: Minority shareholders may not dissolve a close corporation because of a belief that corporate bonuses reduce their return to an unacceptable level.

Kinser v. Coffee [sic] (1982) He

Facts: Claiming oppressive conduct by other shareholders because they were not reelected as directors, minority shareholders (P) sought to dissolve their corporation.

Issue: Does failure to reelect directors constitute oppressive conduct mandating the dissolution of a corporation?

Rule: A single act in breach of a fiduciary duty does not constitute oppressive conduct mandating the dissolution of a corporation unless there has been a disproportionate loss to the minority or those in control can no longer be trusted to manage the corporation fairly in the interests of the shareholders.

Matter of Cristo Bros., Inc. (1985) He

Facts: P brought a successful suit to dissolve a corporation because of irreconcilable differences between 50 percent shareholders who were the only directors of a corporation. The other shareholder (D) claimed the right to buy-out the former's shares.
Issue: May one shareholder buy-out the other in dissolution proceedings?
Rule: Under state law, a shareholder holding more than 20 percent of the stock of a corporation has the right to buy-out the other shares during dissolution proceedings.

Arditi v. Dubitzky (1965) JB

Facts: One of two 50 percent shareholders in a corporation alleged that the other shareholder should be liable for his breach of a joint venture agreement because the corporation was formed only as a means of carrying out the joint venture.
Issue: Are shareholders in a close corporation who adopt the corporate form only as a means of carrying out a joint venture held to obligations of the joint venture?
Rule: If the only intention behind the formation of a corporation is to carry out a joint venture, the parties will be bound to the obligations of the joint venture agreement.

Blount v. Taft (1978) JB

Facts: Minority shareholders sought to enforce an agreement that created an executive committee in charge of employment, claiming that it was a shareholders' agreement permitted under state law.
Issue: Are shareholder agreements enforced like any other contract so as to give effect to the intent of the parties?
Rule: Since shareholder agreements are consensual arrangements, they are enforced according to the intent of the parties like any other

contract, unless enforcement would be inequitable or against public policy.

B. & H. Warehouse, Inc. v. Atlas Van Lines (1974) JB

Facts: Minority shareholders alleged that a corporation had converted their shares by requiring that stock be offered to the corporation at book value before it could be sold.
Issue: May a restriction be imposed on stockholders that requires offering shares to the corporation at book value before selling?
Rule: A requirement that shareholders offer their shares to the corporation at book value before selling may not be imposed on shareholders because it is a restriction broader than necessary to effectuate a valid corporate purpose.

Yeng Sue Chow v. Levi Strauss Co. (1975) JB

Facts: A corporate employee stock purchase plan allowed the corporation to repurchase stock at book value after death or termination of an employee. A minority shareholder, who acquired her shares through the will of an employee, sought rescission of the repurchase option.
Issue: May a corporate employee stock purchase plan grant a corporation an option to repurchase stock at book value?
Rule: Since determination of benefits is a contractual matter, parties may agree to an employee stock purchase plan that allows the corporation an option to repurchase the stock according to a predetermined scheme.

Weil v. Beresth (1966) JB

Facts: Shareholders entered an agreement to vote for each other as directors, amend the bylaws to reduce the number of directors needed for a quorum, and not to further amend the bylaws in regard to their agreement.
Issue: Are shareholder agreements over future voting for directors and limitations on bylaw amendments binding?
Rule: Shareholders can limit the exercise of their powers by agreement, subject to statutory restrictions that may limit the enforceable duration of the agreement.

Tankersley v. Albright (1975) JB
Facts: Beneficiaries of a voting trust claimed that the trustees of a voting trust had breached their fiduciary duty by engaging in self-dealing through voting the trust's shares in favor of amendments to the corporation's bylaws.
Issue: Are the trustees of a voting trust liable to beneficiaries for self-dealing and lack of good faith?
Rule: Trustees in charge of a voting trust must exercise good faith in their capacity or will be liable to the beneficiaries.

Selig v. Wexler (1969) JB
Facts: A voting trust agreement provided for the election of two directors who were to be impartial between the 50 percent shareholders. One of the shareholders (P) claimed that subsequent events proved that the independent directors were not in fact impartial, a sufficient cause to rescind the agreement.
Issue: May a voting trust be terminated if its purpose is frustrated?
Rule: A voting trust may be terminated when its purposes become frustrated and can no longer be carried out as originally envisioned.

In re Jamison Steel Corp. (1958) JB
Facts: Claiming that their corporation could not be managed efficiently because of disagreements within an evenly divided board of directors, two directors sought for the court to appoint a provisional director.
Issue: May a director be appointed by the court to end an equal division within a board of directors?
Rule: Under state law, the court has the power to appoint a provisional director to break a deadlock within a board of directors if there is a danger that the corporation's business will be impaired.

In re Security Finance Co. (1957) JB
Facts: President and 50 percent shareholder (P) managed the operations of a prosperous corporation, and two 25 percent shareholders (D) were in charge of its finances. The articles of incorporation restricted the ability of shareholders to sell their stock without the consent of other shareholders. After attempting to purchase the

140 Close Corporations

stock of Ds or sell them his interest, P sought to dissolve the corporation.
Issue: Does a 50 percent shareholder have the right to dissolve a prosperous corporation?
Rule: A 50 percent shareholder may dissolve a prosperous corporation if his decision is made in good faith.

Triggs v. Triggs (1978) SSB
Facts: A shareholder and director (P) sought to enforce an option to purchase stock after the death of another shareholder and director. The stock option was part of a contract that included an agreement, of questionable legality, to pool votes.
Issue: Is a stock option provision that is part of a contract with a vote pooling agreement of questionable legality enforceable?
Rule: A stock option that is part of a contract with terms that may illegally restrict the freedom of the board remains valid so long as the contract did not result in interference with the operation of the board.

Jones v. Harris (1964) SSB
Facts: The contract of a manager and minority shareholder (P) stated that upon termination he would sell back his corporate shares at book value plus 20 per cent of the depreciation costs. P claimed he should be allowed to sell his shares based on the current market value because the book value was unfairly low.
Issue: May a contractual method that specifies selling stock back to other shareholders according to book value be rescinded as inequitable?
Rule: If a contract provides a method for determining the price that stock will be sold to other shareholders, that method is binding on the parties so long as it was fair when the contract was made.

Vogel v. Melish (1964) SSB, He
Facts: Two shareholders in a close corporation entered an agreement that provided neither would transfer their shares without giving the other the opportunity to obtain them. A shareholder (P) sought to enforce the agreement after the other's death.
Issue: May an agreement to restrict the transfer of stock be enforced after the death of one of the parties if the agreement does not enumerate the rights of the parties in the event of death?

Rule: An agreement to restrict the transfer of stock may not be enforced after the death of one of the parties, without specific language to the contrary, if the entire contract evinces an intention to reach a result based on a personal relationship.

Matter of Kemp & Beatley, Inc. (1984) SSB, CE, He
Facts: Longtime employees (P) acquired a 20 per cent interest in a close corporation (D) with the expectation of receiving a portion of the company's earnings as had been done in the past. After a change of policy eliminated the distribution of earnings to the shareholders, P claimed to have been a victim of oppressive conduct and sought to dissolve the corporation.
Issue: May a corporation be involuntarily dissolved when its directors have been guilty of oppressive actions towards the complaining shareholders?
Rule: Oppressive conduct may require dissolving a corporation if liquidation is the only feasible means to protect the complaining shareholder's expectation of a fair return on his investment, subject to the right of another shareholder to purchase stock at a fair price.

Aron v. Gillman (1955) V
Facts: Two shareholders in a close corporation agreed that when they died their shares would be sold back to the corporation at book value. After the death of the first shareholder, the other (P) claimed the book value was the amount taken literally from the accounting records minus unincluded tax adjustments.
Issue: Is the book value of shares determined literally from the values found in the accounting records?
Rule: Since actual accounting records are to be relied upon only to the extent that they are correct and complete, inventory amounts incorrectly recorded are to be disregarded and taxes must be apportioned monthly in determining the book value of stock.

Jackson v. Nicolai-Neppach Co. (1959) V
Facts: A shareholder brought suit to dissolve a solvent corporation after she and the two other shareholders and directors had been deadlocked for several years on the number of directors needed in the

corporation and proper salary for one shareholder who served as operating manager.

Issue: Do shareholders have an absolute right to dissolve deadlocked close corporations?

Rule: There is no absolute shareholder right to dissolve a deadlocked corporation, but under the state corporation act, deadlocked corporations may be dissolved if the complaining shareholder can establish equitable grounds for its dissolution.

Chapter 6

FINANCIAL MATTERS AND DISTRIBUTIONS

I. THE BALANCE SHEET AND THE INCOME STATEMENT

A. The Balance Sheet Defined

The balance sheet is a "snapshot" of the financial status of a corporation as it stands on a particular day, usually the final day of an accounting period. The current balance sheet is usually displayed alongside the previous term's balance sheet for comparison purposes. The balance sheet is divided into two sides: the left (debit) side shows assets and the right (credit) side shows liabilities and owners' equity. The two sides must always be in balance; that is, assets minus liabilities must equal owners' equity.

B. Assets

Listed under the assets entry are all the goods and property owned by a business as well as claims against others yet to be collected.

1. Current Assets
Also called working assets, current assets include cash and other assets that can reasonably expected to be converted into cash within a year of the date of the balance sheet. The entries under current assets are:

a. Cash
Petty cash and funds on deposit in the bank.

b. Marketable Securities
Investments of excess cash, usually in readily marketable securities such as commercial paper and government securities.

c. Accounts Receivable
The amount not yet collected from customers for goods shipped prior to payment, minus a percentage to account for bad debts.

d. Inventories
Includes raw materials, partially finished goods, and finished goods. Inventory is valued at cost or at market value, whichever is lower.

   i. Operating profits are determined by subtracting from revenues the cost of goods sold plus selling and administrative costs.

   ii. Cost of goods sold is determined by adding the amount of purchases during the year to the opening inventory and then subtracting the closing inventory, which is the figure under the "Inventory" entry on the balance sheet.

   iii. Hence, the lower the (closing) inventory, the lower the profit.

e. Prepaid Expenses
Payments or purchases made in advance in exchange for which the company has not yet received benefits or goods.

2. Fixed Assets
Assets intended for use in the company's business, rather than for sale. Fixed assets commonly include land, buildings, machinery, equipment, and vehicles.

3. Accumulated Depreciation
A theoretical calculation of the decline in the value of assets over time due to wear and tear or technological obsolescence, arrived at by spreading the cost of acquiring an asset over its expected useful life. The accumulated depreciation charge, representing the depreciation of all fixed assets other than land, is an expense that is deducted from the fixed assets figure, thus, reducing profits.

4. Deferred Charges
Expenditures incurred for which the benefit will be reaped over future years. These include such items as the introduction of a new product or the moving of a manufacturing plant to a new location. Deferred charges are gradually written off over several years, rather than being fully charged off in the year payment is made.

5. Intangibles
Assets that have no physical existence, but still have worth to the company (e.g., goodwill).

C. Liabilities

Liabilities represent the debts of the business.

1. Current Liabilities
Current liabilities include all debts that fall due within the coming year. Payments are made on current liabilities from current assets.

   a. Accounts Payable
   The amounts owed by a company to its regular business creditors.

   b. Notes Payable
   Loans by banks and other lenders that are evidenced by promissory notes of a term of up to one year.

   c. Accrued Expenses Payable
   The accumulated obligations of the company that have not yet matured (e.g., employee wages, interest on loans, rent, or pensions) and remain unpaid as of the date of the balance sheet.

   d. Federal Income Tax Payable
   Simply, an additional accrued expense that is listed separately due to accounting conventions.

2. Long-Term Liabilities
Long-term liabilities represent all debts falling due after one year from the date of the report.

   a. Deferred Income Taxes
   A charge representing what taxes would be without certain accelerated write-offs that the government allows businesses for certain investments and expenses.

   b. Debentures
   A note issued by the borrower as evidence of a loan that calls for payment of the principal at some set date in the future and annual interest payments at a specified rate until the principal becomes due and secured by the general credit of the issuing business.

   c. First Mortgage Bonds
   A note similar to a debenture, but secured against the assets of the issuing business.

D. Owners' Equity

Also called stockholders' equity when appearing on corporate (as opposed to partnership or sole proprietorship) balance sheets, owners' equity represents the total ownership interest that stockholders have in the corporation.

1. Capital Stock
Also called authorized capital, stated capital, or paid-in capital, capital stock is the product of the par value of shares issued to shareholders and the number of authorized and outstanding shares. This entry is usually broken down according to the classes of preferred and common stock issued.

2. Capital Surplus
Also called capital in excess of par value stock or paid-in surplus, capital surplus is the amount paid in by shareholders for their shares in excess of par value.

3. Earned Surplus
   Also called accumulated retained earnings, earned surplus is the surplus equal to a corporation's aggregate profits, income, gains and losses from the date of its incorporation or the date on which a deficit was eliminated, minus any dividends or other distributions.

E. What the Balance Sheet Shows

The balance sheet is an indicator of the overall worth and economic health of a corporation. Data listed in the balance sheet are used by accountants to compute the following figures:

1. Working Capital
   The difference between current assets and current liabilities, sufficient working capital is necessary for a company to expand its volume and explore new ventures.

2. Current Ratio
   An index of the sufficiency of a corporation's working capital, the current ratio is calculated by dividing current assets by current liabilities. Accountants generally take a current ratio of at least 2:1 (i.e., that current assets are at least twice as large as current liabilities) as a sign of financial health.

3. Liquidity Ratio
   The ratio of "quick assets" (i.e., current assets minus inventory) to current liabilities, the liquidity ratio is an indicator of a corporation's ability to cover a sudden financial emergency.

4. Inventory Turnover
   A measure of the sufficiency and balance of a corporation's inventory, inventory turnover is calculated by dividing sales by inventory.

5. Inventory as a Percentage of Current Assets
   Another measure of the sufficiency and balance of a corporation's inventory, inventory as a percentage of current assets for

a given corporation is usually compared with the same figures for other companies within the same industry.

6. Net Asset Value
Also called net book value, the net asset value of a corporation's equity or debt securities represents the amount of corporate assets backing the security. Hence, accountants speak of net asset value per bond (omitting intangible assets from the calculation), net asset value per preferred stock share (omitting intangible assets, current liabilities, and long-term liabilities), and net asset value per share of common stock. Net asset value is not always a reliable indicator of the market value of a corporate security, since many profitable companies show a low net asset value but enjoy substantial earnings.

7. Capitalization Ratio
The capitalization ratio represents the proportion of each kind of security issued by a corporation and is calculated by dividing the face value of the security in question by the total value of bonds, capital stock, capital surplus, and earned surplus. An excessively high ratio of debt to equity, as evidenced by the capitalization ratio, can reduce the attractiveness of the preferred and common stock.

F. The Income Statement Defined

Also called the profit-and-loss statement or the statement of the results of operations, the income statement shows how profitable a company is. Though income statements vary in detail, they all end with the "bottom line," which shows how much the company earned or lost during the period of the statement. While a balance sheet is a "snapshot" of a corporation's financial situation at a given time, the income statement shows how a corporation has developed over time. Like the balance sheet, however, an income statement for the current term will be displayed alongside the statement for the previous term for comparison purposes. The following entries appear on an income statement.

1. Net Sales
   The most important source of revenue.

2. Cost of Goods Sold
   Includes the cost of materials and labor directly attributable to the manufacture of the product.

3. Depreciation
   The means by which the costs associated with the decline in the value of fixed assets are allocated.

4. Amortization
   The means by which the costs associated with the decline in the useful value of intangible assets (e.g., patents, licenses) are allocated.

5. Selling and Administrative Expenses (e.g., advertising costs, sales commissions)

6. Operating Profit
   Operating profit is the difference between net sales and the aggregate of cost of goods sold, depreciation, amortization, and selling and administrative expenses.

7. Other Income
   Income composed of dividends and interest on money invested in bank accounts and securities.

8. Total Income
   Total income is the sum of operating profit and other income.

9. Interest Expense
   Interest representing the cost of capital borrowed from bondholders.

10. Federal Income Tax

11. Net Profit
Net profit is the "bottom line" of an income statement, calculated by subtracting from total income the aggregate of interest expense and federal income tax.

G. What the Income Statement Shows

Accountants derive the following figures from the income statement:

1. Operating Margin of Profit
Represents the portion of each dollar of sales remaining as gross profit from operations. The operating margin of profit is calculated by dividing the operating profit by sales. This figure can be compared with figures for previous years to track the profitability of a firm over time.

2. Operating-Cost Ratio
The complement of the operating margin of profit, the operating cost ratio represents the portion of each dollar of sales that went to operations expenses.

3. Net-Profit Ratio
Represents the portion of each dollar of net sales that went to the corporation. The net-profit ratio is calculated by dividing net profit by net sales. This figure can be compared with the net profit ratio for previous years and with that of other companies to determine the financial evolution of the corporation.

II. CORPORATE SECURITIES

A. Securities Defined

Corporate securities are contracts whose terms, including those prescribed in the articles of incorporation, can be modified at the will of the corporation. Investors in a corporation receive an ownership interest in the corporation through the ownership of securities. Ownership interest in a corporation consists of three basic powers or rights:

1. Control over the management of the corporation;

2. Right to income derived from the corporation's operations; and

3. Right to a share of the corporation's assets.

B. Classes of Corporate Securities

Corporate securities are categorized into different classes based on the attendant risk and degree of control.

1. Equity Securities
In connection with securities, equity has come to be synonymous with ownership, and an equity security entitles its holder to the assets and income remaining in a corporation after the principal and interest payments due on any corporate indebtedness have been paid.

   a. Common Stock
   By law, every corporation must have common stock. Common stock carries with it the highest degree of risk, since its holders participate in the income of the corporation through dividends, which may or may not be declared at the broad discretion of the board of directors. Although common stock usually carries with it all the voting power of the corporation, entitling its holders to select or remove directors and approve certain basic corporate transactions, it is last in line for a share of the assets of the corporation in the event of bankruptcy.

   b. Preferred Stock
   A corporation has the choice of whether to issue preferred stock. The ownership rights of holders of preferred stock are superior to those of common shareholders, since the right of preferred shareholders to receive dividends super-

sedes that of common shareholders. The standard dividend preference provision states that no dividends will be paid on the common stock until the preferred shareholders have received their dividends. Other features separating preferred from common stock include:

i. Redeemability
Preferred stock is redeemable if the corporation has the option to repurchase the stock at a stipulated price.

ii. Dividend Preference
While the amount of the dividend paid out to holders of common stock lies within the discretion of the board of directors, the dividend preference to which preferred shareholders are entitled is stated in the articles of incorporation either as a set dollar amount or as a percentage of the par value of the stock.

iii. Cumulative Rights
If a yearly dividend due on cumulative preferred stock is not paid on schedule, it accumulates, and the past dividends in arrears must be paid in addition to current dividends before any dividends are paid out to holders of noncumulative and common stock.

iv. Participation
Preferred stock is deemed participating if its holders are entitled to share in any dividends paid out to common shareholders in addition to the preferred dividend.

v. Liquidation Preference
Holders of preferred shares may be entitled to receive a specified amount of the assets of a bankrupt corporation before any distributions are made to common stockholders.

vi. Convertibility
Preferred stock may be converted to common stock at a specified ratio at the option of the preferred shareholder.

c. Issuance of Shares
Authorized shares are those shares created in the articles of incorporation. These authorized shares are "issued" when they are sold to investors. Issuance of new stock is a power vested in the board of directors. Under the corporation statutes, however, power to authorize stock beyond that initially authorized requires amendment of the articles of incorporation and thus the approval of the shareholders.

   i. Issued and outstanding shares are authorized shares that have been sold to, and are still in the hands of, shareholders.

   ii. Treasury shares are authorized and issued shares that have been repurchased and held by the issuing corporation.

   iii. Authorized but unissued shares are shares that have been authorized by the corporate charter but not yet sold to shareholders.

d. Underwriters
Underwriters are securities dealers who take stock from an issuing corporation and handle its sale to the investing public. The underwriting process is subject to the same stringent regulations under SEC and state laws applicable to the issuing corporation.

2. Derivative Securities
There are additional securities that derive their value from the equity interest in common stock:

a. Warrants
A warrant is a security issued by the corporation, usually bundled with a debt security (e.g., a debenture or bond), that gives the holder the right to purchase the corporation's stock up to a specified future date at a specified price. Warrants

are usually detachable; that is, they can be sold separately from the security with which they were bundled.

  b. Options
  An option is a right to purchase stock up to a specified future date at a specified price.

   i. Call Option
   A call option is a right to purchase stock in the future at a price slightly higher than market price that is procured by an investor who believes that the value of the stock will rise even higher.

   ii. Put Option
   A put option is a right purchased by a shareholder, who believes that the value of the stock could fall dramatically, to sell his shares at a price slightly lower than market value.

3. Debt Securities
Debt securities are given in exchange for long-term loans made to a corporation. The loans contribute to the permanent capital structure of a corporation and represent an ongoing interest in the corporation's future. The holders of debt securities are known as creditors.

  a. Bonds and Debentures

   i. Bonds are debt securities that are secured by a mortgage on corporate assets and have long maturity periods (twenty years or more).

   ii. Debentures are debt securities that are backed by the general credit of the corporation and have shorter maturity periods (10–20 years).

  b. Indentures
  Debt securities are issued pursuant to the terms of a complex contract known as an indenture. The parties to the

indenture are the corporation, the bondholders, and a large bank. The bank, known as the indenture trustee, has a fiduciary duty to protect the interests of the bondholders and oversees compliance by the corporation with the terms of the indenture.

c. Interest on Debt
Unlike dividends on stock, which are paid at the discretion of the board of directors, interest on debt must be paid as scheduled. Failure to pay interest is a default on the loan and may prompt the creditor to initiate bankruptcy proceedings against the corporation.

d. Sinking Fund
An indenture may require the indenture trustee to establish a sinking fund, to which the corporation must make periodic payments to retire the debt in an orderly fashion and avoid the prospect of having to pay the entire indebtedness in one lump sum on the maturity date.

e. Debt securities may be redeemable by the corporation (usually when interest rates decline and short-term low-interest borrowing becomes more attractive than long-term high-interest loans) and may be convertible into common stock, giving the debt holders the choice of becoming equity holders in the corporation.

f. Hybrid Securities
Hybrid Securities combine elements of debt and equity in one instrument. Common hybrid securities include convertible debentures (a debt security with the convertibility rights of an equity security), income bonds (where interest payments are contingent upon whether the corporation has actually earned the amount of interest due), and debentures with voting rights.

g. Registered Bonds and Bearer Bonds

   i. A company may issue securities known as registered bonds in the name of a particular owner, which will be entered into the corporate records. Since interest payments on registered bonds are sent to the registered owner, the name of the new owner must be registered by the corporation when a registered bond is sold.

   ii. Bearer bonds belong to whoever has possession of the actual instrument. Interest is paid by detaching a coupon affixed to the instrument and redeeming it with the corporation or a bank acting as its agent.

h. Issuance of Debt Securities
Issuance of long-term debt securities almost always requires the authorization of the board of directors. In contrast, short-term loans require no such authorization.

i. Tax Aspects
Tax law draws a significant distinction between payments made on debt and those made on equity. While payments made on equity (i.e., dividends and other distributions) are taxable against both the corporation and the recipient, interest payments on debt are taxable only against the recipient. This tax savings is the most common reason that corporations choose debt securities over equity securities as a means of securing needed capital.

4. Leverage
A stock is highly leveraged if the corporation that issued it has a large ratio of bonds and preferred stock outstanding in relation to the amount of stock.

5. Thin Capitalization
A corporation is considered to be thinly capitalized when it has too little equity and too much debt. Thin capitalization often results where a close corporation has abused the tax advantages of debt and has characterized an inappropriate proportion of

the capital contributed by its promoters as debt. Thin capitalization can result both in the disregard of corporate entity and the personal liability of shareholders and in the subordination of shareholder claims against a bankrupt corporation in favor of the claims of general unsecured creditors.

   a. Courts have formulated the following tests for adequate capitalization:

      i. Whether a reasonably prudent person with a general knowledge of the corporation's business would consider the capital amount reasonable in light of any special circumstances that existed at the time of incorporation;

      ii. Whether, in the opinion of a skilled financial analyst, the capital amount was definitely sufficient for the type of business in question in light of the circumstances existing at the time of incorporation; or

      iii. Whether, at the time that the capital was contributed, the corporation could have borrowed a similar amount from an informed outside source.

   b. Though thin capitalization is a persuasive ground for disregard of corporate entity, most courts require additional evidence of fraud or improper motive.

C. Preemptive Rights

1. Dilution of Interest
A shareholder's interest in a corporation is determined by the number of shares he holds in relation to the holdings of others. A shareholder's interest can be diluted if the corporation alters his proportionate share in the corporation by issuing additional shares to other investors.

158 Financial Matters and Distributions

2. **Consequences of Dilution of Interest**
   A shareholder's interest in a corporation takes two forms: economic interest (i.e., the market value of shares held) and voting interest (i.e., a one share one vote say in corporate matters). While the issuance of additional shares at market price or where there is an active market for the trading of such shares does not pose a serious threat to either of these interests, the issuance of additional shares at a discount or within the context of a close corporation has damaging consequences for both the economic interests and voting power of shareholders.

3. **Preemptive Rights Defined**
   Where a shareholder faces a dilution of his interest due to a corporation's issuance of additional stock, he may claim a preemptive right to purchase his proportionate share of the new issue. At common law, preemptive rights were thought to attach only to common stock, but courts have also found that issuances of preferred stock are subject to preemptive rights. While at common law, preemptive rights were extended by implication to every holder of common stock, today they can be abrogated in a corporation's corporate charter.

   a. Some courts have denied stockholders preemptive rights in the following situations:

      i. Where the newly issued shares are part of the stock originally authorized by the corporation's shareholders; or

      ii. Where the new shares were issued pursuant to employee stock plans.

   b. Courts have also permitted the issuance of new stock at prices out of reach of the original stockholders, provided that the original stockholders were offered the opportunity to purchase their share of the new stock and the high price is justified by some legitimate business reason.

   c. Courts are more willing to grant preemptive rights to shareholders in a close corporation. While a shareholder in a large public corporation has to be content with warrants issued to him pursuant to his preemptive rights on the ground that the warrants can be traded should the shareholder not wish to purchase his pro rata share of the new issue, warrants on stock issued by close corporations have no real market value.

d. Courts have found that directors have a fiduciary duty to treat existing shareholders equally, even where preemptive rights have been expressly abolished in the corporate charter. Proof of fraud or improper motive is not required.

e. Shareholders asserting their preemptive rights may either sue for damages, measured by the market value of their proportionate share of the new issue, or specific performance (i.e., compelling the corporation to sell to them their proportionate share of the new issue).

III. INITIAL PUBLIC OFFERINGS

A. Securities Act of 1933 (the "'33 Act")

With respect to initial public offerings, the '33 Act provides federal control based on the federal power to regulate interstate commerce. The Act contemplates a system of registration of public offerings for the purpose of encouraging full disclosure of all relevant facts to protect the uninformed and unsophisticated investor.

B. Relevant Provisions

1. Section 5 permits the interstate sale of only those securities that have been registered with the SEC.

2. Section 12 imposes liability on any person who knowingly sells securities in interstate commerce using misleading methods or who sells securities in interstate commerce using methods he should have known were misleading. The extent of liability is

160   Financial Matters and Distributions

the cost of the security plus interest, less the amount of income the buyer gained from the security.

3. Section 17 makes it unlawful to employ fraudulent or misleading methods in the interstate sale of securities or to engage in any interstate transaction of securities with the intent to defraud.

4. Section 3 establishes the scope of the '33 Act. Only in-state transactions are exempt from this federal statute. The right is reserved to add to the provisions of the Act any new class of securities, and a maximum of $5 million is stipulated for exempt transactions.

5. Section 4 sets forth certain exemptions:

   a. Section 4(1) states that the registration requirements of § 5 do not apply to transactions by persons other than issuers, underwriters, or dealers.

   b. Section 4(2) states that the registration requirements of § 5 do not apply to offerings other than public offerings.

   c. Section 4(6) exempts from the registration requirements of § 5 transactions between issuers and accredited investors (as defined by § 2 of the Act), provided that the transaction is under the maximum exemption amount in § 3, there is no advertising in connection with the transaction, and proper notice has been filed by the issuer with the SEC.

IV. LEGAL CAPITAL

A. The concept of legal capital has its roots in the attempt to accommodate the often conflicting interests of corporate creditors and shareholders.

   1. Creditor Interests
      The creditor often looks for the following in a corporation:

      a. Sufficient assets in the corporate coffers at the time the creditor extends credit and afterwards;

      b. A minimal number of prior creditors with whom it may have to share assets in the event of corporate insolvency;

      c. Corporate assets that are free and unencumbered by any lien by a prior secured creditor; and

      d. Some sort of insurance that junior creditors and shareholders will not be entitled to a share of the corporate assets until senior creditor claims are satisfied.

   2. Shareholder Interests
      Creditors take relatively small risks compared with shareholders. The shareholder sacrifices the secure prospect of periodic interest payments and eventual payment of the principal in exchange for the hope of greater profits through periodic returns on his investment, called dividends, which are paid out of assets from the corporate treasury.

   3. Given the conflict between a creditor's desire to preserve his hierarchical claim to a corporation's assets and the shareholder's desire to see some of those assets distributed as dividends, the concept of legal capital has emerged as a means of addressing the question of what portion of corporate assets may be distributed to shareholders without injuring the senior interest of the creditors.

B. Subscription for Shares

During the nineteenth century, promoters in search of capital for a proposed enterprise would solicit from potential investors a commitment to purchase a stipulated amount of stock if the promoter could sell to other investors the total number of contemplated shares. This commitment was a formal, legally enforceable agreement known as a subscription contract.

C. Par Value

1. Origin
Par value arose out of the subscription process, which required that a mathematical relationship be established between the monetary amount to be invested by an individual subscriber and the total number of shares to be issued.

2. Par Value Defined
The par value of a stock is the fixed dollar value of each share as stated on the face of the share certificate. The par value traditionally represented the amount that each investor agreed to pay per share pursuant to the subscription agreement. The corporation statutes require corporations to state the par value, if any, of the stock in their articles of incorporation.

D. Traditional View of Legal Capital

Since par value in theory represented the price for each share, legal capital was calculated by multiplying the par value by the number of shares issued. This figure represented the total assets of the corporation, upon which a creditor could determine the amount he could safely extend as credit.

1. Watered Stock
Watered stock is stock issued by a corporation in return for consideration less than the stated par value.

2. Bonus Stock
Bonus stock is stock issued for no consideration. Common stock given away free with the purchase of preferred shares constituted a typical form of bonus stock.

E. Shareholder Liability

Creditors (and shareholders) were led to believe that legal capital equalled the total assets of the corporation, based on the assumption that each shareholder paid the par value for each share purchased. If a corporation that had issued watered or bonus stock to shareholders went bankrupt and its creditors discovered that the legal capital, aside from being insufficient to pay off the corporation's obligations, did not accurately reflect the total assets of the corporation, the shareholders of that corporation were held to be liable to creditors for the difference between the par value of the shares held and the actual price paid.

F. The Transformation of Legal Capital

1. The Illusion of Par Value
Par value came to be of limited use due to shareholder liability to creditors. Promoters began to issue low-par stock—i.e., stock with a low par value and a higher subscription price—causing confusion over which legal doctrine to apply in creditor suits in the event of corporate insolvency: the obligation of the shareholder to pay par value or the shareholder's obligation to pay the price stated in the subscription agreement.

2. No-Par Stock
No-par stock required a corporation's board of directors to declare a figure, known as stated capital, as the capital for the corporation. This figure would be at most equivalent to the amount paid by initial stockholders for their stock. No-par stock has negative tax consequences and is rarely used.

3. Due to the proliferation of low-par stock as a means of avoiding watered stock liability, the legal capital figure has ceased to be

an accurate indicator of the assets held by a corporation and is now used by lawyers merely as a benchmark to be compared to the total assets entry on the corporate balance sheet to determine whether a proposed corporate distribution to shareholders is valid, legal, and creates no liabilities.

4. The RMBCA does away with notions of par value, legal capital, and watered stock liability. Shares may be issued at any price fixed in accordance with the sound business judgment of the board of directors.

V. CONSIDERATION AND VALUATION

A. Consideration for Par Value Shares

1. Quantity of Consideration
   Originally, adequate consideration for issued shares was considered to be the par value of the shares. With the practice of stock watering came various theories setting forth the functions of consideration and legal capital:

   a. Trust Fund Theory
      Stock watering injures creditors because the capital of the corporation (i.e., the aggregate par value of all outstanding shares) constitutes a trust fund for the benefit of creditors. Reliance need not be shown. This theory gained currency during the mid-nineteenth century, but proved to be too great of a legal fiction for later judges and was eventually discarded.

   b. Fraud/Misrepresentation Theory
      This has also been called the "holding out" theory. In order for a creditor to compel shareholders to pay in the par value of their shares, the creditor must show (1) that the acts of the stockholders in representing that the legal capital has been paid constituted a fraud on his rights, and (2) that he relied on the misrepresented legal capital amount in extending credit. See *Hospes v. Northwestern Manufacturing Co.*

c. Statutory Obligation
Some states prohibit by statute the receipt by investors of watered stock and hold recipients strictly liable for the difference between par value and price paid, irrespective of creditor reliance. This approach is based on the rationale that the contributions of stockholders substitute for their personal liability. See Del.G.C.L. § 162.

2. Quality of Consideration
All states allow cash or property to be furnished in exchange for stock. Forms of property acceptable as consideration include:

a. Services rendered by a promoter on behalf of a contemplated corporation during the pre-incorporation period (acceptable in New York and California and under the RMBCA, but unacceptable under the Model Business Corporation Act).

b. An executory contract to render future services valuable to the corporation (acceptable under the RMBCA, but unacceptable under many state corporation statutes).

c. Promissory notes (acceptable under the RMBCA and acceptable, if secured, under California law).

d. Trade secrets (unacceptable in some jurisdictions).

B. Valuation of Assets

To determine whether consideration paid for stock is adequate, it is necessary to arrive at a valuation of a corporation's assets.

1. As a general rule, absent fraud or improper motive, the good-faith determination of the board of directors is determinative as to the valuation of a corporation's assets. See Del.G.C.L. § 152.

2. Prospective profits cannot lawfully be included in a valuation of corporate assets. See *See v. Heppenheimer.*

3. In a transfer of a business in exchange for stock, goodwill may lawfully be included as an asset for valuation.

C. Liability

Most jurisdictions have statutes that hold liable the holder of shares for which the legal consideration has not been paid. Under RMBCA § 6.22, the shareholder is liable to the corporation for the amount below the legal consideration not paid, and if the corporation is insolvent, to the corporate creditors.

VI. DIVIDENDS

A. Dividends Defined

A dividend is any distribution of cash or property to shareholders based on their equity interest.

B. Types of Dividends

1. Cash Dividends
   Cash dividends are the most common form of distribution. Because payment of cash dividends can affect the financial condition of the corporation, every state corporation statute regulates the sources out of which cash dividends can be paid.

2. Stock Dividends
   Dividends paid in stock do not involve the distribution of corporate assets and are thus subject to fewer limitations than cash dividends. Stock dividends can dilute shareholders' interests, however, and are therefore subject to preemptive rights.

VII. LEGAL SOURCES OF DIVIDENDS

A. Senior Interests

With respect to dividend payments, the senior interests of preferred shareholders and creditors often conflict with the subordinate interests of common shareholders. Creditors do not want to see corporate assets drained through dividend payments to common shareholders, while preferred shareholders want to maintain their preferred status and reduced risk in relation to common shareholders. Conversely, common shareholders usually look to the corporation for regular dividend payments.

B. Legal Protections

1. To protect creditor and senior shareholder interests, nearly all corporation statutes prohibit the payment of dividends when the corporation is "insolvent." Section 6.40 of the RMBCA contains two interpretations of insolvency:

    a. Equity Sense
    When a corporation is insolvent in the equity sense, it means that the corporation is unable to pay its debts in the usual course of business. The Act leaves to the discretion of the directors the determination of whether a solvent corporation will be able to pay its debts.

    b. Bankruptcy Sense
    When a corporation is insolvent in the bankruptcy sense, it means that the total assets of the corporation are less than the total liabilities plus any sum that would be paid to preferred shareholders in the event of liquidation. This "balance sheet test" does not require adherence to any professional accounting concepts, but does prescribe fair valuation and other reasonable methods.

2. Contained in some corporation statutes is an alternative formulation intended to protect senior interests by permitting

dividends to be paid only when there is an earned surplus (commonly defined as the aggregate profits accumulated during the life of the business). A more lenient version of this provision allows payment of dividends out of "surplus," be it earned or capital surplus (i.e., any amount exceeding the legal consideration paid by shareholders for their stock).

3. Some states permit payment of dividends out of current net earnings (also called current net profits). These distributions, known as nimble dividends, are paid out of the corporation's earnings for the relevant accounting period, even though they might impair the corporation's legal capital. See *United States v. Riely.*

4. Wasting Asset Corporations
Many corporation statutes have specific dividend provisions for wasting asset corporations, whose main business involves the exploitation of natural resources (e.g., coal mines, oil wells). Wasting asset corporations are permitted to avoid a depletion (depreciation) reserve; that is, they are permitted to pay dividends out of such a reserve. This amounts to a return in the form of dividends of some of the capital initially invested by shareholders. California, however, prohibits such dividend payments unless adequate provision is made for debts and the liquidation preferences of preferred shares.

C. Excessive Dividends

1. Despite the complex limitations on dividend payments prescribed in the corporation statutes, protection of the senior interests of creditors and preferred shareholders often fails due to the centrality of the troublesome concept of legal capital:

   a. Directors can designate any amount as a corporation's legal capital and in doing so often try to accommodate the interests of the shareholders who elect them.

b. Many state corporation statutes have discarded the earned surplus requirement for distributions in favor of payment out of any surplus, including capital surplus.

c. Though most corporation statutes stipulate that accounting be performed in accordance with "generally accepted accounting principles," these principles have not necessarily been designed to safeguard senior interests.

d. In a few jurisdictions, courts have held that corporations may legally "revaluate" assets that have risen in market value, thereby creating additional surplus available for dividend payments. See *Randall v. Bailey*.

2. The RMBCA attempts to resolve the problems inherent in a system of regulating distributions based on legal capital by abandoning the concept of legal capital altogether. Instead, § 6.40(c) stipulates that in order for a dividend to be legal, the corporation must be able, following the payment of the dividend, to pass both the bankruptcy and equity tests of solvency set forth in VI.B.1.a. and b. above.

D. Share Repurchases

1. A corporation may choose to repurchase issued shares in the following situations:

a. The corporation is overcapitalized (i.e., it possesses liquid assets that it cannot put to productive use);

b. The shareholders in a close corporation have concluded a stock transfer restriction agreement;

c. The corporation is undergoing a merger or other major structural change and shareholders opposing the change have exercised their right of appraisal; or

d. The corporation is fighting a takeover bid.

2. Share repurchases have the same effect on a corporation's creditors as a distribution of dividends and are thus subject to the same kinds of restrictions under the corporation statutes:

   a. Del.G.C.L. § 160 permits repurchase of common stock only if the transaction would not impair the corporation's capital.

   b. The RMBCA defines share repurchases as distributions in § 1.40(b) and subjects them to the provisions of § 6.40.

   c. New York permits repurchases only out of surplus, although redeemed shares may be paid for out of capital.

VIII. LIABILITY FOR UNLAWFUL DISTRIBUTIONS

A. Courts are extremely hesitant to compel boards of directors to declare and pay a dividend upon a suit by shareholders. In the absence of bad faith, fraud, or abuse of discretion on the part of board members, courts leave decisions whether to make a distribution of corporate assets to the directors' sound business judgment.

   1. In connection with the refusal to declare a dividend, bad faith means the directors' shaping of corporate policy and use of corporate profits for their own, rather than corporate, ends.

   2. Absent an allegation of bad faith, a plaintiff in a suit to compel payment of a dividend will face an uphill battle, even if he has shown that the corporation had the funds sufficient to pay a dividend, that the corporation was using its surplus to pay its directors fat bonuses, and there existed hostile relations between directors and other stockholders. See *Gottfried v. Gottfried*.

B. Where courts have found that the intention of the directors was to conduct the affairs of the corporation for the benefit of third parties rather than shareholders, courts have used their powers in equity to compel a dividend distribution. These cases are, however, extremely rare. See *Dodge v. Ford Motor Co.*

CASE CLIPS

Randall v. Bailey (1942) CE, CCM, He, JB

Facts: The trustee in bankruptcy of Bush Terminal Company (P) sued the directors of the corporation to recover what he claimed were illegally paid dividends. P argued that the capital surplus from which the dividends were paid was illusory, based on the inclusion in the corporate books of an overvalued goodwill figure and a write-up of the corporation's assets reflecting unrealized appreciation. The relevant statute prohibited a corporation from making dividend payments "while its capital or capital stock is impaired."

Issue 1: Can a corporation lawfully include goodwill among its assets to create a surplus for dividend payment?

Rule 1: Absent fraud, a corporation may include elements of value in addition to physical assets, such as goodwill, among its assets to create a surplus for dividend payment, and the judgment of the directors as to the value of the goodwill is controlling.

Issue 2: Can a corporation increase the value of its physical assets to reflect unrealized appreciation to create a surplus for dividend payment?

Rule 2: A corporation may increase the value of its physical assets to reflect unrealized appreciation to create a "revaluation surplus" for dividend payment, so long as it also incorporates in its calculations reductions due to unrealized depreciation.

Morris v. Standard Gas & Electric Co. (1949) CE

Facts: Standard Gas & Electric Co. (D) was sued by one of its shareholders (P), who wished to enjoin D's payment of a nimble dividend on its senior stock out of net profits. P claimed that D had not complied with the relevant statute, which required that the value of D's assets equal or exceed the amount of D's outstanding stock, because D had not carried out an accurate appraisal of its assets.

Issue: Are directors free to choose the standard to be applied in the valuation of corporate assets pursuant to statutory requirements?

Rule: Absent fraud or bad faith, directors have reasonable latitude in choosing the standard to be applied in the valuation of corporate assets pursuant to statutory requirements, with reasonability to be determined on a case-by-case basis.

Reilly v. Segert (1964) CE
Facts: The directors of Deerfield Lumber & Fuel Co., Inc. authorized the purchase of Deerfield shares from five of its shareholders (D) at a time when Deerfield was insolvent. The receiver (P) of Deerfield subsequently sued to recover the amount paid for the stock. D claimed that § 42 of the Business Corporation Act, which imposed on directors liability to creditors for distributions during insolvency, repealed shareholder liability to creditors.
Issue: Where a statute imposes on directors liability to creditors for distributions during periods of corporate insolvency, is common-law shareholder liability for these distributions repealed?
Rule: Where a statute imposes on directors liability to creditors for distributions during periods of corporate insolvency, common-law shareholder liability is preserved unless the statute expressly provides an exclusive remedy.

Berwald v. Mission Development Co. (1962) CE, CCM
Facts: Mission Development Co. (D) was a holding company the sole asset of which was a block of shares of Tidewater Oil Company. Both Tidewater and D were owned by the same corporation, and when Tidewater announced that it was discontinuing dividend payments, thereby depressing both the value of D's shares and D's growth potential, D's minority shareholders (P) sought the liquidation of D and the distribution of its assets, claiming that Tidewater's dividend policy was designed to further the personal interests of its owner.
Issue: Can a corporation adopt a dividend policy that benefits controlling shareholders at the expense of minority shareholders?
Rule: A corporation can adopt a dividend policy that benefits controlling shareholders at the expense of minority shareholders if the policy was adopted in furtherance of its own corporate interest, rather than the selfish interest of the majority.

Sinclair Oil Corp. v. Levien (1971) CE
Facts: A shareholder in a subsidiary brought an action to hold the subsidiary's parent liable for excessive distribution of dividends. P

asserted that the parent bore the burden of proving that its dealings with the subsidiary had been intrinsically fair.
Issue: Does a parent corporation, in defending an alleged breach of fiduciary duty, bear the burden of proving that its dealings with its subsidiary were intrinsically fair?
Rule: A parent corporation defending against an alleged breach of fiduciary duty to a subsidiary bears the burden of proving that its dealings were intrinsically fair only if there is self-dealing that allows the parent to receive something to the detriment of the subsidiary's minority stockholders.

Neimark v. Mel Kramer Sales, Inc. (1981) CE, CCM
Facts: Prior to his death, Kramer, the founder and majority shareholder of D, caused a stock redemption agreement to be executed between D and its shareholders. The agreement required D to purchase the shares of a deceased shareholder for a specified price. If D was unable to pay for the shares out of its surplus or retained earnings, the agreement stipulated that the remaining shareholders would contribute the necessary capital. Additionally, the agreement stated that the parties were entitled to specific performance. Kramer's estate refused to redeem Kramer's shares, and another shareholder (P) brought suit to compel specific performance of the redemption agreement. D argued that redemption would render it insolvent in violation of the statutory provisions regarding the right of a corporation to purchase its own shares.
Issue: What are the criteria for determining whether a company is financially capable of redeeming its shares?
Rule: The criteria for determining whether a corporation is financially capable of redeeming its shares are the insolvency test, which examines the corporate balance sheet both at the time of purchase and, where payment is made in installments, at the time of each installment payment to determine whether the corporation is insolvent in the equity sense, and the surplus cutoff test, which examines the balance sheet at the time of purchase to determine whether the corporation retains earned surplus equal to the cost of the redeemed shares.

Corporate Distributions

Old Dominion Copper Mining & Smelting Co. v. Lewisohn (S.Ct. 1908) CE, JB

Facts: D and Bigelow were promoters who established and made themselves the principal shareholders in a corporation (P) for the purpose of selling to it property that they had purchased. The sale resulted in excessive profits for both D and Bigelow, who then directed P to issue to the public shares of common stock to fund P's purchase of the land. When subsequent shareholders learned of the profits from the land sale, which D and Bigelow had kept secret, P sued for rescission of the sale contract or repayment of D's profits.

Issue: Can a promoter establish a corporation and use it for his personal financial gain without breaching his fiduciary duty to the corporation?

Rule: (Holmes, J.) A promoter may establish a corporation and use it for his personal financial gain without breaching his fiduciary duty to the corporation if the shareholders have full knowledge of, and give corporate approval to, the director's actions.

Old Dominion Copper Mining & Smelting Co. v. Bigelow (1909) CE, JB

Facts: D and Lewisohn were promoters who established and made themselves the principal shareholders in a corporation (P) for the purpose of selling to it property that they had purchased. The sale resulted in excessive profits for both D and Lewisohn, who then directed P to issue to the public shares of common stock to fund P's purchase of the land. When subsequent shareholders learned of the profits from the land sale, which D and Bigelow had kept secret, P sued for rescission of the sale contract or repayment of D's profits.

Issue: Can a promoter establish a corporation and use it for his personal financial gain without breaching his fiduciary duty to the corporation?

Rule: A promoter who establishes a corporation and uses it for his personal financial gain breaches his fiduciary duty where the financial gain is concealed from shareholders who are originally contemplated as part of the fully established corporation, but who have not yet subscribed for shares.

Miller v. San Sebastian Gold Mines, Inc. (1976) CE
Facts: Miller and Rojas organized San Sebastian Gold Mines, Inc. (D) to lease a mine to be used in a gold-mining venture. Miller, his wife (P), and Rojas each invested $75,000 in D, in return for which they received a share of D's stock. P also received an additional share for no consideration. D later recapitalized and offered its shares to the public, after which D's board sued in an Rule 10b–5 action to cancel the share that P received without consideration.
Issue: Can a corporation assert a claim as a seller of stock under Rule 10b–5 of the Securities Exchange Act of 1934 where the promoters have issued stock to themselves without consideration and only subsequent stockholders would be injured?
Rule: A corporation can assert a claim as a seller of stock under Rule 10b–5 of the Securities Exchange Act of 1934 where the promoters have issued stock to themselves without consideration and only subsequent stockholders would be injured; provided, however, that the corporation bears the burden of proving bad faith or fraud.

Hospes v. Northwestern Mfg. & Car Co. (1892) CE, CCM, V
Facts: Semyour, Sabin & Co., a profitable corporation, established Northwestern Manufacturing & Car Co. (D) and transferred to D most of its assets in exchange for preferred stock of equal value. In addition to this preferred stock, Semyour, Sabin & Co. caused D to transfer to its organizers a large amount of bonus common stock, thereby sending D into debt. D subsequently went bankrupt, and the assignee of D's original creditors (P) sued to compel the recipients of the common stock to pay for their shares.
Issue: Can a creditor of a bankrupt corporation compel the recipients of bonus stock to pay for their shares?
Rule: A creditor of a bankrupt corporation can compel the recipients of bonus stock to pay for their shares if the creditor extended credit to the bankrupt corporation in reliance on the corporation's representations that all outstanding stock had been paid for.

Bing Crosby Minute Maid Corp v. Eaton (1956) CE
Facts: Bing Crosby Minute Maid Corp. (P) extended credit to Eaton (P), who had formed a frozen food corporation and issued to himself par value shares totalling $45,000 for a consideration of $34,780. P's

corporation went bankrupt, and P sued as creditor for the difference between the par value of D's stock and the price D actually paid. At trial, P conceded that it was aware of D's financial situation prior to its extension of credit and that it had not relied on the par value of D's shares.

Issue: Where there is a statutory prohibition of watered stock, can a creditor compel the holder of watered stock to make good on the difference between the price actually paid and the par value of the stock, even where the creditor has not relied on the par value of the stock in deciding to extend credit?

Rule: A statutory prohibition of watered stock does not change the creditor's need to establish that it relied on the par value of the stock in extending credit to hold the holder of watered stock liable for the obligations of the bankrupt.

Providence and Worcester Co. v. Baker (1977) CE

Facts: The corporate charter of Providence and Worcester Co. (D) contained certain restrictions on the voting power of shareholders. Baker (P), Penn Central Transportation Company's trustee in bankruptcy, sued D, challenging the voting restrictions under § 151(a) of the Delaware General Corporation Law.

Issue: Under Delaware law, can a corporation's articles of incorporation prescribe voting rights different from a "one share-one vote" standard?

Rule: Although Delaware law prescribes a "one share-one vote" standard, it does not prohibit a corporate charter from weighting or restricting voting rights.

Stokes v. Continental Trust Co. of City of New York (1906) CE, Ha

Facts: P owned 221 out of 5,000 outstanding shares of D. D received a proposal from Blair & Co. that suggested that D double the number of outstanding shares, the additional shares to be purchased by Blair in exchange for Blair's right to appoint new members to D's expanded board of trustees. Though the majority of D's shareholders approved Blair's plan, P demanded that D sell him the number of new shares required to maintain his proportionate interest. D refused P's demand and sold all the new shares to Blair.

Issue: Does a shareholder possess the preemptive right to purchase the number of newly issued shares sufficient to maintain his proportionate interest in the corporation?

Rule: A shareholder has the preemptive right, resting in property law, to subscribe for and take the number of newly issued shares sufficient to maintain his proportionate interest in the corporation.

Ross Transport, Inc. v. Crothers (1946) CE

Facts: Crothers (P) was a former director and minority stockholder of Ross Transport, Inc. (D), a close corporation. D initially issued at $20 par value only 1,035 of its 1,500 authorized shares, which were distributed in various amounts among D's board, but after six months of profitable operations, issued to select board members an additional 365 authorized shares at the same $20 par value price. P was not offered a chance to purchase any of the additional shares and sued to set aside the additional issuance, claiming that D's board violated his preemptive right as a stockholder.

Issue: To bring an action against directors who have authorized an issue of stock to themselves, thereby diluting the proportionate share held by other shareholders, must the complaint assert a violation of a shareholder's preemptive right?

Rule: Directors who have authorized an issue of stock to themselves, thereby diluting the proportionate share held by other shareholders, are presumed to have breached their fiduciary duty and bear the burden of showing that the issuance was fairly conducted, and a violation of a shareholder's preemptive right need not be asserted to bring an action against them.

Bodell v. General Gas & Electric Corp.
(1926) CE (abridged), CCM

Facts: General Gas & Electric Corp. (D) implemented a capital-raising plan under which holders of Class A stock could use their dividends to purchase additional newly issued Class A shares for $25, a substantial discount below the market price. Holders of D's Class B stock (P) sued to restrain the issuance of the new shares since it would unfairly enable Class A shareholders to purchase at a bargain price securities with a high market value.

Issue: Can the directors of a corporation authorize the sale at a discount of additional newly issued shares to one class of stockholder to the exclusion of another?
Rule: The directors of a corporation can authorize the sale at a discount of additional newly issued shares to one class of stockholder to the exclusion of another if, in the exercise of their broad powers of discretion, they determine that such a sale would be in the best interests of the corporation.

See v. Heppenheimer (1905) CCM, V
Facts: A group of promoters (D) bought 39 straw paper mills for $2,250,000 and organized a new company, Columbia Straw Company, to which they sold the mills for a total consideration of $5,000,000 in stock and bonds. D forecasted that their purchase of the mills would create a monopoly in straw paper, and used the anticipated profits from the venture to justify placing a value of $5,000,000 on assets purchased for only $2,250,000. D's venture went bankrupt, and D's creditors sued D for the unpaid consideration for their stock.
Issue: Can prospective profits be treated as property for purposes of valuation of business assets for a stock issuance?
Rule: Prospective profits cannot be treated as property for purposes of valuation of business assets for a stock issuance.

Bailes v. Colonial Press, Inc. (1971) CCM
Facts: Twitty (D) acquired Colonial Press (D) for $6,000, and one year later established American Southern Publishing Company, Inc. and caused it to issue to D approximately half of its authorized shares in exchange for D's assets, which were stated to be worth $412,000. In actuality, D was bankrupt and had no assets of value. American Southern subsequently went bankrupt, and its trustee in bankruptcy (P) sued Colonial and its promoters for damages under Rule 10b–5. The lower court dismissed the action because every stockholder and officer of American Southern knew at the time of the transaction that D was insolvent.
Issue: Is it necessary for a complaint alleging fraud under Rule 10b–5 of the Securities Exchange Act of 1934 to state specific fraudulent transactions involving specific victims?
Rule: If the activity that is the subject of a complaint under Rule 10b–5 contemplates a continuing scheme to deceive various unidenti-

fied persons who rely upon the good faith of the fraudulent entity, it is not necessary for the complaint to state specific fraudulent transactions involving specific victims.

Pipelife Corp. v. Bedford (1958) CCM
Facts: The promoters (D) of Pipelife Corp. obtained a license to exploit pipeline-cleaning technology. Though D paid nothing for the license, they placed a value of $367,000 on it and used it as consideration in the issuance to themselves of 367,000 shares of Pipelife stock. D then proceeded to issue an additional 100,000 shares of Pipelife to the public, the prospectus for which stated that D had paid nothing for the license and stock. Control of Pipelife subsequently changed, and its current board of directors (P) sued to cancel the shares issued to the promoters based on the inadequacy of the license as consideration.
Issue: In the sale of the stock of a corporation to its directors, are the directors bound to a good-faith standard in the valuation of the consideration paid for the stock?
Rule: Where the directors of a corporation have sold stock to themselves, they are bound to a good-faith standard in the valuation of the consideration paid for the stock.

Thomas Branch & Co. v. Riverside & Dan River Cotton Mills, Inc. (1924) CCM
Facts: D's shareholders and directors voted to issue as a stock dividend 20,000 new shares of common stock to the holders of common stock in proportion to their respective holdings. The holders of D's preferred stock sued to obtain their proportionate share of the new stock issue. D argued that preferred shareholders were limited in their participation in the earnings of the company to the rate of interest prescribed for preferred shares and were not entitled to any further dividends.
Issue: Upon the issuance of new stock, do holders of preferred shares possess the same preemptive rights to subscribe for their proportionate share as do holders of common stock?
Rule: Absent any statutory limitation or limiting provision in the corporation's articles, holders of preferred shares possess the same

preemptive rights to subscribe for their proportionate share of a new stock issue as do holders of common stock.

Katzowitz v. Sidler (1969) CCM, Ha

Facts: P, Sidler (D) and Lasker (D) were the directors and stockholders of Sulburn Holding Corp., a close corporation. Relations between P and D had deteriorated to where D successfully ousted P from any management role in Sulburn, although P still enjoyed the same shareholder benefits as D. At the time of P's withdrawal from Sulburn, Sulburn owed each of its directors $2,500. As a substitute for cash payment of the debt, D caused Sulburn to offer to its shareholders for $100 per share stock with a book value of $1,800 per share. P turned down the stock offer, while D purchased their allotment, resulting in a dilution of P's interest in Sulburn. Sulburn was subsequently dissolved, and its assets were distributed in proportion to the number of shares held, resulting in P's receipt of a substantially smaller payment. P sued to compel an equal distribution of Sulburn's assets.

Issue: Can a shareholder in a close corporation void an issuance of new shares where the new shares are offered at a price markedly below book value and the issuance results in a dilution of his interest in the corporation?

Rule: A shareholder in a close corporation can void an issuance of new shares where the new shares are offered at a price markedly below book value for no good business reason and the issuance results in a dilution of his interest in the corporation.

Excelsior Water & Mining Co. v. Pierce (1891) CCM

Facts: P sought to hold one of its directors liable for the payment of a $241,629 dividend out of capital. P, a hydraulic mining company, operated at a profit until the courts enjoined all hydraulic mining operations in the area. P asserted that its surplus profits totalled a mere $98,000, basing its calculations on the inclusion of certain capital outlays as current working expenses. D argued that P improperly included these outlays as expenses and that if the outlays were capitalized, P's surplus profits would total $457,416.

Issue: Where a corporation's business activities have been shut down under circumstances that prevent the writing down of capital outlays over the anticipated time period, can the corporation convert such

capitalized outlays to current working expenses to avoid payment of a dividend out of annual earnings?
Rule: Where a corporation's business activities have been shut down under circumstances that prevent the writing down of capital outlays over the anticipated time period, the corporation cannot convert such capitalized outlays to current working expenses to avoid payment of a dividend out of annual earnings.

Dodge v. Ford Motor Co. (1919) CCM, Ha, SSB
Facts: In 1916, D anticipated an annual profit of $60,000,000. In the same year, the company announced that it would not pay dividends so that it could pay for the construction of a smelting plant and implement a business plan that called for enhancing the public welfare through the creation of jobs and reductions in car prices. P, a shareholder of D, sued to compel payment of the 1916 annual dividend.
Issue: Can a corporation's board legally conduct the corporation's business affairs in a manner that would benefit third parties at the expense of shareholders' interests?
Rule: A board of directors of a corporation may not legally conduct the business affairs of the corporation for the merely incidental benefit of shareholders and for the primary purpose of benefitting third parties.

Smith v. Atlantic Properties, Inc. (1981) CCM, He
Facts: P, D, and two others each held a quarter interest in Atlantic Properties, Inc. The articles of incorporation of Atlantic contained a provision giving any one of the four veto power over any vote of the board of directors. D consistently used this veto power to withhold a declaration of dividends, resulting in the assessment of a tax penalty by the IRS against Atlantic. P and the other shareholders sued for a declaration of dividends, removal of D as a director, and reimbursement for the tax penalties.
Issue: Does a minority shareholder possessing a veto power over the actions of the board of directors owe a fiduciary duty to his fellow board members to exercise that veto power in a reasonable way?
Rule: A minority shareholder possessing a veto power over the actions of the board of directors owes a fiduciary duty to his fellow

board members to exercise that veto power in a reasonable way so as not to cause serious or unjustified risk of injury to the corporation.

Alco Products, Inc. v. White Motor International Corp. (1978) CCM

Facts: D bought the assets of P and its subsidiaries. As consideration for P, both parties agreed that payment would be made in cash and cumulative preferred stock with a redemption requirement and a sinking fund rather than notes, thereby making P a shareholder of D rather than a creditor. After the initial scheduled redemption, D did not redeem any of the stock held by P as required by the agreement and subsequently sold all of P's assets to a third party, using the proceeds to pay off its creditors. P sued to compel redemption of its shares in D, and D argued that it was prohibited from redeeming P's shares due to a prior indenture agreement.

Issue: Where a seller has chosen to accept as payment preferred cumulative stock with a redemption requirement instead of an installment note or other form of unsecured debt, are the seller's claims junior to those of a prior creditor?

Rule: In choosing to accept as payment preferred cumulative stock with a redemption requirement instead of an installment note or other form of unsecured debt, a seller becomes a stockholder rather than a creditor, and its claims are subordinated to those of prior creditors.

Camp v. Genesco, Inc. (1978) CCM

Facts: Genesco (D) bought companies belonging to the Camp family (P) under an agreement that provided for payment in Genesco Series B stock, which was to be exchangeable for Genesco 6.5 percent debentures. D's corporate charter contained a provision that prohibited D from paying any dividend or distribution if it was in arrears in the payment of dividends to senior classes of stock. Genesco decided to halt the payment of dividends on P's stock and senior stock and to withdraw P's exchange privilege pursuant to the provisions of pre-existing loan agreements. P sued to compel D to renew P's exchange privilege, claiming that the provision in D's corporate charter was excluded by the parol evidence rule. D argued that the terms of its corporate charter must be read into subsequent agreements as a matter of law.

Issue: Should agreements entered into by a corporation be construed in light of the terms of the corporation's charter?
Rule: Agreements entered into by a corporation must be construed in light of the terms of the corporation's charter; provided, however, that where prohibited by statute, a corporation cannot raise the terms of the corporate charter as part of an *ultra vires* defense.

Karfunkel v. USLIFE Corp. (1982) CCM
Facts: Six percent of the stock of USLIFE Corp. was acquired by another company over a four-year period. D bought back these shares at a price higher than market rate but lower than book value. One of D's shareholders sued, alleging that the purpose of the stock purchase was to protect the position of D's board and demanding that D purchase his shares for the same price.
Issue: Where a corporation purchases the shares of one of its shareholders, is it obligated to make a pro rata offer to all of its other shareholders at the price offered to the initial seller?
Rule: Where a corporation purchases the shares of one of its shareholders, it is not obligated to make a pro rata offer to all of its other shareholders. Absent fraud, impairment of capital, or harm to creditors, the board may authorize any stock purchase it deems beneficial to the corporation.

Zahn v. Transamerica Corporation (1947) CCM
Facts: A corporate charter provided that directors had the option to redeem Class A stock. Another corporation (D) acquired 80 percent the corporation's stock and through its control of the board of directors redeemed the Class A stock before liquidation of the corporation for its own benefit.
Issue: Are self-interested votes taken by majority shareholders acting as directors voidable by minority shareholders?
Rule: When voting as a directors, majority shareholders represent all shareholders in the capacity of a trustee and actions taken for personal benefit may be voided by minority shareholders in equity.

Kaufmann v. Lawrence (1975) CCM
Facts: The directors (D) of Wells, Rich, Greene, Inc. issued to themselves in the two years after incorporation approximately two

million shares of WRG stock. They thereafter sold much of their stock pursuant to a public offering, from which they realized considerable profits. The stock market took a turn for the worse, however, and WRG stock fell significantly, prompting WRG's directors to institute an exchange offer whereby public owners of stock would sell their shares to WRG for cash and debentures. A WRG shareholder (P) sued to enjoin the exchange offer, claiming that WRG's prospectus contained misleading statements, thereby violating §§ 10(b) and 14(e) of the Securities Exchange Act of 1934.
Issue: Does a plan under which a public corporation goes private because the stock market's depressed state enables the corporation to repurchase its stock at bargain rates violate federal securities regulations?
Rule: Though a plan under which a public corporation goes private because the stock market's depressed state enables the corporation to repurchase its stock at bargain rates may raise public policy questions, it does not violate federal securities laws.

Teschner v. Chicago Title & Trust Co. (1974) CCM
Facts: Lincoln National made exchange offers to shareholders of Chicago Title & Trust Co. (D) and eventually managed to purchase all but a small percentage of D's publicly held stock. D thereafter caused its shareholders to pass an amendment to D's corporate charter authorizing a 600:1 reverse stock split, with D reserving the option to purchase fractional shares for cash. One of D's shareholders (P), who did not choose to take D's exchange offer, voted against the amendment and sued to preserve her status as a shareholder of D.
Issue: To what extent may a shareholder limit a corporation's amendment of its own corporate charter to reclassify its own shares?
Rule: A shareholder may limit a corporation's amendment of its own corporate charter to reclassify its own shares to the extent that the amendment complies with the state corporation statute as it existed at the time the shareholder acquired his shares.

Slappey Drive Indus. Park v. United States (1977) Ha
Facts: To carry out residential and industrial development projects, a real estate developer (P) caused six corporations to be formed by close family members. Though these family members provided funds to the corporations as loans under announced repayment plans, these

funds were not paid back according to schedule because the family members preferred to wait until the corporations had "plenty of cash." The Government (D) treated these loans for tax purposes as shareholder contributions to corporate capital.

Issue: Can a court look beyond the form of the transfer and the intent of the parties to determine whether a transfer of funds from shareholders to a corporation should be treated for tax purposes as a bona fide debt or as equity?

Rule: A court can look beyond the form of the transfer and the intent of the parties to factors such as the return expected from the transaction and the actual manner in which the parties structured their relationship to determine whether a transfer of funds from shareholders to a corporation should be treated for tax purposes as a bona fide debt or as equity.

Securities and Exchange Comm'n v. Ralston Purina Co. (S.Ct. 1953) Ha, V

Facts: D had a policy of offering for sale to "key employees" authorized but unissued shares of its stock. This offering was performed without registering the stock pursuant to § 5 of the Securities Act of 1933, and the stock was sold to employees acting on their own initiative without any solicitation by D. The SEC sought to enjoin D's stock offering, and D claimed that the offering was exempt because it involved D's employees only and thus fell within the offering exception prescribed in § 4(2) of the Securities Act of 1933.

Issue: Does an offer by a corporation of its own stock to its employees fall within the exceptions to the stock registration requirements set forth in § 4(2) of the Securities Act of 1933?

Rule: (Clark, J.) An offer by a corporation of its own stock to its employees does not fall within the exceptions to the stock registration requirements set forth in § 4(2) of the Securities Act of 1933, since the protections provided in the act extend to any potential purchasers lacking the knowledge required to make informed investment decisions.

Smith v. Gross (1979) Ha

Facts: D induced P through a newsletter advertisement to establish a worm-growing enterprise, guaranteeing profits by promising to buy

back at higher-than-market prices any worms that P raised. D reneged on his promise of quick profits, and P sued, charging that the interest purchased from D was an investment contract and that D's breach was a violation of federal securities laws. A lower court dismissed P's suit on the ground that the transaction between P and D involved no security.
Issue: What are the criteria for determining whether an investment scheme constitutes an investment contract for the purposes of the securities statutes?
Rule: An investment scheme constitutes an investment contract for the purposes of the securities statutes if it involves an investment of money in a common enterprise with profits to come through the essential managerial efforts of a party other than the investor.

Gottfried v. Gottfried (1947) Ha
Facts: P was a minority stockholder in Gottfried Baking Corporation, a close family corporation. Gottfried Baking enjoyed a earned surplus, but it had not paid dividends on its common stock in the fourteen years prior to P's suit, although it had paid annual dividends on its preferred stock and occasional dividends on its "A" stock. P sued to compel payment of dividends on the common stock, claiming that the majority stockholders (D) intended to force P to sell his stock to them at a loss.
Issue: Absent a showing of bad faith, can a minority shareholder compel the majority to pay a dividend where the corporation possesses the requisite surplus capital?
Rule: A minority shareholder must prove that the majority shareholders acted in bad faith in withholding dividends to compel payment of dividends where the corporation possesses the requisite surplus capital.

Herbert G. Hatt (1969) Ha
Facts: Hatt (D) married Dorothy Echols, the president and majority stockholder in Johann, a funeral home corporation, and pursuant to an antenuptial agreement obtained a majority interest in Johann and became its president. Hatt then gave himself a generous salary and bonuses, purchased and operated a yacht and two airplanes, and employed his mother as a corpse dresser. The Commissioner of the IRS (P) disallowed Johann's deduction as business expenses of the

salaries of Hatt and Hatt's mother and the cost of operating the boat and the planes.
Issue: What expenses can a corporation deduct from its gross income as business expenses?
Rule: A corporation can deduct from its gross income as business expenses only those expenses that are ordinary and necessary, as shown by the evidence.

Wilderman v. Wilderman (1974) Ha
Facts: D and his wife (P) formed Marble Craft Company, Inc., an installer of marble and tile facings. P and D each had a half interest in Marble Craft, and D served as president while P was designated vice-president, secretary, and treasurer. D looked after most of Marble Craft's affairs, while P performed the bookkeeping. P and D divorced, and P sought to have D return to the company large bonuses that he paid to himself to avoid corporate taxation without the authorization of Marble Craft's board.
Issue: Can a corporate officer pay to himself large salary and bonus payments without the authorization of the board of directors?
Rule: Absent board authorization, corporate officers bear the burden of showing that the amount of compensation that they pay themselves is reasonable.

Donahue v. Rodd Electrotype Co. (1975) Ha
Facts: A minority shareholder (P) in a close corporation claimed the board of directors breached its fiduciary duty to her by refusing to purchase her stock at the price paid to another shareholder.
Issue: When purchasing the stock of one shareholder, must a close corporation afford all shareholders the opportunity to sell their stock at the same price?
Rule: The strict fiduciary duty of majority shareholders in a close corporation requires that equal opportunity be provided to all in the purchase of shareholders' stock by the corporation.

John Kelley Co. v. Commissioner of Internal Revenue
Talbot Mills v. Commissioner of Internal Revenue
(S.Ct. 1946) He

Facts: Both John Kelley Co. and Talbot Mills were close corporations where shareholders were members of a family group. Both corporations wished to reorganize and issued "hybrid" securities that authorized "interest" payments to their holders. Kelley issued transferable debenture bonds that specified an annual payment and a maturity date. Talbot issued registered notes, which provided for fluctuating payments, solely in exchange for stock. The Tax Court, noting the differences in the debt instruments, found that the payments in Kelley were interest on indebtedness and thus deductible and that the payments in Talbot were dividends and thus taxable.

Issue: Is the Tax Court authorized to look beyond the form of the instrument and formulate its own criteria for determining whether "hybrid" securities constitute debt or equity?

Rule: (Reed, J.) Congress intended to leave to the final determination of the Tax Court all tax issues that were not clear-cut cases of law, and the question of whether "hybrid" securities represent debt or equity is one for the Tax Court to resolve using criteria it deems significant.

Dissent: (Rutledge, J.) Distinguishing between debt and equity poses a clear-cut question of law, and a taxpayer who has issued "hybrid" securities should bear the burden of proving by a substantial preponderance of the evidence that he should be exempt from tax liability.

Keough v. St. Paul Milk Co. (1939) He

Facts: P was a minority stockholder in D. D had accumulated a large earned surplus, which its directors transferred to D's capital account over the objections of P, who wanted a dividend declared. P sued, claiming that D's capitalization of the earned surplus was fraudulent and constituted a breach of the directors' fiduciary duties.

Issue: Can the directors of a corporation refuse to declare a dividend where the corporation has amassed excessive earnings?

Rule: Absent a valid corporate need justifying the withholding of dividends, directors may not refuse to declare a dividend where the corporation has amassed excessive earnings.

Martin v. Schuler (1977) JB

Facts: The trustee (P) of a bankrupt company seeking reorganization sued the principal officers of the corporation (D) for the price of new stock issued to them by the corporation. P claimed that the sale was a pre-incorporation subscription for shares. D argued that the sale was pursuant to an executory contract, which was not enforceable.

Issue: Is an agreement to purchase new stock to be issued an executory contract or a subscription for shares?

Rule: If an agreement to purchase new stock is in proper statutory form and the proceeds therefrom are added to the corporation capital, it is a subscription for shares and binds its signatories.

Hidell v. International Diversified Investments (1975) JB

Facts: P entered into a subscription agreement for the purchase of D's shares. The agreement provided that P would not be bound until D had subscribed 20,000 shares. D later omitted this provision with the approval of P and the other subscribers and commenced operations with only 6,000 shares subscribed. Seven months after P's stock purchase, P learned that D signed a repurchase agreement with another subscriber and sought to conclude a similar agreement with D. D refused, and P sued D and its officers for damages for violation of SEC Rule 10b–5.

Issue: If in the solicitation of subscription agreements a corporation concludes a repurchase agreement with one of its subscribers, is it obligated to disclose this fact to its other subscribers?

Rule: Under SEC Rule 10b–5, a corporation has an affirmative duty to disclose a repurchase agreement that it concludes with one of its subscribers to its other subscribers if a reasonable investor would have attached importance to it.

Frink v. Carman Distributing Co. (1935) JB

Facts: P bought preferred stock in the Zott Company. Under the stock purchase plan, P received one share of common stock free with every share of preferred stock purchased. Zott subsequently went bankrupt. State law permitted the creditors of a bankrupt corporation to claim the corporate indebtedness against the corporation's stockholders up to the value of the stockholders' unpaid stock. A creditor of Zott (D) claimed against P.

190 Corporate Distributions

Issue: Can a stockholder who receives bonus unpaid stock in a corporation be held liable for the debts of that corporation up to the value of the unpaid stock?
Rule: A stockholder who receives bonus unpaid stock in a corporation is liable for the debts of that corporation up to the value of the unpaid stock held, and par value is the measure.

Eastern Oklahoma Television Co., Inc. v. Ameco, Inc. (1971) JB
Facts: Eastern Oklahoma was a corporation organized to secure broadcast rights and establish and operate a television station. Its board of directors, composed of three veterans of the broadcast industry, issued two types of stock and subscribed for all the shares of the senior type of stock in consideration for various services rendered to the corporation. A subscriber for the junior type of stock (P) sued for damages, claiming that the services provided did not constitute adequate consideration.
Issue: Can services or property be considered valid consideration for the issuance of par value stock?
Rule: Services or property within the meaning of the state constitution can be considered valid consideration for the issuance of par value stock.

Cahall v. Lofland (1922) JB
Facts: The directors of Lewes Fisheries Company (D) issued shares of stock to themselves. As consideration for the stock, each director gave a promissory note in which Lewes was the payee. Partial payment on the notes was made through dividends, but a portion remained unpaid when Lewes was liquidated and its assets distributed among its creditors and shareholders. Lewes' receiver (P) sued to recover both the balance on the promissory notes and funds distributed to the directors upon Lewes' liquidation.
Issue: Is a promissory note valid consideration for the issuance of stock?
Rule: A promissory not does not constitute valid consideration for the issuance of stock.

Hooper v. Mountain States Securities Corp. (1960) JB
Facts: D cooperated in a fraudulent scheme to cause Consolidated American Industries, Inc. to issue 700,000 shares of its stock to a sham

corporation established by D in exchange for two contract rights of inflated value. Consolidated's trustee in bankruptcy sued under Rule 10b–5 of the Securities Exchange Act of 1934, claiming that for purposes of the Rule, Consolidated was a "seller" and its issuance of stock a "sale."

Issue: Where a corporation is induced through a fraudulent scheme to issue stock in exchange for property of inflated value, is the corporation a "seller" and the stock issue a "sale" for purposes of Rule 10b–5 of the Securities Exchange Act of 1934?

Rule: Given the legislative purposes upon which Rule 10b–5 was based, a corporation is a "seller" and a stock issue is a "sale" for purposes of the Rule where the value of the property received for the value of the stock is inflated.

Spencer v. Anderson (1924) JB

Facts: The judgment creditor (P) of Medical Building Corporation, a bankrupt company, sued to enforce his judgment against the unpaid balance on a subscription contract concluded between Medical Building and D.

Issue: In an action to recover upon stockholders' unpaid subscriptions, does a creditor have a direct right of recovery?

Rule: In an action to recover upon stockholders' unpaid subscriptions, a creditor's right of recovery is based on his status as equitable assignee of a debtor corporation and is not a direct right.

Caplin v. Marine Midland Grace Trust Co. of New York (S.Ct. 1972) JB

Facts: D executed an indenture with Webb & Knapp, a company in financial trouble, that provided for the issuance of debentures. Webb & Knapp subsequently went bankrupt, and its reorganization trustee (P) found upon investigation that D had failed to fulfill its obligations as an indenture trustee. P sued on behalf of the debenture holders, seeking to recover from D the outstanding amount of the debentures.

Issue: Under Chapter X of the Bankruptcy Act, does a reorganization trustee have standing to hold an indenture trustee liable for misconduct on behalf of debenture holders?

Rule: (Marshall, J.) Since the legislative intent behind Chapter X of the Bankruptcy Act is silent on this point, a reorganization trustee

does not have standing to hold an indenture trustee liable for misconduct on behalf of debenture holders.
Dissent: (Douglas, J.) By not permitting the reorganization trustee from suing on behalf of debenture holders, the majority locks out one class of creditors and hampers the reorganization trustee's ability to formulate an equitable reorganization plan.

In re Stirling Homex Corp. (1978) JB

Facts: Stirling Homex, a maker of prefabricated housing, attracted investors (P) by concealing adverse information. Homex became insolvent and initiated reorganization proceedings. The reorganization trustee in bankruptcy determined that the claims of shareholders would be subordinated to those of Homex's general creditors. D argued that its claims should be treated equally with those of Homex's creditors, since they were induced to purchase Homex stock through fraudulent means.
Issue: Should the claims of defrauded shareholders be subordinated to those of general unsecured creditors in a corporate reorganization proceeding?
Rule: The claims of defrauded shareholders should be subordinated to those of general unsecured creditors in a corporate reorganization proceeding to preserve "the general rules of equity."

Fuller v. Krough (1962) JB

Facts: P and D formed Cormier Corp. and were its sole stockholders, each initially possessing an equal number of shares. Cormier's fortunes began to fail, however, and only D was able to contribute the additional capital necessary to keep the business going. In return for his contribution, D received additional stock in Cormier, increasing his holding in the company to twice that of P. P claimed that he had preemptive rights to the additional stock issued by Cormier and sought to have Cormier issue the number of shares required to equalize his holding with that of D.
Issue: Where stock has been issued in payment of a preexisting debt, can preemptive rights attach to the issue?
Rule: Preemptive rights can attach where stock has been issued in payment of a preexisting debt.

Adelman v. Conotti Corp. (1975) JB

Facts: The board of directors of Libbie Rehabilitation Center, Inc. was divided into two camps: the first, represented by P, controlled the voting rights for a majority of shares, while the second (D) owned a majority of shares but possessed voting rights for a minority share only. P's camp obtained a needed loan for Libbie that required that P put up a personal guaranty. As collateral for the loan, P arranged that Libbie's board vote to issue him 80,000 new shares of Libbie stock. D, who was not present at the board meeting and had no knowledge of the loan, became aware of the new share issue and offered to supply the guaranty itself. When this offer was refused, D sued to rescind the new share issue.

Issue: If a director withholds information relevant to the issuance of stock, does he breach his fiduciary duty to the shareholders and invalidate the issuance?

Rule: A director who withholds information relevant to the issuance of stock breaches his fiduciary duty to the shareholders and voids the issuance.

Schwartz v. Marien (1975) JB

Facts: A director of Superior Engraving Co. (D) caused the board of directors to sell to him treasury shares of Superior Engraving stock, thereby giving him voting control of the board. Another director (P) objected, claiming that the planned stock sale was concealed from her, that it diluted her interest in Superior Engraving, and that D had breached his fiduciary duty to other shareholders by selling himself treasury shares without offering them to her.

Issue: Is a director's sale of treasury stock to himself without offering it to other shareholders a breach of his fiduciary duty?

Rule: A director's sale of treasury stock to himself without offering it to other shareholders is a breach of fiduciary duty unless he proves that the sale served a significant business purpose that could not be accomplished through other means that would not disturb the positions of the other shareholders.

Goodnow v. American Writing Paper Co. (1908) JB

Facts: P sued to have a dividend on D's preferred stock declared unlawful. P claimed that D's capital stock was issued primarily for

over-valued property, that dividends should only be paid when D's net profits exceeded the par value of its shares, and that payment of dividends before then constituted an unlawful reduction of D's capital stock. D argued that because its balance sheet showed profits sufficient to pay a dividend, it should be allowed to do so.
Issue: Can a corporation lawfully distribute as dividends profits in excess of capital stock actually paid in?
Rule: A corporation can lawfully distribute as dividends profits arising from the business of the company in excess of capital stock actually paid in.

United States v. Riely (1948) JB
Facts: Pierce Oil Corporation, a Virginia corporation, earned a profit in 1937, but did not pay dividends and was consequently forced to pay an undistributed earnings tax. The relevant tax statute was later amended to exempt from the undistributed earnings tax those corporations that were prevented from distributing dividends by state law. Pierce Oil's receiver sued for a tax refund, claiming that Virginia state law prohibited the payment of dividends for corporations in Pierce's financial condition.
Issue: Can a corporation pay dividends from its net earnings over expenses for a given period, even when these net earnings fall short of the corporation's authorized capital stock?
Rule: A corporation can pay dividends from its net earnings over expenses for a given period, even when these net earnings fall short of the corporation's capital stock.

Miller v. Magline, Inc. (1977) JB
Facts: A minority shareholder, director, and former corporate officer (P) of Magline (D), a close corporation, sued to compel D to declare and pay a dividend. D, which had enjoyed several profitable years in a row, refused, citing, among other things, working capital shortages and inadequate reserve funds. P pointed to the generous profit distribution plan extended to corporate officers as proof of D's breach of fiduciary duty to its minority shareholders.
Issue: Is a corporation's refusal to pay dividends a breach of its fiduciary duty to its minority shareholders?

Rule: Where a corporation has a surplus of net profits, its refusal to pay dividends is a breach of its fiduciary duty to its minority shareholders.

Snyder v. Memco Engineering & Mfg. Co., Inc. (1965) JB
Facts: P held preferred stock in D, which was redeemable at a price stipulated in its articles of incorporation. Over a two-year period, D made separate purchases of blocks of its preferred stock at less than the prescribed redemption price. P sued for damages, seeking the full redemption price for his shares.
Issue: Can a corporation that has included a redemption price for its preferred stock in its articles of incorporation elect to forego redemption and instead buy back its preferred stock in separate purchases for a lower price?
Rule: A corporation that has included a redemption price for its preferred stock in its articles of incorporation can elect to forego redemption and instead buy back its preferred stock in separate purchases for a lower price.

Lewis v. H.P. Hood & Sons, Inc. (1954) JB
Facts: P was a director and shareholder of D. On three separate occasions, P approved board resolutions amending D's articles of incorporation so as to provide D with the authority to call for purchase the shares of any of its shareholders. Although it was common for members of D's board voluntarily to sell their shares back to D upon retirement, P did not do so when he retired, and D subsequently called for purchase half of D's shares.
Issue: Is a provision in a corporation's articles of incorporation that allows the corporation to call for purchase the shares of an individual shareholder enforceable?
Rule: A provision in a corporation's articles of incorporation that allows the corporation to call for purchase the shares of an individual shareholder is enforceable.

In re National Tile & Terrazzo Co., Inc. (1976) JB
Facts: A shareholder of National Tile (P) sold her shares back to National Tile in exchange for a note secured by a deed of trust on National Tile's property. After paying a portion of the amount due

196 Corporate Distributions

on the note, National Tile became insolvent, and P filed a claim of lien against the trustee in bankruptcy (D). D argued that since National Tile was insolvent and the note underlying P's lien had consequently become invalid, P's claim was not enforceable.

Issue: In a stock purchase transaction, can a lien against an insolvent corporation be enforced even where the note underlying the lien has failed?

Rule: In a stock purchase transaction, a lien against an insolvent corporation is not invalidated by the unenforceability of the underlying note.

Moore v. Bay (1931) JB

Facts: D executed a mortgage that was admitted to be void due to improper execution as to creditors who were such at the date of the mortgage and those who became creditors after the date of the mortgage but prior to its recordation. In bankruptcy, a question was raised whether the mortgage was void as to those who became creditors after recordation.

Issue: Should the assets marshalled by the trustee of a bankrupt estate be distributed equally among all creditors with valid claims?

Rule: The assets marshalled by the trustee of a bankrupt estate should be distributed equally among all creditors with valid claims, except where there are creditors with priority or secured claims.

Maley v. Carroll (1967) JB

Facts: D sold his business in exchange for secured notes that would defer payment over twenty years. With the sale completed, D had nothing more to do with the business. At the time of the sale, D's business was a going concern, but after four years under new ownership, it became insolvent. D filed a claim against the trustee in bankruptcy (P) for the amount due on the notes. P countered by bringing an action against D to void the sale, claiming that the transaction was a ruse to enable D to redeem his stock and that the corporate form of the new business should be disregarded.

Issue: Can corporate form be disregarded to hold a previous owner of a now insolvent corporation personally liable for the corporation's debts?

Rule: Corporate form cannot be disregarded to hold a previous owner of an insolvent corporation personally liable for the corporation's debts where there is no evidence of bad faith or fraud in the transaction between the previous and present owners.

Minton v. Cavaney (1961) JB
Facts: P obtained a tort judgment against Seminole Hot Springs Corporation. Cavaney, D's husband, was Seminole's attorney, and conducted the incorporation of Seminole, served as one of Seminole's three directors, and kept Seminole's records at his office. When P could not enforce its judgment against Seminole, which was undercapitalized, it sought to hold D personally liable as executor of Cavaney's estate under the "alter-ego" doctrine.
Issue: Can a director of a corporation that he knows to be undercapitalized be held personally liable for the obligations of the corporation?
Rule: Undercapitalization of a corporation is an abuse of corporate privilege, resulting in the personal liability of those directors who actively participate in the conduct of its business.

DeWitt Truck Brokers, Inc. v. W. Ray Flemming Fruit Co. (1976) JB
Facts: D operated and served as president of a corporation that sold fruit on commission for growers. The corporation was undercapitalized, failed to adhere to required corporate formalities, and was dominated by, and operated for, the personal benefit of D. D defaulted on payments to P, which provided D with transportation services, and P sought to hold D personally liable for the debt.
Issue: In the absence of fraud, is disregard of corporate entity supported where the corporation is insufficiently capitalized and is dominated by, and used for the personal benefit of, the principal shareholder?
Rule: In the absence of fraud, disregard of corporate entity is supported where the corporation is insufficiently capitalized, is dominated by, and used for the personal benefit of, the principal shareholder, and where preserving the corporate form would produce injustice or inequity.

198   Corporate Distributions

Stodd v. Goldberger (1977) JB
Facts: M.I.I. Corp entered into a joint venture with Goldco, a limited partnership run by D. M.I.I. went bankrupt, leaving no assets. M.I.I.'s trustee in bankruptcy claimed against D, alleging among other things that D created M.I.I. as an "alter ego" and should be held liable for its debts.
Issue: Can a trustee in bankruptcy maintain an action against corporate shareholders under an "alter ego" theory without allegations giving rise to a cause of action for the bankrupt corporation?
Rule: In the absence of any allegation of injury to the bankrupt corporation, a trustee in bankruptcy cannot maintain an action against corporate shareholders under an "alter ego" theory. This cause of action belongs only to the corporate creditors.

In re Mader's Store for Men, Inc. (1977) JB
Facts: Gelatt (D) was the half-owner of Mader's Store for Men, Inc. At the time D purchased his half-share, Mader's capitalization was $65,000. Mader's encountered financial difficulty, and D made four advances to Mader's totalling $45,000. Mader's subsequently declared bankruptcy, and the trustee subordinated D's claim to those of Mader's general unsecured creditors.
Issue: Can claims arising from shareholder loans to a bankrupt corporation be subordinated to the claims of general unsecured creditors where the corporation was adequately capitalized?
Rule: Absent fraud, claims arising from shareholder loans to a bankrupt corporation will be treated at parity with the claims of general unsecured creditors where the corporation was adequately capitalized and the loan was not intended to become part of the corporation's financial structure.

Walkovsky v. Carlton (1966) JB
Facts: P was struck by a taxi cab owned by Seon Cab Corporation, one of ten taxi cab companies established by D as separate entities to minimize liability insurance costs. P brought a tort action against each cab company and its shareholders, alleging that D operated all of the companies as a single entity. D moved for dismissal of the pleadings for failure to state a cause of action.
Issue: Where a complaint alleges that ownership of assets has been deliberately broken up and intermingled among several corporations,

each insufficiently capitalized to ensure adequate recovery in a tort suit, is a cause of action sufficient to support disregard of corporate entity and personal liability of individual shareholders established?
Rule: To support disregard of corporate entity and hold shareholders personally liable, a complaint must allege that the separate corporations were undercapitalized, their assets have been intermingled, and the shareholders used the corporations in their personal capacities for purely personal rather than corporate ends.

In re Fett Roofing & Sheet Metal Co., Inc. (1977) SSB
Facts: P incorporated his sole proprietorship, became its sole stockholder and president, and provided it with an insufficient amount of paid-in capital. On three separate occasions, P took out bank loans and made the funds available to the corporation in exchange for promissory notes. Just prior to the corporation's bankruptcy, P recorded deeds of trust on the assets of the corporation to secure the notes and upon bankruptcy sought to claim at parity with other creditors. The bankruptcy court subordinated P's claim, finding that the transfer of funds from P to the corporation constituted a contribution to capital rather than a loan.
Issue: Can a bankruptcy court use its equitable powers to look beyond the form of the transfer and the intent of the parties to determine whether a transfer of funds from shareholders to a corporation should be treated as a bona fide debt or as equity?
Rule: A bankruptcy court can use its equitable powers to look beyond the form of the transfer and the intent of the parties to factors such as the adequacy of the initial capitalization, the debt-to-equity ratio, and interest payments to determine whether a transfer of funds from shareholders to a corporation should be treated as a bona fide debt or as equity.

Kamin v. American Express Co. (1976) SSB
Facts: D had purchased Donaldson, Lufkin and Jenrette, Inc. (DLJ), and D's directors had planned to distribute DLJ's stock to its shareholders rather than sell it publicly. Minority stockholders (P) in D sued to rescind the distribution, alleging that by not selling DLJ's stock publicly, D was passing up a tax savings of $80 million. D

moved for dismissal of P's complaint for failure to state a cause of action.
Issue: Absent a showing of fraud or bad faith, can a minority shareholder prevent the majority from paying a distribution where it would have been to the corporation's financial advantage to withhold the distribution?
Rule: A minority shareholder must prove that the majority shareholders acted fraudulently or in bad faith in the pursuit of a given policy within their discretion to make out a cause of action.

G. Loewus & Co. v. Highland Queen Packing Co. (1939) V
Facts: The certificate of incorporation of Highland Queen Packing Co. (D) authorized its directors to issue no-par shares and set the consideration for the purchase of the shares. Highland Queen issued stock worth $6,000 to three investors (D) in exchange for payments totalling $2,550 and subsequently went bankrupt. Highland Queen's receiver (P) sought to assess against the three stockholders the difference between the stated consideration for the stock and the price they actually paid.
Issue: Where by statute it is provided that purchasers of par value shares at less than par will be liable for the difference in the event of corporate insolvency, can purchasers of no-par shares be held liable for the difference between stated consideration and the price actually paid?
Rule: In the case of insolvency, the principles that govern the liability to creditors of the holders of par value shares apply to the liability to creditors of the holders of no-par shares.

Costello v. Fazio (1958) V
Facts: D was a partner in a plumbing supply company and had contributed a considerably larger sum of capital to the partnership than had the other two partners. After the company's business started to fail, D and the other partners decided to incorporate the company, and D withdrew most of the partnership capital from the corporation by converting it into debt evidenced by a promissory note, leaving the corporation with inadequate capital. The corporation subsequently went bankrupt, and D filed creditor's claims with the trustee in bankruptcy (P) for payment of the note. P objected to the claims,

arguing that they should be subordinated to the claims of general unsecured creditors.

Issue: Can a bankruptcy court subordinate a claim brought against the bankrupt corporation by one of its shareholders as creditor?

Rule: A bankruptcy court can subordinate a claim brought by a shareholder where the shareholder has exercised control of the corporation for his personal and private benefit, has inadequately capitalized the corporation, and if honoring the claim would do injustice to innocent creditors.

Gilligan, Will & Co. v. Securities and Exchange Commission (1959) V

Facts: Elliott & Company offered for purchase to Gilligan (D) $300,000 of Crowell-Collier 5 percent convertible debentures, which Crowell-Collier wished to sell privately, without registration. Gilligan agreed to purchase $100,000 of debentures for his own account. Although as part of the sale, Gilligan signed a statement that he had no present intention of distributing the debentures, he sold to two others half of the debentures he had purchased, and placed the remainder in the trading account of Gilligan, Will & Co. (D). Gilligan later agreed to find purchasers for an additional issue of Crowell-Collier debentures, for which Gilligan, Will & Co. received 50,000 stock warrants. The SEC determined that D had violated § 5 of the Securities Act of 1933, in response to which D claimed an exemption based on the private nature of the offering.

Issue: Where a party has purchased unregistered securities with a view towards distributing them to a small group of select buyers, do the purchase and distribution constitute a public offering requiring registration under § 5 of the Securities Act of 1933?

Rule: Wherever a small group of eventual buyers of securities lack the knowledge required to make informed investment decisions, the purchase of unregistered shares for purposes of distribution constitutes a public offering requiring registration under § 5 of the Securities Act of 1933.

Kaiser-Frazer Corp. v. Otis & Co. (1952) V

Facts: P concluded a contract with Otis & Co. (D) and two other firms under which D and the others would purchase and underwrite

202 Corporate Distributions

the distribution of 900,000 of P's shares. The sales contract provided that if P's registration statement or prospectus contained any misleading statements, or if P was involved in any material litigation, D could reject the securities. On the day of the closing of the sale, D and one other firm rejected the securities on the basis of litigation initiated that day by one of P's shareholders seeking to enjoin the sale. As an alternative reason for refusing the stock, D claimed that P's registration statement contained misleading statements.

Issue: If the registration statement or prospectus produced in connection with an issuance of securities contains misleading statements, can an underwriting agreement between the issuer and the underwriter be enforced?

Rule: An underwriting agreement is unenforceable if the registration statement or prospectus produced in connection with the issuance of securities contains misleading statements.

Hyman v. Velsicol Corp. (1951) V

Facts: Velsicol Corp. (D) was organized by P, a research chemist and inventor, and Regenstein (D), who through Arvey and Transco Corporations (D) provided the capital required to produce P's inventions. D became a director and the president of Velsicol, and P served as both a director and vice president. Eighty shares of Velsicol stock went to Arvey and Transco, while P received forty shares. Relations between P and the other Velsicol directors soured, leading P to resign as a board member and officer and start his own company. Velsicol subsequently implemented a recapitalization plan under which the par value of Velsicol's stock would be decreased and the number of shares issued would be increased. Though P was offered the chance to exercise his rights to purchase his pro rata share of the new stock, he sued to enjoin the recapitalization plan, claiming that its purpose was to dilute his interest in Velsicol and that it represented a violation of the fiduciary duty of Velsicol's board toward its stockholders.

Issue: Where the board of directors of a corporation has, for legitimate business reasons, implemented a recapitalization plan under which the pro rata share of the new stock offered to shareholders is prohibitively expensive, has the board violated its fiduciary duty toward its shareholders?

Rule: Absent a showing by a shareholder of bad faith on the part of the board of directors, the fiduciary duty of the board of directors towards shareholders is not violated where it implements, for legitimate business reasons, a recapitalization plan under which the pro rata share of the new stock offered to shareholders is prohibitively expensive.

Bennett v. Breuil Petroleum Corp. (1953) V

Facts: Bennett (P) and Breuil (D) established Breuil Petroleum Corp. (D), with P holding 423,500 shares and Breuil holding 567,000. Relations between P and Breuil deteriorated, and Breuil made two unsuccessful attempts to buy out P's share in the corporation. Breuil thereafter caused the shareholders of Breuil Petroleum to decrease the par value of existing shares, increase the number of authorized shares, and deny preemptive rights to the new shares. Though P was offered the chance to purchase his pro rata share of the new stock, P sued to cancel the issuance of the new shares, claiming that the motive behind the sale of the new shares was improper and the price of the new stock was unfairly low.

Issue: Can the board of directors authorize the issuance of new stock for the primary purpose of "freezing out" a minority stockholder, even where the price of the new stock is fair?

Rule: The board of directors cannot authorize the issuance of new stock for the primary purpose of "freezing out" a minority stockholder, even where the price of the new stock is fair.

United States Trust Co. v. First Nat. City Bank (1977) V

Facts: First National City Bank (D) served as trustee for itself and three other banks under an indenture agreement with Equity Funding for the issuance of debentures. At the same time, D provided loans to, and was a creditor of, Equity Funding under a "Revolving Credit Agreement" secured by a promissory note. Equity Funding went bankrupt, and D resigned as trustee and was replaced by P. Section 613(a) of the Trust Indenture Act required a trustee to hold in account for the benefit of both the trustee and debenture holders any payments or property paid on the debentures or as security on the trustee's individual creditor claim, while § 613(b) exempted securities acquired by the trustee. P sued, claiming that the payments on the

204 Corporate Distributions

promissory note securing the "Revolving Credit Agreement" should have been subject to § 613(a)'s sharing provision, and that by favoring its claims as creditor over its obligation as trustee, D breached its fiduciary duty to the debenture holders. D claimed that the note was a security for purposes of § 613(b) and was therefore exempt from the provisions of § 613(a), and that as a trustee it had no fiduciary duty to the debenture holders.

Issue: Does a bank acting both as a lender to a debtor and as an indenture trustee for debt securities issued by the same debtor have a fiduciary duty as trustee to the holders of the debt securities?

Rule: A bank acting both as a lender to a debtor and as an indenture trustee for debt securities issued by the same debtor has a fiduciary duty as trustee to the holders of the debt securities, and a violation of this fiduciary duty occurs where the trustee has an interest in the debtor that involves a material conflict with the interests of the holders of the debt securities.

Polk v. Good (1986) V

Facts: Texaco (D) took over Getty Oil Company and was having trouble refinancing the debt incurred. Texaco feared that the Bass Group (D), which owned stock comprising approximately 10 percent of Texaco, would push to acquire a greater share in Texaco, leading eventually to a tender offer and a corporate raid. Bass offered Texaco its Texaco stock for a price 3 percent higher than market price, and Texaco, acting on the advice of its bankers and counsel, repurchased the stock from Bass to avoid further trouble with Bass. A group of Texaco's stockholders (P) sued, claiming that Texaco's purchase of its own stock at higher-than-market price constituted economic waste

Issue: Can a corporation acquire its own shares from a hostile shareholder?

Rule: Unless the primary purpose is to perpetuate the directors in office, the acquisition by a corporation of its own shares from a hostile shareholder is permissible if the board had a justifiable belief that there existed a reasonable threat to corporate enterprise.

Chapter 7

SECURITIES REGULATION

I. INTRODUCTION

Why Regulate Securities?

1. Public distrust of securities market has serious economic consequences.

2. A great proportion of people in the United States invest in securities.

3. Lack of self-help remedies.

II. THE DISCLOSURE SYSTEM

A. The Securities Act of 1933 ('33 Act)

1. Applies to the initial public distribution of securities.

2. Creates a system of mandatory disclosure.

3. Expanded definition of actionable fraud:

   a. The issuer is strictly liable for material misstatements.

   b. The officers and directors and others who participate in the offering are liable and have the burden of proving reasonable diligence.

4. Registration Statement

The registration statement is the '33 Act's critical instrument of disclosure, containing the prospectus distributed to potential investors.

   a. Must be approved by the SEC.

   b. No other promotion is allowed until the registration statement is approved and becomes effective.

   c. Standard forms promulgated by SEC (S–1, S–2, and S–3) are used to prepare the registration statement.

   d. Includes:

      i. Any risk factors that make the offering speculative;

      ii. Detailed information about the issuer's line of business; and

      iii. Management's assessment of recent business trends, projected capital needs, firm liquidity, and the reasons for any fluctuations in profits and revenues.

5. Liability for Material Misstatements

   a. Strict liability for the issuer.

   b. Negligence liability for secondary participants; must prove "due diligence" defense. (see below III.B.5.a)

B. Securities Exchange Act of 1934 ('34 Act)

1. A continuous disclosure system focussing on the secondary market.

2. Aimed at improving the market's efficiency by informing the professional investor.

3. A corporation must enter into continuous disclosure system if:

   a. Its securities are listed on a national securities exchange (§ 12(b));

   b. At least five hundred persons hold any class of its equity securities and the corporation has gross assets of over a specified level (presently five million dollars) (§ 12(g)); or

   c. The corporation files a '33 Act registration statement that becomes effective (§ 15(d)).

4. Periodic Reports to be Filed

   a. 10–K: annual report
   b. 10–Q: quarterly report
   c. 8–K: material development

5. Rule 14A–3 requires "reporting" companies to provide, along with proxy statements, annual reports containing audited financial information covering a two-year period and the Management's Discussion and Analysis of Financial Condition and Results of Operations, a "basic information package" consisting of certain essential financial information and a qualitative discussion of recent earnings performance. Most shareholders will then receive a summarized version of the data required by the '34 Act.

C. Integrated Disclosure

   1. Abbreviated Registration Statements

      Allows incorporation by reference material from '34 Act filings into '33 Act registration statements.

      a. Form S–3: Most abbreviated form for corporations that the SEC has determined are sufficiently traded to respond to the '34 Act information:

i. Companies whose public "float" (i.e., the aggregate market value of outstanding voting stock held by non-affiliates) exceeded $150 million; or

ii. Companies whose public "float" exceeded only $100 million but whose annual trading volume exceeded three million shares.

b. Form S–2: For companies who have experience in the '34 Act reporting system by:

i. Having been a reporting company under the '34 Act for the preceding twelve months;

ii. Having made timely fillings of all reports for the last twelve months; and

iii. Having not defaulted on debt or preferred stock dividends since its most recently filed audited financial statements.

c. Standard S–1 is used by companies not subject to the '34 Act or those who have recently become a reporting company.

2. Efficient Capital Market Hypothesis (ECMH)

a. Theory: The security price reflects all available relevant information and changes immediately with new information because of competition by market professionals.

b. Shifts focus of disclosure requirements from individual investor to the market as a whole.

3. Shelf Registration
Rule 415 allows an issuer to sell securities without advance notice when market conditions are right for up to two years. This is done by registering stock for future sale by filling a

registration statement that automatically incorporates by reference subsequently filed '34 Act reports.

D. "Blue Sky" Regulation: State Securities Regulation

1. Various state statutes have followed three basic regulatory approaches:

    a. Imposing state licensing requirements on securities dealers (brokers, dealers, salesmen, and investment advisers);

    b. Prohibiting fraudulent practices; and

    c. Requiring registration of securities to be sold in-state.

2. Most states have adopted the Uniform Securities Act, introduced in 1956, that affords three methods of securities registration:

    a. Notification
    Registration by notification is available for seasoned issuers and only requires a modest amount of information;

    b. Coordination
    Registration by coordination is available for issuers who have registered with the SEC under the '33 Act and uses same documents filed under the '33 Act, and it becomes effective along with the federal registration absent an administrative action to the contrary.

    c. Qualification
    Registration by qualification is available in states where notification and coordination do not exist or when corporations do not qualify for them and requires similar information to that of a '33 Act federal registration.

210 Securities Regulation

3. While federal regulation is based on disclosure, state administrators attempt to ascertain the substantive merits of a particular securities issue.

E. Disclosure Requirements of Self-Regulatory Organizations

Self-regulatory organizations, such as the New York Stock Exchange (NYSE), the American Stock Exchange (ASE), or the National Association of Securities Dealers Quotation System (NASDAQ), create an affirmative duty for corporations under their listing agreements to disclose material information to the public. Unlike the periodic reports required under the '34 Act, these rules call for timely disclosure of material information on a continuing basis.

F. When Does a Duty to Disclose Arise?

1. When a corporation is not itself trading, federal law imposes no affirmative duty to disclose, but only a duty not to make false statements.

2. A company has no duty to disclose, correct or verify, or halt trading when rumors are influencing its stocks price unless those rumors can be attributed to the company or scienter is otherwise established.

3. For a delay in the disclosure of an earnings decline by a corporation to be considered improper, it must be shown, using a subjective business judgment approach, that the corporation, acting in bad faith, failed to issue the special earnings statement when sufficient information was available for an accurate release or could have been collected by the exercise of due diligence. Information may be withheld until it is "ripe" for publication; that is, the data have been verified sufficiently so that officers and directors of the corporation have full confidence in their accuracy.

III. LIABILITIES IN SECURITIES ISSUANCES AND TRADING

A. Civil Liabilities in Public Offerings

There are four provisions for liability contained in the '33 Act:

1. Section 11 creates liability for false statements in a registration statement.

    a. Anyone who has purchased the stock may bring suit and need not prove reliance.

    b. The issuer is subject to strict liability, but other defendants may raise the "due diligence defense."

2. Section 12(1) imposes liability for violation of § 5 of the '33 Act, most often an unregistered public offering.

3. Section 12(2) imposes a general liability for fraudulent statements or omissions in connection with the sale of securities, not limited to those on registration statements.

4. Section 17(a) imposes liability for "any device, scheme, or artifice to defraud" in connection with the sale of securities. This section does not express a civil remedy.

B. Section 10(b) and Rule 10b–5

1. Section 10(b) of the Securities Exchange Act of 1934 makes it unlawful to "use or employ, in connection with the purchase or sale of any security registered on a national securities exchange or any security not so registered, any manipulative or deceptive device or contrivance in contravention of such rules and regulations as the Commission may prescribe as necessary or appropriate in the public interest or for the protection of investors."

2. With respect to the purchase or sale of any security, Rule 10b–5 makes it unlawful to:

   a. Employ any device, scheme or artifice, to defraud;

   b. Make any untrue statement of a material fact or to omit to state a material fact necessary in order to make the statements made, in the light of the circumstances under which they were made, not misleading; or

   c. Engage in any act, practice, or course of business which operates or would operate as a fraud or deceit upon any person.

3. Courts have found an implied private right of action in Rule 10b–5 since investors trading in securities are members of the class that the rule was designed to protect.

4. The Elements of a Cause of Action Under Rule 10b–5

   a. Standing

      i. The Birnbaum Doctrine
         The plaintiff must be a purchaser or seller of the company's stock. Those who have been discouraged from purchasing or selling due to fraud are not covered by the statute.

      ii. Exceptions to the Birnbaum Doctrine:

         (1) Injunctive Relief has been permitted to those allegedly injured by violations of Rule 10b–5 who where neither purchasers nor sellers and therefore could not ask for damages.

         (2) Those becoming "forced sellers" from mergers, recognized as sales for securities law purposes, may sue for damages even though they still hold their shares.

b. **Materiality**
The defendant must have misrepresented a material fact. A fact is material if there is a substantial likelihood that a reasonable investor would consider it important in deciding whether to make a transaction. Materiality will depend at any given time upon the balancing of both the indicated probability that the event will occur and the anticipated magnitude of the event in light of the company's activity.

c. Causation
Accepting the "fraud-on-the-market" theory that all publicly available information is reflected in the market price, an investor's reliance on any public material misrepresentations may be presumed for the purposes of a Rule 10b–5 action. Reliance provides the requisite causal connection between a defendant's misrepresentation and a plaintiff's injury.

d. Scienter

   i. A private cause of action for damages may not lie under § 10 or Rule 10b–5 in the absence of an alleged intent to deceive, manipulate, or defraud.

   ii. Although the Supreme Court has still not spoken on this issue, all courts of appeals that have considered it have found recklessness sufficient to satisfy the scienter requirement.

e. Damages
A reasonable investor is entitled to an amount which offsets any loss he suffered by a deceitfully induced sale, to be decided on a case-by-case basis. Damages recoverable from a Rule 10b–5 action need not be limited to the net economic harm suffered by the plaintiff.

i. "Out of Pocket" Damages
This usual form of relief available for a Rule 10b–5 violation awards the difference between the price paid and the actual value received in the transaction.

ii. Rescission
Frequently awarded in cases involving privately held corporations where the "out of pocket" measure is difficult to calculate because no active market exists. Some argue that this remedy protects investors too much, but others say that the need for deterrence, the language of § 29 of the '34 Act providing that any contract made in violation of the Act "shall be void," and that it is more appropriate to give the defrauded party the benefit of windfalls than the fraudulent party justify its use.

iii. The "Cover" Measure
This gives the plaintiff a reasonable period after disclosure of the fraud to determine whether or not to reinvest or "cover."

iv. In cases where a plaintiff can prove that losses were proximately caused by the defendant's misrepresentations, some courts have allowed recovery of consequential damages.

5. Defenses Based on the Plaintiff's Conduct

   a. Due Diligence
   Defendant claims that even though he might be at fault, his actions would have had no effect if the plaintiff had used due care.

   b. *In Pari Delicto*
   Defendant claims, rarely successfully, that the plaintiff was at equal fault as himself and that barring the suit would not interfere with the proper enforcement of securities laws.

6. Corporate Mismanagement

   a. Section 10(b) bars deceptive devices and contrivances in the purchase or sale of securities whether conducted in the organized markets or face to face.

   b. A claim of fraud and fiduciary breach constitutes a cause of action under § 10(b) or Rule 10b–5 only if the conduct alleged can be fairly viewed as "manipulative or deceptive" within the meaning of the statute. If, however, the facts concerning the sale of shares to a parent that were not disclosed or were misleadingly disclosed to the shareholders by the officers of a corporation breaching their fiduciary duty were material and reliance can be shown, perhaps in the form of missed opportunities to take injunctive action, then those who were misled have a cause of action under Rule 10b–5.

   c. Where approval by the shareholders is not necessary, full disclosure to a disinterested board of directors is equivalent to full disclosure to the shareholders. However, where shareholder approval is required, full disclosure must be made.

7. The sale of 100 percent of the stock in a corporation, although actually the sale of the business itself, is still considered the sale of securities subject to the antifraud provisions of the federal securities laws.

IV. INSIDER TRADING

Federal antifraud securities regulations prohibit any person in a position giving access, directly or indirectly, to information intended to be available only for a corporate purpose and not for the personal benefit of anyone, particularly officers, directors, or controlling stockholders, otherwise known as "insiders," from taking advantage of such information knowing it is unavailable to those with whom he is dealing.

A. Possible Harms and Benefits of Insider Trading

1. Harms of Insider Trading

a. Corporate Harm
Insider trading harms the corporation whose confidential plans are revealed. Efficiency might also be affected if officials waste time searching for undisclosed material information or restrict access to information, thereby restricting information flow within the firm, which could deprive the firm of internal dialogue, advice, and criticism. The corporation might also suffer harm to its reputation that could affect its sales or sales of its securities.

b. Delayed Disclosure and Inefficiency
If the disclosure of material nonpublic information is delayed by insiders, some firms will trade at prices that are either too high or too low on an inefficient capital market. Some corporations will have a cost of capital that does not accurately reflect their true risks and prospects as a result of this distortion in stock prices. This will result in inefficient investment decisions and allocative inefficiency of the economy's resources.

c. Investor Injury
Investors who sell to an insider before the disclosure of good news and buy from an insider before the release of bad news are harmed. However, the insider's action may have a slight effect on the market price, making the investor better off than if he had bought or sold without insider trading. Only those who trade during the period of non-disclosure and would have behaved differently if there had been no insider trading are actually harmed.

2. Ostensible Benefits of Insider Trading

   Four basic arguments are made in favor of insider trading.

   a. *Claim:* Insider trading enhances market efficiency since hidden information will be reflected in the market.
   Counter: Insider trading, an indirect and ambiguous signal, is probably a relatively inefficient way to cause information to be reflected in prices and is far less efficient than disclosure in causing the market to respond rapidly and accurately. In addition, securities dealers will have to widen their bid/asked differential, making securities trading more expensive to investors and weakening market efficiency.

   b. *Claim:* Insider trading is compensation for entrepreneurs and provides incentives to managers to take risks.
   Counter: Managers are not systematically undercompensated and insiders who could profit from nonpublic material information cannot usually be considered entrepreneurs. Insiders can still profit on adverse inside information and this would cause an inefficient compensation scheme.

   c. *Claim:* Corporations have generally not taken steps to prohibit insider trading themselves.
   Counter: Firms probably do not try to prohibit insider trading because it is already criminal and prohibitions are enforced by public authorities. Private detection and enforcement are not practically feasible since firms do not have the investigative means available to public authorities.

   d. *Claim:* Insider Trading is too costly to prohibit.

B. Enforceability: Who is Covered

   1. The duty to disclose under § 10(b) does not arise from the mere possession of nonpublic information; there can be no fraud from nondisclosure absent a duty to speak. Insiders usually have a

fiduciary duty to speak, but might give an outsider, who has no duty, the information.

2. A tippee (one who receives inside information—a tip—from an insider) assumes a fiduciary duty to shareholders of a corporation not to trade on material nonpublic information only when the insider has breached a fiduciary duty to his shareholders by disclosing the information to the tippee and the tippee knows or should know that there has been a breach. An insider has breached his fiduciary duty if he will personally benefit, directly or indirectly, from his disclosure. A tippee may sue a tipper since tippees are not as responsible, their duty is derivative from the insider's duty, and it would aid in enforcement of the securities laws. In such a case, the tipper may not raise the *in pari delicto* defense.

3. Misappropriation Theory
Persons who trade based on inside information in a security of a corporation to which they do not owe a fiduciary duty are still liable under Rule 10b–5 if the information is "misappropriated" from a party to whom a duty is owed. For example, an employee may not misappropriate material nonpublic information from his employer in connection with a scheme to purchase and sell securities.

4. Rule 14–3
An SEC rule adopted in 1980 that prohibits trading on nonpublic information concerning a tender offer, even if no fiduciary duty has been breached.

C. Causation and Damages

1. Causation

a. In silent insider trading cases, the "fraud on the market theory" has little relevance. A plaintiff cannot be said to have relied on information which was never disclosed.

b. A plaintiff must establish a causal connection between the defendants misconduct and his loss. This causal connection does not exist when the defendant only trades with third parties and the plaintiff traded on the impersonal market, otherwise unaffected by the wrongful acts of the insider.

c. The duty to disclose is owed to the class of investors trading contemporaneously with the insider and it is only this group who are the beneficiaries of a relaxed causation standard. Thus, one who sells (buys) on material inside information is liable not only to the purchasers (sellers) of the actual shares sold (bought) by him but to all persons who during the same period purchased (sold) stock in the open market without knowledge of the material inside information.

2. Damages

   a. The "Disgorgement" Measure
   After any purchase or sale based on inside information, any uninformed investor, where a reasonable investor would either have delayed his purchase (sale) or not purchased (sold) at all if he had the benefit of the tipped information, is allowed to recover any post-purchase decline in market value of his shares up to a reasonable time after he learns of the tipped information or after there is a public disclosure of it. Recovery is limited, however, to the amount gained by the tippee as a result of his selling (buying) at the earlier date, rather than delaying his sale until the parties could trade on an equal informational basis.

   b. Racketeer Influenced Corrupt Organizations (RICO)
   Treble damages can be sought in a private suit under the RICO statute if the securities law violation was part of a "pattern of racketeering activity" and the plaintiff can demonstrate an injury to his "business or property." In addition to treble damages, RICO can also be used when there would otherwise be standing limitations for the plaintiff. The success in use of RICO by plaintiffs in this

way has been limited, but the statute does provide extra leverage in settlement negotiations.

D. Section 16(b) and "Short-Swing" Profits

Section 16(b) of the '34 Act states an automatic rule that anyone who is an officer, director, or a beneficial owner of more than 10 percent of a public corporation's shares cannot buy and sell any amount of the corporation's stock within a six month period, and doing so would make him liable to the corporation for any profits realized on the transaction in a federal suit brought by the corporation or shareholder derivative action.

1. What is an Officer?

   a. Rule 3b–2 under the '34 Act defines "officer" as a "president, vice president, secretary, treasurer or principal financial officer, comptroller or principal accounting officer, and any person routinely performing corresponding functions with respect to any organization whether incorporated or unincorporated."

   b. Liability under § 16(b) is not based simply upon a person's title within his corporation; rather, liability follows from the existence of a relationship with the corporation that makes it more probable than not that the individual has access to inside information.

   c. Deputization

      1. When a representative of one corporation sits as an officer or director of a second corporation in whose shares the representative's corporation trades, his corporation can be liable for violating § 16(b) under a "deputization theory."

      2. While under § 16(b) a partnership can be a "director, officer, or 10 percent shareholder" when it has a member

acting as such for a corporation whose shares the partnership trades, a partnership is not absolutely liable under the statute in such a situation. Absent evidence of deputization and use of inside information, only that partner "inside" can be held accountable for his shares of the profits made by the partnership on a short swing transaction.

2. What is a Beneficial Owner?

   a. Section 16(b) covers a person who owns 10 percent or more of any class of the company's stock, not just those who hold 10 percent of the corporation's total equity.

   b. Convertible securities (preferred stocks or bonds that are convertible into common stock) are most often treated as if they were already converted in determining the percentage held.

   c. Attribution
   Under § 16(b), a person can be the owner if he is "directly or indirectly the beneficial owner." Courts may treat two people as one for this purpose, making one's ownership the indirect ownership of the other or one's transactions the transactions of the other. A person will generally be regarded as the beneficial owner of his spouse's or minor children's securities, but most often not his adult children.

      i. The exercise of control by an insider over his spouse's investment decisions would justify treating the insider as the beneficial owner of his spouse's securities for the purposes of § 16(b).

      ii. The profit realized by a corporate insider, as stated in §16(b), means direct pecuniary benefit to the insider; it is not enough that ties of affinity or consanguinity between the nominal recipient and the insider make it likely that the insider will experience an enhanced sense of well-being as a result of the receipt, or will be lead to reduce his gift giving to the recipient.

3. Timing Under 16(b): Beneficial Owner

   a. Section 16(b) does not apply if the "beneficial owner was not such both at the time of the purchase and sale, or the sale and purchase, of the security involved."

      i. The effect of this is that the initial purchase that brings him over the 10 percent mark is not subject to the statute. He must only account for profits from a transaction if he was already the beneficial owner of more than 10 percent of the stock before the purchase of the additional shares.

      ii. The sale of stock bringing a beneficial owner below the 10 percent mark is, however, considered a sale falling under § 16(b). The reasoning behind this is that the person was over 10 percent owner with access to inside information at the time he decided to sell.

   b. Under § 16(b), a statutory insider might sell enough shares to bring his holdings below 10 percent, and later, but still within six months, sell additional shares free from liability.

4. Timing Under 16(b): Officer or Director

   a. One need only be a director or officer of a corporation at the time of either his purchase or sale of its securities to fall under § 16(b) liability.

   b. For the purposes of § 16(b), an officer is presumed to have continued access to confidential information during the period between the tender of his resignation and when it becomes effective, and the officer must prove substantial evidence to overcome this presumption and escape liability for short-swing profits.

c. It has been held that a person who engages in a short-swing transaction in shares of a corporation that he has recently retired from as an officer or director is not liable under § 16(b).

d. It is unclear under § 16(b) whether liability would attach to a person who, within a six-month period, first purchases shares, then becomes an officer or director, then resigns, and then sells the shares.

5. What is a Purchase or Sale?

In order for a transaction that is not definitively a "purchase" or "sale", such as a merger or the execution of an option, to be considered a "purchase" or "sale" for the purposes of § 16(b), the transaction must (1) be voluntary (i.e., not mandated by state law), and (2) must serve as a vehicle for the evil that congress sought to prevent (i.e., the realization of profits based on inside information). A defendant must show that both of these criteria were not present in order prevent his disposal from being considered a § 16(b) sale.

6. Damages Under § 16(b): Computation of Profits

Under § 16(b) liability, a defendant must forfeit to the corporation all his profits realized in his short-swing transactions. To solve the ambiguity of calculating profits in the case of multiple purchases or sales, courts generally take the lowest price paid and the highest price sold and attribute those prices to all the purchases and sales. This simple method of calculation yields the highest profit figure possible and, therefore, provides the most deterrence. Under this method, it is possible to attribute a profit to a defendant who has actually lost money.

E. Common Law

1. Shareholder Suits

a. Shareholders may bring common-law actions of deceit against insider traders. This traditional tort claim requires the plaintiff to prove that he justifiably relied to his detriment on a misrepresentation of a material fact made by the defendant with the requisite culpability (i.e., knowledge of its falsity or reckless disregard of its truth with the intent that the plaintiff rely.)

b. In suits by shareholders for breaches of fiduciary duty by an officer or director who trades with them having inside knowledge, most courts have held that the officer's or director's fiduciary duty of disclosure does not extend beyond the corporation to the individual shareholders. This is true for both open-market and face-to-face transactions. Where a director or officer personally seeks a stockholder for the purpose of buying his shares without making disclosure of material facts within his particular knowledge and not within reach of the stockholder, however, the transaction will be closely scrutinized and relief may be granted in appropriate instances.

2. Corporation as Plaintiff

a. Harm to the Corporation
There is a lack of case law in this area, but it is generally agreed that a corporation would be able to recover from an officer or director who, by using material inside information, considered a corporate asset, has breached his duties and harmed the corporation.

b. No Harm to the Corporation
Courts have split on whether to award a corporation that has brought suit against an officer or director for trading on material inside information but has not suffered a direct loss. See *Diamond v. Oreamo*, which is the leading case holding

that the corporation can still recover absent any direct loss based on a breach of the fiduciary duty owed to them by the officer or director. No other state court has accepted the rationale of *Diamond*, and all who have decided the issue would deny recovery to a corporation that has not suffered a direct loss.

CASE CLIPS

Goodwin v. Agassiz (1933) CE, Ha, SSB, V
Facts: Ds, both officers and directors of Cliff Mining Company, bought shares of Cliff Mining from P on the open market without disclosing a theory that Cliff Mining might have been the owner of land with an abundance of copper deposits.
Issue: Do the officers and directors of a corporation have a duty to disclose inside information before purchasing stock in the corporation?
Rule: Where a director personally seeks a stockholder for the purpose of buying his shares without making disclosure of material facts within his particular knowledge and not within reach of the stockholder, the transaction will be closely scrutinized and relief may be granted in appropriate instances; however, fiduciary obligations of officers and directors are not so onerous as to preclude hard bargains made between competent parties without fraud.

In the Matter of Cady, Roberts & Co. (1961) CE, CCM
Facts: Cowdin, a director of Curtis-Wright Corp. who was also associated with the brokerage firm of Cady, Roberts & Co., was informed at a Curtis-Wright board meeting that Curtis-Wright was about to cut its dividends. He then caused Cady to sell its customers' stock in Curtis and also sell short before the information was publicly released.
Issue: What constitutes insider trading?
Rule: Federal antifraud securities regulations prohibit any person in a position giving access, directly or indirectly, to information intended to be available only for a corporate purpose and not for the personal benefit of anyone, particularly officers, directors, or controlling

stockholders, otherwise known as "insiders," from taking advantage of such information knowing it is unavailable to those with whom he is dealing.

SEC v. Texas Gulf Sulfur (1968) CE, CCM, Ha, JB, V

Facts: Texas Gulf did not disclose promising test results and its subsequent purchase of land around the tested site in eastern Canada to the public before corporate officers had a chance to purchase stock on the open market.

Issue: Is it a violation of securities law if potentially price-altering information is not disclosed by a corporation until after insiders have had a chance to purchase stock?

Rule: (Waterman, J.) Any potentially material fact, i.e., one that in reasonable and objective contemplation might affect the value of the corporation's stock or securities, must be disclosed before corporate insiders can trade the stock. Materiality will depend at any given time upon a balancing of both the indicated probability that the event will occur and the anticipated magnitude of the event in light of the totality of the corporation's activity.

Concurrence: (Friendly, J.) A rule requiring a minor officer to reject a stock option plan that a directors' committee proposes of its own initiative to make options available to the officers at a time when they know that the option price, geared to the market value of the stock, did not reflect a substantial increment likely to be realized in short order and was therefore unfair to the corporation would not comport with the realities either of human nature or of corporate life.

Basic, Inc. v. Levinson (S.Ct. 1988) CE, CCM, Ha, SSB

Facts: While in negotiations with Combustion Engineering, Basic (D) made three public denials of their talks. Levinson (P) sold Basic stock between the first denial and the actual merger. P filed suit claiming that the statements made by D violated Rule 10b–5.

Issue 1: Is it a violation of Rule 10b–5 if a corporation publicly denies merger negotiations that are actually taking place?

Rule 1: (Blackmun, J.) To violate Rule 10b–5, a corporation must misrepresent a material fact to the public. A fact is material if there is a substantial likelihood that a reasonable investor would consider it important in deciding whether to make a transaction.

Issue 2: Must an investor claiming a violation of Rule 10b–5 prove individual reliance on a corporation's material misstatements?
Rule 2: (Blackmun, J.) Accepting the "fraud-on-the-market" theory that all publicly available information is reflected in market price, an investor's reliance on any public material misrepresentations may be presumed for the purposes of a Rule 10b–5 action.
Dissent to Rule 2: (White, J.) The Court's embrace of the fraud-on-the-market theory represents a departure in securities law that we are ill-suited to commence and even less suited to control as it proceeds.

Blue Chip Stamps v. Manor Drug Stores (S.Ct. 1975)
CE, CCM, Ha, V

Facts: Blue Chip Stamp Co. became Blue Chip Stamps (D) as a result of a consent decree in response to an antitrust prosecution against it. Under the reorganization plan, the new Blue Chip Stamps offered retailers who had used its service a chance to buy stock at a low price. Manor Drug Stores (P) claimed that Blue Chip violated Rule 10b–5 by issuing false and misleading reports for the purpose and having the effect of discouraging the low-priced purchases. D argued that Rule 10b–5 claims are restricted to those who have actually bought or sold securities, and not those who have simply lost an opportunity to purchase units of stock.
Issue: Can a party bring an action on Rule 10b–5 without having either bought or sold the securities described in the allegedly misleading prospectus?
Rule: (Rehnquist, J.) Rule 10b–5 applies only to frauds upon purchasers or sellers of securities, and not those discouraged from purchasing or selling securities as a result of fraud.
Concurrence: (Powell, J.) Rule 10b–5 which states "purchase or sale" must be limited to such or else wide opportunities for fraud would be opened up.
Dissent: (Blackmun, J.) The essential test of a valid Rule 10b–5 claim must be the showing of a logical nexus between the alleged fraud and the sale or purchase of a security. If the purpose of the fraud is to prevent one from acquiring the status of "purchaser," it is anomalous to deny suit based on the plaintiff's failure to fit into that mechanistic category.

Ernst & Ernst v. Hochfelder (S.Ct. 1976) CE, CCM, Ha, JB

Facts: Hochfelder (P) was the victim of a securities fraud scheme perpetrated by the president of the small brokerage firm, First Securities, that handled his investments. P tried to recover from Ernst & Ernst, the accounting firm retained by First Securities, for negligently failing to uncover the escrow account fraud scheme.

Issue: May a private cause of action for damages lie under § 10 and Rule 10b–5 in the absence of "scienter"?

Rule: (Powell, J.) In the absence of an alleged intent to deceive, manipulate, or defraud, a private cause of action for damages may not lie under § 10 or Rule 10b–5.

Dissent: (Blackmun, J.) Requiring scienter in civil actions under Rule 10b–5, where victims are harmed equally by negligent and intentional fraud, is contrary to congressional intent that securities legislation enacted for the purpose of avoiding frauds be construed "not technically and restrictively, but flexibly to effectuate its remedial purposes."

Santa Fe Industries, Inc. v. Green
(S.Ct. 1977) CE, CM, Ha

Facts: Santa Fe (D) merged with Kirby Lumber, of which it was the majority shareholder, to buy out the minority shareholders. After a complete audit and full disclosure, the minority shareholders (P) were offered $150 per share. P claims that the merger took place without prior notice to minority stockholders and that the purpose of the merger was to appropriate the difference between the offered price of $150 per share and the $772 per share value of Kirby's assets, as valued by P. P brought the action in federal court alleging a violation of Rule 10b–5, in that D employed a "device, scheme or artifice to defraud" in the securities transaction.

Issue: Is a breach of fiduciary duty, without any deception, misrepresentation, or nondisclosure, a violation of § 10(b) and Rule 10b–5?

Rule: (White, J.) A claim of fraud and fiduciary breach only constitutes a cause of action under § 10(b) or Rule 10b–5 if the conduct alleged can be fairly viewed as "manipulative or deceptive" within the meaning of the statute.

Concurrence: (Stevens, J.) The facts alleged in the complaint do not constitute "fraud" within the meaning of Rule 10b–5.

Chiarella v. United States (S.Ct. 1980) CE, Ha, SSB, V
Facts: Chiarella (D) worked for Pandick Press, a financial printer servicing an acquiring corporation. D ascertained from documents the names of target corporations. Without disclosing his knowledge, D purchased stock in the target companies and sold the shares immediately after the takeover attempts were made public.
Issue: Does a person who learns from the confidential documents of one corporation that it is planning an attempt to secure control of a second corporation violate § 10(b) of the Securities Exchange Act of 1934 if he fails to disclose the impending takeover before trading in the target company's securities?
Rule: (Powell, J.) The duty to disclose under § 10(b) does not arise from the mere possession of nonpublic information; there can be no fraud from nondisclosure absent a duty to speak.
Concurrence: (Stevens, J.) A criminal conviction cannot rest on the theory that a nonexistent duty was breached. This does not, however, place a stamp of approval on P's actions.
Concurrence: (Brennan, J.) A person violates § 10(b) whenever he improperly obtains or converts to his own benefit nonpublic information which he then uses in the purchase or sale of securities, regardless of duty; however, impropriety was not an element of the instructions to the jury.
Dissent: (Burger, J.) An absolute duty to disclose or refrain from trading arises from the very act of misappropriating nonpublic information.
Dissent: (Blackmun, J.) Persons having access to confidential material information that is not legally available to others generally are prohibited by Rule 10b–5 from engaging in schemes to exploit their structural informational advantage through trading in affected securities.

Dirks v. SEC (S.Ct. 1983) CE, CCM, Ha, He, SSB, V
Facts: Dirks (D) received material nonpublic information concerning undiscovered fraudulent corporate practices resulting in overvalued assets from an insider of a corporation with which he had no connection who wanted him to expose the fraud. He disclosed this information to investors who relied on it in trading in the shares of the

corporation. He also tried to get the *Wall Street Journal* to expose the illegalities, but they refused.

Issue: When is a tippee's use of material inside information a violation of federal antifraud securities regulations?

Rule: (Powell, J.) A tippee assumes a fiduciary duty to the shareholders of a corporation not to trade on material nonpublic information only when the insider has breached his fiduciary duty to the shareholders by disclosing the information to the tippee and the tippee knows or should know that there has been a breach. An insider has breached his fiduciary duty if he will personally benefit, directly or indirectly, from his disclosure.

Dissent: (Blackmun, J.) The addition of an improper purpose element to a breach of fiduciary claim is an undue limitation of the scope of an insider's fiduciary duty to shareholders. The duty is addressed not to the insider's motives, but to his actions and their consequences on the shareholder.

United States v. Carpenter (1987) CE

Facts: Winans, a *Wall Street Journal* columnist, leaked confidential information before it was published to brokers for the profit of himself and others. Carpenter (D), Winans' roommate, aided and abetted the scheme by acting as a messenger between the conspirators.

Issue: Must one be a corporate insider or "quasi-insider" or misappropriate material nonpublic information from an insider or "quasi-insider" in order to violate § 10(b) and Rule 10b–5?

Rule: Section 10b–5 and Rule 10b–5 proscribe an employee's unlawful misappropriation of material nonpublic information from his employer in connection with a scheme to purchase and sell securities.

Carpenter v. United States (S.Ct. 1987) CE, CCM, Ha

Facts: See above.

Issue 1: Can liability be imposed under Rule 10b–5 for releasing securities information from a journalistic publication before it is published, with the intent to profit therefrom?

Rule 1: (White, J.) See above.

Issue 2: Can it be a violation of federal mail and wire fraud laws to disclose information from a journalistic publication before it is published?

Rule 2: (White, J.) Information to be printed in a journalistic publication is property and private use of such information prior to publication may be a violation of federal mail and wire fraud laws.

Gratz v. Claughton (1951) CE, JB
Facts: A shareholder of the Missouri-Kansas-Texas Railroad Company (P) brought suit against D for violating § 16(b) of the Securities Exchange Act of 1934. D challenged the constitutionality of the rule and the calculation of profits.
Issue 1: Is § 16(b) of the Securities Exchange Act of 1934 constitutionally valid?
Rule 1: Section 16(b) of the Securities Exchange Act of 1934 is constitutional.
Issue 2: How may damages be calculated under § 16(b) of the Securities Exchange Act of 1934?
Rule 2: Section 16(b) declares that "any profit realized . . . from any purchase and sale, or any sale and purchase . . . within any period of less than six months . . . shall inure to and be recoverable by the issuer." Matching sales and purchases in such a way as to increase the profits to the greatest possible amount is a valid method of damage calculation under § 16(b) of the Securities Exchange Act of 1934.

Kern County Land Co. v. Occidental Petroleum
(S.Ct. 1973) CE, CCM
Facts: As a result of an unsuccessful tender offer, D had more than 10 percent of the shares in P. Tenneco was to merge with P, converting P's stock to shares of Tenneco. D executed an option with Tenneco for the sale of D's interest in P after six months had passed.
Issue: Is the execution of an option a "purchase" or "sale" for the purposes of § 16(b)?
Rule: (White, J.) In order to be considered a "purchase" or "sale" for the purposes of § 16(b), a transaction must serve as a vehicle for the evil that Congress sought to prevent; i.e., the realization of profits based upon access to inside information.
Dissent: (Douglas, J.) The public interest and the interest of the investors are better served in this area by the unrestricted, objective operation of § 16(b). By its own terms, § 16(b) subsumes all transactions that are technically purchases and sales and is applicable

irrespective of any actual or potential use of inside information to gain a trading advantage.

Diamond v. Oreamuno (1969) CE, CCM, Ha, JB, SSB
Facts: Ds, chairman of the board and president of Management Assistance, Inc. (MAI), aware of a sharp decrease in earnings due to extra expenses, sold shares in MAI before the public disclosure of this information, which had a detrimental effect on the stock price. P, shareholder of MAI, claimed that Ds profits from the sale of MAI stock rightfully belonged to the corporation.
Issue: Can a derivative suit be maintained against officers and directors of a corporation for profits realized on the securities market by an abuse of their position of trust and confidence even if their employer suffers no loss?
Rule: The officers and directors of a corporation breach their fiduciary duties owed to the corporation by trading in its stock on the basis of material nonpublic information acquired by virtue of their official positions and, although the employer might not suffer a direct loss, should reimburse their corporations for their profits from the transactions, possibly by a successful derivative suit.

Landreth Timber Co. v. Landreth (S.Ct. 1985) CE, CCM
Facts: D sold 100 percent of the stock of Landreth Timber, allegedly without adequately disclosing the consequences of a fire that had damaged the timber mill that was the principal asset of the corporation. P sued under Rule 10b–5 for rescission.
Issue: Is the sale of all the stock of a company a securities transaction subject to the antifraud provisions of the federal securities laws?
Rule: (Powell, J.) The sale of 100 percent of the stock in a corporation, although actually the sale of the business itself, is still considered the sale of securities subject to the antifraud provisions of the federal securities laws.

Securities and Exchange Comm'n v. Ralston Purina Co. (S.Ct. 1953) CE, He
Facts: D had a policy of offering for sale to "key employees" authorized but unissued shares of its stock. This offering was performed without registering the stock pursuant to § 5 of the Securities Act of 1933, and the stock was sold to employees acting on

their own initiative without any solicitation by D. The SEC sought to enjoin D's stock offering, and D claimed that the offering was exempt because it involved D's employees only and thus fell within the offering exception prescribed in § 4(2) of the Securities Act of 1933.
Issue: Does an offer by a corporation of its own stock to its employees fall within the exceptions to the stock registration requirements set forth in § 4(2) of the Securities Act of 1933?
Rule: (Clark, J.) An offer by a corporation of its own stock to its employees does not fall within the exceptions to the stock registration requirements set forth in § 4(2) of the Securities Act of 1933, since the protections provided in the act extend to any potential purchasers lacking the knowledge required to make informed investment decisions.

Escott v. BarChris Construction Corp. (1968) CE, SSB
Facts: BarChris, a builder of bowling alleys, issued debentures as part of a capital-raising plan. The prospectus prepared pursuant to the registration requirement of § 11 of the Securities Act of 1933 and issued by BarChris to potential debenture holders had several false statements and omissions, which resulted in a portrayal of BarChris's financial situation as being far healthier than it actually was. BarChris subsequently went bankrupt, and the holders of its debentures sued BarChris's board, the underwriters of the debentures, and BarChris's auditors, claiming that all were liable for the misleading statements under § 11 of the '33 Act.
Issue: What is the burden of proof placed on defendants other than the issuer raising a due diligence defense as provided in § 11 of the Securities Act of 1933?
Rule: Under § 11 of the Securities Act of 1933, defendants other than the issuer raising a due diligence defense in an action based on a misleading registration statement must show that they made a reasonable investigation into the entries in the statement and that as a result of the investigation, they had reasonable grounds to believe and did believe that the statement was true and contained no omissions.

Financial Industrial Fund, Inc. v. McDonnell Douglas Corp. (1973) CCM

Facts: A mutual fund (P) purchased 80,000 shares of McDonnell Douglas in the open market two days before D announced a sharp earnings decline. P alleged that public disclosure of this decline had been delayed improperly in order that the defendant corporation could proceed with a planned public offering of its debentures to other persons.

Issue: What constitutes an improper delay by a corporation of a public disclosure of an earnings decline?

Rule: For a delay in the disclosure of an earnings decline by a corporation to be considered improper, it must be shown, using a subjective business judgment standard, that the corporation, acting in bad faith, failed to issue the special earnings statement when sufficient information was available for an accurate release or could have been collected by the exercise of due diligence. Information may be withheld until it is "ripe" for publication; that is, the data has been verified sufficiently so that officers and directors of the corporation have full confidence in their accuracy.

J.I. Case Co. v. Borak (S.Ct. 1964) CCM, Ha

Facts: Directors of J.I. Case Co.(D) released a proxy statement with allegedly false information to get shareholder approval of a merger being discussed at the time. The merger being subsequently executed with narrow approval by the shareholders, Borak (P), a shareholder, brought suit claiming a violation of § 14 of the Securities Exchange Act of 1934. D said the '34 Act gave no private right of action.

Issue: Does § 27 of the Securities Exchange Act of 1934 authorize a federal cause of action for rescission or damages to a corporate stockholder with respect to a consummated merger that was authorized pursuant to the use of a proxy statement alleged to contain false and misleading statements violative of § 14(a) of the Act?

Rule: (Clark, J.) Private parties have a right under § 27 to bring suit for violation of § 14(a) of the Securities Exchange Act of 1934.

Touche Ross & Co. v. Redington (S.Ct. 1979) CCM

Facts: Touche Ross (D), an accounting firm, did not find falsehoods in reports filed by Weiss Securities pursuant to § 17(a) of the

Securities Exchange Act of 1934. Investors, including Redington (P), not aware of Weiss' poor financial condition, lost money.

Issue: Do customers of securities brokerage firms that are required to file certain financial reports with regulatory authorities by § 17(a) of the Securities Exchange Act of 1934 have an implied cause of action for damages under § 17(a) against accountants who audit such reports, based on misstatements contained in such reports?

Rule: (Rehnquist, J.) Absent legislative intent, no implied private cause of action can be found enabling customers of brokerage firms to bring suit against third-party professionals who prepare reports pursuant to § 17(a) of the Securities Exchange Act.

Flynn v. Bass Bros. Enterprises, Inc. (1978) CCM

Facts: P, former minority shareholders, made a successful tender offer for National Alfalfa at a price of $6.45 per share. A third party had prepared appraisals with the corroboration of National Alfalfa officials that estimated that (1) $12.40 per share could be realized in an "orderly liquidation" of the target and (2) $16.40 per share represented National Alfalfa's "going concern value." P charged that D, also including the management of National Alfalfa, violated Rule 10b–5 and Section 14(e) of the Securities Exchange Act of 1934 for failing to disclose the asset appraisals when the offer was made.

Issue: Must asset appraisals be disclosed by a corporation in response to a tender offer?

Rule: Courts should determine on a case-by-case basis whether asset appraisals and other soft information are material and if there is a duty to disclose such information by weighing the potential aid such information will give a shareholder against the potential for harm, such as undue reliance, if the information is released with a proper cautionary note. The factors a court must consider in making such a determination are: the facts upon which the information is based; the qualifications of those who prepared or compiled it; the purpose for which the information was originally intended; its relevance to the stockholders' impending decision; the degree to which the information is unique; and the availability to the investor of other more reliable sources of information.

Affiliated Ute Citizens v. United States (S.Ct. 1972) CCM

Facts: First Security Bank acted as the transfer agent for the Ute Distribution Corp. (UDC), distributing shares in its assets, which consisted largely of oil, gas, and mineral rights, to "mixed-blood" descendants of the Ute Indian Tribe. Gale and Haslem (D), employees of First Security, purchased shares from the stockholders without disclosing to the mixed-blood sellers that nontribal members were trading UDC shares at higher prices than defendants were offering. D's behavior constituted a "scheme to defraud" under Rule 10b–5, but the court of appeals said that there was insufficient evidence of reliance by the plaintiffs on any statements or conduct by D and, therefore, narrowed their liability to the shares they purchased themselves and did not include those purchases they arranged for others.
Issue: Must there be evidence of reliance on material fact misrepresentations made by a defendant in order to prevail on a Rule 10b–5 claim?
Rule: (Blackmun, J.) Positive proof of reliance is not a prerequisite to recovery on a Rule 10b–5 claim that primarily involves a failure to disclose, as long as the facts withheld are material in the sense that a reasonable investor might have considered them important in making a decision. The obligation to disclose and the withholding of a material fact establish the requisite element of causation in fact.

Mitchell v. Texas Gulf Sulfur Co. (1971) CCM, JB

Facts: D misinformed the public about a substantial mineral ore find on April 12th and then gave a more accurate account on April 16th. P, relying on the April 12th statement, sold their shares in D short. P claimed that D's failure to disclose and subsequent false press release cost P profits they would have realized if they would have kept the stock instead of selling on April 22nd and 23rd.
Issue: How are damages calculated when a corporation violates Rule 10b–5 by issuing false and misleading statements, unfairly causing investors to lose money?
Rule: A reasonable investor is entitled to an amount that offsets any loss he suffered by a deceitfully induced sale, to be decided on a case-by-case basis.

Randall v. Loftsgaarden (S.Ct. 1986) CCM

Facts: After three years as limited partners in partnership with D taking deductions on the losses, P brought suit under both Rule 10b–5 and § 12(2) of the Securities Act of 1933, alleging that the offering brochure had misrepresented key facts. The district court found that P's investments were worthless at the time they discovered the fraud and granted rescission under § 12(2). On appeal, the Eight Circuit upheld the finding of liability, but reversed the rescissionary award because the district court had not reduced the damage award by the tax losses that the petitioners deducted.

Issue: Does § 28(a) require a rescissionary recovery under § 12(2) or § 10(b) to be reduced by tax benefits received from a tax shelter investment?

Rule: (O'Connor, J.) Section 28(a) does not require that every recovery on an express or implied right of action under the 1934 Act must be limited to the net economic harm suffered by the plaintiff. Therefore, actions under § 10(b) or § 12(2) need not be offset by prior tax deductions of the losses resulting from the bad investments.

Superintendent of Insurance v. Bankers Life & Casualty Co. (S.Ct. 1971) CCM

Facts: Manhattan Casualty Co., represented here by P, was sold by D to Begole for five million dollars. Begole received a check from Irving Trust Inc. to pay for the stock and backed the check with Manhattan's own assets after acquiring control of the firm.

Issue: Is § 10(b) limited to preserving the integrity of the open securities market?

Rule: (Douglas, J.) Section 10(b) bars deceptive devices and contrivances in the purchase or sale of securities whether conducted in the organized markets or face-to-face.

Goldberg v. Meridor (1977) CCM

Facts: Minority shareholders (P) of Universal Gas & Oil Company (UGO) alleged that the officers of UGO issued shares to UGO's parent for inadequate consideration, failed to disclose the fraudulent nature of the transaction to the minority shareholders, and put out several press releases falsely stating that the deal was beneficial to UGO.

Issue: Can nondisclosure and misrepresentations by officers of a corporation regarding the sale of securities to its parent be the basis of a Rule 10b–5 claim by the corporation's minority shareholders?

Rule: If the facts concerning the sale of shares to a parent corporation that were not disclosed or were misleadingly disclosed to the subsidiary's shareholders by the officers of the subsidiary breaching their fiduciary duty were material and reliance can be shown, perhaps in the form of missed opportunities to enjoin the action, then those who were misled may claim a violation of Rule 10b–5.

Maldonado v. Flynn (1979) CCM

Facts: Four members of the board of directors of Zapata voted unanimously to allow the other four members to move up the date of their options to before Zapata made a tender offer for its own shares. This maneuver allowed the four optionees to gain at the expense of the firm by avoiding a large tax liability in exchange for the loss by the firm of an equivalently large expense deduction. The four directors who voted were legally disinterested parties. These modifications were never submitted to the shareholders, whose approval was unnecessary.

Issue: When the approval of the shareholders is not required, must a disinterested board of directors disclose to shareholders information regarding decisions it has made?

Rule: Where approval by the shareholders is not necessary, full disclosure to a disinterested board of directors is equivalent to full disclosure to the shareholders.

Fridrich v. Bradford (1976) CCM

Facts: D purchased 1,225 shares of Old Line Life Insurance on an inside tip from his father and sold the shares three months later for a thirteen-thousand-dollar profit. In the interim, Ps bought and sold Old Line's stock, making a slight profit. As a result of an SEC investigation and subsequent consent decree, D was forced to give up the profit. Ps claim that they would not have sold the shares if they were aware of the impending merger.

Issue: Is the private civil remedy for violations of § 10(b) and Rule 10b–5 coextensive in its reach with the reach of the SEC, which under the Act was designated by Congress as the primary vehicle of enforcement?

Rule: (Engel, J.) In a private civil action under Rule 10b–5, a plaintiff must establish a causal connection between the defendant's misconduct and his loss; this causal connection does not exist when the defendant trades with third parties and the plaintiff traded on the impersonal market, otherwise unaffected by the wrongful acts of the insider.
Concurrence: (Celebrezze, J.) The duty to disclose is owed to the class of investors trading contemporaneously with the insider and only this group can be beneficiaries of the relaxed causation standard of *Affiliated Ute*. Non-contemporaneous traders do not suffer the disadvantage of trading with someone who has superior access to information.

Elkind v. Ligget & Myers, Inc. (1980) CCM, SSB

Facts: Shareholders brought a class action against D for wrongful tipping of inside information about an earnings decline to certain persons who then sold Ligget's shares on the open market.
Issue: How are damages calculated when a defendant is found guilty of selling on inside information and is held liable to those who bought on the open market and sustained substantial losses during the period of insider trading?
Rule: After a tippee sells on inside information, any uninformed investor, where a reasonable investor would either have delayed his purchase or not purchased at all if he had had the benefit of the tipped information, is allowed to recover any post-purchase decline in market value of his shares up to a reasonable time after he learns of the tipped information or after there is a public disclosure of it, but his recovery is limited to the amount gained by the tippee as a result of his selling at the earlier date rather than delaying his sale until the parties could trade on an equal informational basis.

Merrill Lynch, Pierce, Fenner & Smith, Inc. v. Livingston (1978) CCM

Facts: D, an employee of P, had the honorary title of Vice President while still working as a securities salesman. P, alleging a violation of § 16(b) of the Securities Exchange Act of 1934, attempted to recover the profit D made on a short-swing transaction.

Issue: Does § 16(b) impose strict liability on any person who holds the title of "officer" and who has access to information about his company that is not generally available to the members of the investing public?
Rule: Liability under § 16(b) is not based simply upon a person's title within his corporation; rather, liability follows from the existence of a relationship with the corporation that makes it more probable than not that the individual has access to insider information.

CBI Industries, Inc. v. Horton (1982) CCM

Facts: D, a director of P, realized a profit for his children's trust by trading shares of P on the open market.
Issue: Does the "him" of § 16(b), referring to a corporate insider, also include the insider's grown children when they are beneficiaries of a trust of which the director is a co-trustee?
Rule: The profit realized by a corporate insider, as stated in § 16(b), must be a direct pecuniary benefit to the insider; it is not enough that ties of affinity or consanguinity between the nominal recipient and the insider make it likely that the insider will experience an enhanced sense of well-being as a result of the receipt, or will be led to reduce his gift giving to the recipient.

Reliance Electric Co. v. Emerson Electric Co.
(S.Ct. 1972) CCM

Facts: Having acquired 13.2 percent of the outstanding common stock of Dodge Manufacturing Co. in an unsuccessful attempt to take it over, Emerson followed a plan to dispose of enough shares to bring its holdings below 10 percent, in order to immunize the disposal of the remainder from liability under § 16(b).
Issue: Can liability be imposed under § 16(b) simply because the investor structured his transaction with the intent of avoiding liability?
Rule: (Stewart, J.) Under § 16(b), a statutory insider might sell enough shares to bring his holdings below 10 percent, and later, but still within six months, sell additional shares free from liability.
Dissent: (Douglas, J.) Section 16(b) is a "prophylactic" rule whose wholesome purpose is to control those insiders whose access to confidential information gives them unfair advantage in the trading of their corporate securities. The statute should be construed as allowing a rebuttable presumption that any such series of dispositive transac-

tions will be deemed to be part of a single plan of disposition and treated as a single "sale" for the purposes of § 16(b).

Freeman v. Decio (1978) CCM, JB, SSB
Facts: Officers of the Skyline Corporation traded in its securities with knowledge that its material costs were significantly understated and its earnings overstated.
Issue: Under Indiana law, can shareholders of a corporation sustain a derivative action against certain officers and directors of that corporation for allegedly trading in the stock of the corporation on the basis of material inside information?
Rule: A corporate insider does not ordinarily violate his fiduciary duty to the corporation by dealing in the corporation's stock, unless the corporation was thereby harmed.

Winston v. Federal Express Corporation (1988) Ha
Facts: Winston (D) resigned as Senior Vice-President of Electronic Products and ceased performing any of his duties on August 27, 1985, but remained on the payroll until September 30, the date his resignation became effective. Prior to September 30, D took options out to purchase 8,298 shares of Federal Express stock, which he exercised on that date. (The "trade date," as opposed to the "settlement date," determines the transaction date for the purposes of securities law.) On March 26, 1986, D sold the shares he purchased on September 30 for a profit in excess of $176,000.
Issue: Is a person considered an officer for the purposes of § 16(b) during the period between the tender of his resignation and the termination of his employment?
Rule: For the purposes of § 16(b) of the Securities Exchange Act of 1934, an officer is presumed to have continued access to confidential information during the period between the tender of his resignation and when it becomes effective, and the officer must prove substantial evidence to overcome this presumption and escape liability for short-swing profits.

C.R.A. Realty Corp. v. Crotty (1989) Ha
Facts: D had the title of a vice-president of United Artists, but he was actually a middle management employee whose duties did not

provide access to any confidential information about the company's financial plans or future operations. D made a short-swing transaction, purchasing 7,500 shares of United Artists on December 19, 1984 and selling 3,500 of the shares on July 24, 1985, realizing a large profit.

Issue: Do an employee's functions, rather than his title, determine whether he is an "officer" within the meaning of § 16(b) of the Securities Exchange Act of 1934?

Rule: The duties of an employee, especially his potential access to inside information, rather than his corporate title, determine whether he is an officer subject to the short-swing trading restrictions of § 16(b) of the Securities Exchange Act of 1934.

Jammies Intern., Inc. v. Lazarus (1989) Ha

Facts: The CEO of Toys "R" Us, Inc. (D) allegedly realized short-swing profits by matching his wife's sale of Toys shares with the execution of his options on shares of common stock.

Issue: May a corporate officer or director be held to have "realized profit" within the meaning of § 16(b) of the Securities Exchange Act of 1934 as a result of a matching of his wife's sales and his own purchase of corporation's securities within the statutory six-month period?

Rule: The exercise of control by an insider over the other spouse's investment decisions would justify treating the insider as the beneficial owner of the other spouse's securities for the purposes of § 16(b) of the Securities Exchange Act of 1934.

Feder v. Martin Marietta Corp. (1970) He

Facts: The CEO of D sat on the board of Sperry Rand, and acted as a deputy of D, a principal holder of Sperry securities. P brought a derivative suit to recover "short-swing" profits realized upon D's purchases and sales of Sperry shares within less than six months.

Issue 1: Can § 16(b) apply to a company that places a deputy on the board of directors of another company in which it has investment interests?

Rule 1: When a director of one corporation sits as an officer or director of a second corporation in whose securities the corporation trades within a six-month period, the corporation is liable for violating § 16(b) under a "deputization theory."

Issue 2: Can § 16(a) liability attach to "short-swing" profits realized after a deputy's resignation from the traded corporation?
Rule 2: As distinguished from the liability of shareholders whose holdings exceed 10 percent, which is conditioned upon their being such both at the time of purchase and at the time of sale, the liability under § 16(b) of corporate directors and officers, including investors with deputies acting as such, extends to profits realized from purchases during their tenure and sales after their resignation or termination from their inside positions.

Sedima, S.P.L.R. v. Imrex Co. (S.Ct. 1985) He
Facts: P and D were parties to a joint venture that provided electronic components to a Belgian firm. P received orders and D obtained the parts in the United States. P became convinced that D was presenting inflated bills and cheating P out of a portion of its proceeds by collecting nonexistent expenses. Along with common-law claims, P filed two counts of alleged RICO violations, one under § 1964(c), based on the predicate acts of mail and wire fraud, and the other for conspiracy to violate § 1962(c).
Issue: Can a private civil RICO action be brought without a criminal conviction and a "racketeering injury"?
Rule: (White, J.) The alleged presence of predicate acts punishable through criminal statutes and sufficiently related to constitute a pattern is sufficient to state a private civil RICO claim.
Dissent: (Powell, J.) Congress never intended the wide scope of the civil RICO statute, which is applied to authorize the types of private civil actions now being brought frequently against respected businesses, to redress ordinary fraud and breach of contract cases.

American Nat'l Bank & Trust Co. v. Haroco, Inc. (S.Ct. 1983) He
Facts: Haroco (P) claimed that American (D) and several of its officers had fraudulently charged excessive interests rates on loans. The complaint alleged that this scheme to defraud, which was carried out through the mails, violated 18 U.S.C. § 1962(c), in that the mailings constituted a pattern of racketeering activity by means of which petitioners operated, or participated in the operation of, the

bank. The only injuries alleged were the excessive interest charges themselves.

Issue: Does a civil claim for treble damages under RICO require that the plaintiff suffer damages by reason of the defendant acquiring, maintaining control or an interest in, or conducting the affairs of an "enterprise" through the commission of statutorily prescribed offenses, as opposed to being damaged solely by reason of the defendant's commission of such offenses?

Rule: (Per Curiam) Injury may result from the predicate acts themselves in order to state a private civil RICO action. The submission that the injury must flow not from the predicate acts themselves but from the fact that they were performed as part of the conduct of an enterprise would be an unfounded restriction on a RICO private action.

Dissent: (Marshall, J.) The RICO statute, § 1964(c), clearly contemplates recovery for injury resulting from the confluence of events described in § 1962 and not merely from the commission of a predicate act.

Strong v. Repide (S.Ct. 1909) JB

Facts: D, director and owner of 75 percent of the stock of Philippine Sugar Estates Development company, bought out P's interest in the company without disclosing his negotiations with the Philippine government for the sale of Philippine Sugar's main assets, secularized church property or "friar lands." Two and one-half months after the sale, the price of P's former holding increased dramatically.

Issue: Does a director of a corporation have a duty to disclose the facts bearing upon, or that might affect the value of, the stock he intends to purchase?

Rule: (Peckham, J.) Although a director's duty to disclose does not rest on his fiduciary relationship with the shareholder from whom he intends to purchase shares, their relationship is one of a number of factors that when taken together may create a duty, the existence of which can only be determined on a case-by-case basis.

Jones v. H.F. Ahmanson & Co. (1969) JB

Facts: A minority shareholder in a Savings and Loan Association brought suit against majority shareholders, alleging that they had breached their fiduciary duty to minority shareholders through the

creation of a holding company that only allowed certain majority shareholders to exchange their shares.
Issue: May majority shareholders dispose of their stock without regard to its effect on minority shareholders?
Rule: Majority shareholders have a fiduciary responsibility to minority shareholders to use their ability to control the corporation in an equitable manner.

Green v. Occidental Petroleum Corp. (1976) JB

Facts: A class of purchasers of D's stock over a five-year period brought a class action suit alleging the dissemination by D of misleading information concerning proper corporate accounting over the five years. The district court granted Federal Rules of Civil Procedure Rule 23(b)(3) (class action) certification based upon the assumption that the rescissory measure of damages would be the proper measure.
Issue: Is it an abuse of the court's discretion to grant class action certification based on the use of the rescissory measure of damages?
Rule: An assumption that the rescissory measure of damages would be used would make certification an abuse of discretion; an assumption that the out-of-pocket measure would be used is within the proper scope of discretion.

Huddleston v. Herman & Maclean (1983) SSB

Facts: Texas International Speedway, Inc., (TIS) sold over four million dollars in securities and then went bankrupt. Ps filed a class action on behalf of themselves and other purchasers of TIS securities alleging claims under § 10(b) of the Securities Exchange Act of 1934 and Rule 10b–5.
Issue: Must a plaintiff prove reliance and causation in a Rule 10b–5 action?
Rule: To prevail on a Rule 10b–5 action, plaintiffs must establish that their economic loss was proximately caused by the fraudulent misstatements and omissions in the prospectus on which they "reasonably relied."

State Teachers Retirement Board v. Flour Corp. (1981) SSB

Facts: On February 28, 1975, D entered into a one billion dollar contract to build a large coal gasification plant in South Africa with a provision for an "embargo" on all publicity about the contract until March 10, 1975. Rumors of the agreement grew, and trading was suspended on March 7 when Flour complied with a New York Stock Exchange suggestion. Between March 3 and March 6, P sold, according to a decision made in January, some $6.4 million worth of Flour stock.

Issue: Does a corporation have a duty to disclose or halt trading when rumors of a large contract are affecting stock prices?

Rule: A company has no duty to disclose, correct or verify, or halt trading when rumors are influencing its stock prices unless those rumors can be attributed to the company or scienter is established.

Brophy v. Cities Service Co. (1949) V

Facts: Kennedy was employed in an "executive capacity" and as a "confidential secretary" to Cities Service and used confidential information to profit on Cities Service stock.

Issue: Is an employee liable to his employer for profits made by trading his employer's stock based on confidential information acquired during his employment?

Rule: An employee who in the course of his employment acquires secret information relating to his employer's business occupies a position of trust and confidence analogous to that of a fiduciary and is accountable for any personal profit made by an abuse of that position, regardless of whether or not his employer suffers a loss.

Blau v. Lehman (S.Ct. 1962) V

Facts: Thomas, member of partnership D, sat on the board of directors of Tidewater. D realized "short swing" profits on Tidewater securities independent of any advice or "inside" knowledge given it by Thomas.

Issue: Does § 16(b) impose absolute liability for "short-swing" profits made by a partnership with a partner acting as a director for the company whose shares are being traded independently of any advice or "inside information" given to it by him?

Rule: (Black, J.) While under § 16(b) a partnership can be a "director, officer, or 10 percent shareholder" when it has a member acting as such for a corporation whose shares the partnership trades, a partnership is not absolutely liable under the statute in such a situation. Absent evidence of deputization and use of inside informa-

tion, only that partner "inside" can be held accountable for his share of the profits made by the partnership on a short swing transaction.
Dissent: (Douglas, J.) The Court's opinion would allow all but one partner to share in the feast which the one places on the partnership table. They in turn can offer feasts to him in the 99 other companies of which they are directors.

Flamm v. Eberstadt (1987) V
Facts: On December 2, 1975, Microdot, then trading at $11 3/4 per share, was approached as a takeover target by General Cable, increasing the price to $18 3/8 per share. Microdot, with D as its CEO, opposed the offer with publicity defending the future of growth companies, while it solicited other offers through Goldman, Sachs & Co., a brokerage house. The stock fell to $17 per share until Northwest Industries made an offer and acquired the stock at $21 on January 26, 1976. P filed a class action on behalf of investors who sold Microdot between December 5, 1975 and January 23, 1975 alleging violations of Rule 10b–5 for failure to disclose negotiations with Northwest, the "White Knight."
Issue: Must a corporation disclose incomplete merger talks?
Rule: For the sake of all the investors, the economic well-being of the corporation, and the chance of success of the negotiations, a corporation need not disclose merger or acquisition negotiations until the parties to the talks have reached an agreement.

Chapter 8

DUTY OF LOYALTY

I. SELF-INTERESTED TRANSACTIONS

The duty of loyalty applies to transactions between a corporation and a director, officer, or majority shareholder.

A. General Rule

A contract between a corporation and one of its directors is subject to judicial scrutiny and will be invalidated if found to be unfair to the corporation.

B. Requirements

Although there is substantial variation among jurisdictions, most courts will permit self-interested transactions that fulfill the following requirements:

1. Disclosure
    The director, officer, or shareholder must disclose his conflict of interest to the corporate decision-maker. The requirement is met if at any time the corporate decision-maker ratifies the transaction.

2. Other Requirements
    One of the following is also necessary:

    a. Fairness
        The transaction is objectively fair to the corporation.

    b. Authorization by Directors
        The transaction is authorized by disinterested directors who reasonably believed it was fair at the time of the authorization.

c. Authorization by Shareholders
The transaction is authorized by disinterested shareholders and does not constitute a waste of corporate assets.

C. Burden

1. General Rule
   A party challenging the transaction normally has the burden of proof.

2. Exception
   A director or senior executive has the burden of proving the fairness of a challenged transaction that was not authorized by disinterested directors or disinterested shareholders.

D. Remedies

The normal remedy is rescission of the contract, if possible, or restitution of losses to the corporation. Unlike violation of the duty of care, violation of the duty of loyalty usually returns the director, officer, or majority shareholder to the position he was in before the violation, and consequently, does not serve as a strong deterrent.

II. COMPENSATION

A conflict of interest issue may arise over compensation awarded to a director or senior executive by the corporation.

A. Forms of Executive Compensation

The basic types of executive compensation include salaries, bonuses, stock-based incentives, pensions, and deferred cash options.

B. Issues Raised by Compensation

Forms of executive compensation may be struck down if they involve self-dealing, lack consideration, or grant "excessive" compensation.

1. **Self-Dealing**
   Compensation plans that involve self-dealing are subject to the same requirements as other self-interested transactions: there must be disclosure to the corporate decision-maker, and the compensation must be objectively fair, or authorized by disinterested directors or shareholders.

2. **Excessive Compensation**
   Courts may strike down compensation agreements as a waste of corporate assets if the level of compensation is excessive.

   a. **Shareholder Approval**
      Even compensation plans approved by disinterested shareholders may be struck down, although ratification shifts the burden from the executive to the complaining party.

   b. **Most Common Test**
      There must be a reasonable relationship between the compensation and the services rendered. A strong case must be presented to strike down a compensation plan as waste, as courts are reluctant to strike down compensation plans.

3. **Consideration**
   Compensation plans granted without consideration are generally struck down.

III. CORPORATE OPPORTUNITY DOCTRINE

A. Use of Corporate Assets

1. **General Rule**
   A director may not use his corporate position to advance his own pecuniary interests if the act would cause reasonably

foreseeable harm to the corporation or allow him to receive a benefit that is not proportionally available to other shareholders.

2. Burden

The burden of proving wrongful use of corporate assets is on the complaining party unless the conduct was neither authorized by disinterested directors nor authorized or ratified by disinterested shareholders.

B. Competition with the Corporation

1. General Rule

A director or senior executive may not make personal economic gains by engaging in competition with his corporation unless:

a. Any reasonably foreseeable harm to the corporation is outweighed by reasonably expected benefits to the corporation;

b. Competition is authorized or ratified by directors; or

c. Competition is authorized or ratified by shareholders.

C. Corporate Opportunity Doctrine

A number of tests have been used to determine if a director or officer has appropriated a corporate opportunity.

1. Interest or Expectancy Test

A director or officer is liable for taking advantage of an opportunity in which the corporation has an interest already existing or has an expectancy growing out of an existing right.

2. Line of Business Test

A director or officer is liable for taking advantage of an opportunity that is logically and naturally adaptable to the corporation's business.

252 Duty of Loyalty

    3. Fairness Test
       A director or officer is liable if his action could be classified as "unfair" under the application of ethical standards to the particular set of facts.

IV. SALE OF CONTROL

A. Usually, controlling shareholders are free to dispose of their shares as they wish, but in certain circumstances courts may intervene.

B. Looting by Purchasers

Sellers of controlling interests may be liable for ensuing losses if they know or have reason to know of the purchaser's intentions to take over the company to convert its assets to his private use. See *Gerdes v. Reynolds*.

C. Diversion of Collective Opportunity

Courts may find that the sale of a controlling interest diverts an opportunity that belongs to the corporation collectively, profiting the sellers to the detriment of the corporation. See *Perlman v. Feldmann*.

V. OTHER DUTIES OF CONTROLLING SHAREHOLDERS

A. Duty of Complete Disclosure

When dealing with minority shareholders, majority shareholders must disclose all information needed by the minority to protect their interests. See *Zahn v. Transamerica Corporation*.

B. Parent and Subsidiary
   Like other controlling shareholders, a parent corporation owes a fiduciary duty to a subsidiary. A parent corporation engaged in self-dealing must show that its actions towards the subsidiary are fair. See *Sinclair v. Oil Corp. v. Levien*.

C. General Fiduciary Duty

Most courts have been reluctant to recognize general duties of controlling shareholders towards the minority in public corporations. A well known exception is *Jones v. H.F. Ahmanson & Co.* in which Chief Justice Traynor enunciated a duty of controlling shareholders to treat the minority equitably.

CASE CLIPS

Lewis v. S.L. & E., Inc. (1980) CE
Facts: A minority shareholder brought an action to hold directors liable for an alleged waste of corporate assets for low rent charged to another corporation, also owned by the board of directors.
Issue: Are corporate directors liable to complaining shareholders if they fail to prove that transactions in which they have a conflict of interest are fair and reasonable?
Rule: Directors are liable to shareholders if they cannot prove that transactions in which they had an interest other than that of their corporation were fair and reasonable.

Talbot v. James (1972) CE
Facts: A corporate director (D) was authorized to sign a construction contract on behalf of his company. He arranged for himself to be the building contractor without disclosing his individual interest to the corporation.
Issue: May a corporation void an undisclosed transaction entered into by a director in his corporate capacity and as an individual?
Rule: A corporation may void a transaction entered into by a director as an individual if there has not been full disclosure to the corporation.

Globe Woolen Co v. Utica Gas & Elec. Co. (1918) CE, V
Facts: Mayard was president, director, and principal shareholder of P corporation and served as director of D corporation. He was

present at a meeting of D's board but did not vote or make any comment on a resolution to contract with P.
Issue: Does the presence of a director common to two contracting parties allow a contract to be voided if the director does not vote or comment on the resolution?
Rule: Silence does not satisfy the duty of a director to see that no advantage is taken to the detriment of his trust, and a contract between corporations with common directors can be voided unless its terms are fair.

Scott v. Multi-Amp Corp. (1974) CE
Facts: A minority shareholder brought suit to enjoin a proposal by directors and majority shareholders to sell assets from their corporation to another in which they had an interest at an allegedly inadequate price.
Issue: May minority shareholders void a contract entered into by corporate directors having a conflict of interest?
Rule: A contract may not be voided by minority shareholders simply because of a conflict of interest among contracting directors, but such contracts may be voided if directors cannot prove it is fair and reasonable.

Beard v. Elster (1960) CE, CCM
Facts: A restricted stock option plan was approved by a disinterested board of directors and a majority of shareholders for employees who remained with the corporation for five years. A shareholder sought cancellation of the plan as an invalid gift.
Issue: Is a restricted stock option plan that seeks to induce employees to remain with the company valid?
Rule: The business judgement of a disinterested board of directors in formulating a restricted stock option plan will receive the utmost consideration by the court, and a plan will be binding on the corporation so long as there is a reasonable relationship between the value of the benefits passing to the corporation and the value of the options granted.

Michelson v. Duncan (1972) CE
Facts: Minority shareholders (P) sought to set aside modifications in a stock option granted by officers and directors to certain key

employees, including those formulating the plan. P alleged that the modifications, which were overwhelmingly but non-unanimously ratified by the shareholders, lacked consideration and were a waste of corporate assets.

Issue: Is a minority shareholder claim of waste of corporate assets precluded by shareholder ratification of the disputed option?

Rule: Although shareholder ratification of an alleged waste of corporate assets does not preclude a complaint of waste of corporate assets, it does shift the burden of proving the inadequacy of consideration from directors to the complaining shareholders.

Lincoln Stores v. Grant (1941) CE

Facts: Two directors of a corporation (D) formed a business in competition with their corporation and secretly used information from the corporation to aid the new business.

Issue: May a constructive trust be established for the benefit of a corporation whose directors form a competing business and secretly rely on information from the corporation?

Rule: A constructive trust will not be imposed on a competing business for the benefit of a corporation unless the corporation had an expectancy to acquire the property of the competing business.

Klinicki v. Lundgren (1985) CE, Ha

Facts: A director in a close corporation brought suit alleging usurpation of a corporate opportunity by another director. Although the other director failed to disclose the opportunity to the close corporation, he claimed not to be liable because the corporation lacked the financial ability to take advantage of the business opportunity.

Issue: May a director in a close corporation be liable for usurping a corporate opportunity if the corporation does not have the financial ability to take advantage of the opportunity?

Rule: A director in a close corporation may be liable for usurping a corporate opportunity, regardless of whether the corporation has the financial ability to take advantage of the situation, based on his obligation to disclose all facts and offer the opportunity to disinterested directors before taking personal advantage of the opportunity.

Zetlin v. Hanson Holdings, Inc. (1979) CE

Facts: A minority shareholder brought suit, claiming that he was entitled to share in a premium price paid for shares of a controlling block of stock that was almost twice the stock's market value.

Issue: Are minority shareholders entitled to the same premium price offered for the purchase of a controlling block of shares of a corporation?

Rule: Minority shareholders do not have the right to share equally in premiums paid for controlling interests of stock.

Gerdes v. Reynolds (1941) CE

Facts: Majority shareholders, directors, and officers of an investment corporation (D), sold their stock to another group at an inflated price. In the same transaction, Ds resigned as directors and elected members of the purchasing group as directors without investigating their financial background or notifying minority shareholders. After the transaction, the new directors began converting the corporation's securities for personal use.

Issue: May directors and officers who hold a controlling interest in a corporation be liable to minority shareholders for sale of their stock to others accompanied by their resignations and the election of others to the board?

Rule: Majority shareholders who are officers and directors owe a fiduciary duty to other shareholders and may be liable for terminating their agency or accepting the resignation of others if the immediate consequences would leave the interests of the corporation without proper protection.

Perlman v. Feldmann (1955) CE

Facts: During a steel shortage, the president, director and dominant shareholder (D) of a steel corporation sold his controlling interest to a group of steel users, who promptly elected their own board of directors. Minority shareholders (P) alleged that consideration paid for the stock included a corporate asset that D held in trust for the corporation: the ability to control the allocation of a corporate product in a time of short supply.

Issue: May a corporate president and dominant stockholder be liable to minority shareholders for profits gained through the sale of his controlling interest?

Rule: If there is a possibility of individual gain by a fiduciary at the expense of his corporation, the fiduciary must establish the fairness of his dealings or is subject to liability.

Caplan v. Lionel Corp. (1964) CE
Facts: A minority shareholder brought suit against a corporation to nullify an agreement that permitted another shareholder to gain voting rights of stock before actual possession of it.
Issue: Is an agreement that transfers the voting rights of stock immediately and defers the actual transfer of the stock valid?
Rule: Management of a corporation is not an area of trade and may not be bought apart from actual stock control.

Essex Universal Corp. v. Yates (1962) CE
Facts: A contract for the sale of an amount of stock usually sufficient to maintain majority control in a public corporation included a clause that granted the purchaser the right to immediately replace the majority of the existing board of directors with the purchaser's nominees. The selling party (D) claimed the contract was illegal per se.
Issue: Is a contract for sale of stock illegal because it includes a clause allowing the purchaser to replace a majority of the existing directors with his own nominees?
Rule: (Lumbard, J.) A contract for the sale of stock that permits the immediate transfer of management is not invalid unless the party attacking the transaction can establish that the block of stock does not carry majority control.
Concurrence 1: (Clark, J.) There is no reason to declare a contract that permits the immediate transfer of management illegal on its face, regardless of hypothetical findings on control.
Concurrence 2: (Friendly, J.) A contract that permits the immediate transfer of management is illegal unless seller owns more than 50 percent of the stock.

Zahn v. Transamerica Corporation (1947) CE, Ha
Facts: A corporate charter provided that directors had the option to redeem Class A stock. Another corporation (D) acquired 80 percent of the corporation's stock and through its control of the board of

258 Duty of Loyalty

directors redeemed the Class A stock for its own benefit before liquidation of the corporation.
Issue: Are self-interested votes taken by majority shareholders acting as directors voidable by minority shareholders?
Rule: When voting as directors, majority shareholders represent all shareholders in the capacity of a trustee and actions taken for personal benefit may be voided in equity by minority shareholders.

Sinclair Oil Corp. v. Levien (1971) CCM, Ha
Facts: A shareholder in a subsidiary brought an action to hold the subsidiary's parent liable for excessive distribution of dividends. P asserted that the parent bore the burden of proving that its dealings with the subsidiary had been intrinsically fair.
Issue: Does a parent corporation, in defending an alleged breach of fiduciary duty, bear the burden of proving that its dealings with its subsidiary were intrinsically fair?
Rule: A parent corporation defending against an alleged breach of fiduciary duty to a subsidiary bears the burden of proving that its dealings were intrinsically fair only if there is self-dealing that allows the parent to receive something to the detriment of the subsidiary's minority stockholders.

Jones v. H.F. Ahmanson & Co. (1969) CE, He
Facts: A minority shareholder in a Savings and Loan Association brought suit against majority shareholders, alleging that they had breached their fiduciary duty to minority shareholders through the creation of a holding company that only allowed certain majority shareholders to exchange their shares.
Issue: May majority shareholders dispose of their stock without regard to its effect on minority shareholders?
Rule: Majority shareholders have a fiduciary responsibility to minority shareholders to use their power to control the corporation in an equitable manner.

State ex. rel. Hayes Oyster Co. v. Keypoint Oyster Co. (1964) CCM
Facts: A corporate president (D) arranged a sale to another corporation through which he was able to personally profit. The sale was approved by the shareholders without knowledge of the presid-

ent's interest. After D left the corporation, the corporation (P) sought to recover profits obtained by the president through the transaction.
Issue: May a corporation recover profits obtained by an officer through a transaction in which he held a personal interest unknown to the corporation?
Rule: A corporation may recover secret profits obtained by a corporate officer, since whatever a director or officer acquires by virtue of his fiduciary relationship belongs not to the individual but the company.

Case v. New York Central R.R. (1965) CCM
Facts: Minority shareholders (P) of a subsidiary corporation sought to rescind a tax agreement with their parent company that allowed the parent company to save over $3.5 million while benefitting the subsidiary corporation less than three hundred thousand dollars.
Issue: May an agreement that benefits a parent corporation to a greater extent than its subsidiary be rescinded on grounds of unfairness?
Rule: The receipt of greater profits by a parent through an agreement with its subsidiary is not alone sufficient to demonstrate unfairness worthy of judicial intervention.

Adams v. Smith (1963) CCM
Facts: A board of directors resolved to make payments to the widows of two deceased employees. A shareholder sought to rescind their agreement.
Issue: May a board of directors authorize payments, without consideration, to surviving spouses of employees?
Rule: Unless the corporate charter provides otherwise, a board of directors has no authority to give away the corporation's money without consideration.

Osborne v. Locke Steel Chain Co. (1966) CCM
Facts: A board of directors of a corporation (D) resolved to pay a sum to its retiring chairman in exchange for his agreement to be available for consultation.

260   Duty of Loyalty

Issue: May a board of directors execute an enforceable agreement that provides benefits to a director?
Rule: An agreement of the board that provides benefits to a director is valid so long as the director demonstrates that his personal dealings with the board were fair, in good faith, and for adequate consideration.

Eliasberg v. Standard Oil Co. (1953) CCM
Facts: A shareholder asserted an action to declare invalid a restricted stock option plan approved by the board of directors and shareholders, claiming the directors failed to adequately inform their shareholders of the consequences of the text of the plan, which was included with the proxy statements.
Issue: For a restricted stock option plan to be valid, must the directors demonstrate that their shareholders were adequately informed in approving the submitted plan?
Rule: Directors have no obligation to explain to shareholders the consequences of a restricted stock option plan submitted for approval.

Irving Trust Co. v. Deutsch (1934) CCM
Facts: Defending a charge of violating their fiduciary duty, corporate directors asserted that their personal purchase of stock was permissible because their corporation was unable to purchase the stock itself and their personal ownership permitted the corporation access to the accompanying patents.
Issue: May directors personally acquire stock that their corporation is unable to acquire if it appears that their possession of the stock may benefit the corporation in some way?
Rule: Directors may not personally acquire stock that their corporation is unable to acquire because they may not put themselves in a position where their personal interest might conflict with the interest of the corporation.

Burg v. Horn (1967) CCM
Facts: D, a director, claimed that other directors were guilty of taking a corporate opportunity by failing to direct an opportunity to purchase real estate to the corporation.
Issue: May a director personally accept an offer in his corporation's area of business if the offer was made to him as an individual?

Rule: A director may personally accept an offer in his corporation's area of business so long as there were no grounds for the corporation to expect to profit from the particular agreement.

Karrigan v. Unity Savings Assn. (1974) CCM

Facts: Directors of Unity, Inc. (D) organized another corporation whose business benefitted from referrals from Unity. Ds believed Unity could not legally engage in the business of the corporation they formed.
Issue: Are directors protected from liability for usurping a business opportunity if they believe that their corporation was legally barred from taking advantage of the opportunity?
Rule: To be shielded from liability for usurping a business opportunity directors are under a duty fully to disclose pertinent facts to their corporation so it can decide whether it wishes to enter into a business that is reasonably incident to its operations.

Aero Drapery of Ky., Inc. v. Engdahl (1974) CCM

Facts: A corporate director (D) was aware that a number of employees intended to resign in the near future to form a competing company and that these employees copied corporate materials for use in their new business, but did not disclose his awareness to the corporation.
Issue: Does a director violate his fiduciary duty by withholding useful information from his corporation?
Rule: The fiduciary duty of a director requires full disclosure of all material information to the corporation.

Marciano v. Nakash (1987) Ha

Facts: Corporate directors (D) personally arranged for a large loan to their corporation. Another group of directors (P) claimed that self-dealing by the others voided the corporation's debt.
Issue: May a transaction engineered by self-interested directors be voided by the corporation notwithstanding its fairness?
Rule: Interested transactions are subject to close judicial scrutiny but may only be voided if they cannot be shown to be intrinsically fair.

Duty of Loyalty

Heller v. Boylan (1941) Ha

Facts: Seven stockholders out of sixty two thousand brought suit to recover bonuses paid to certain officers based on corporate earnings, in accordance with bylaws nearly unanimously approved by the stockholders. P claimed the payments bore no relation to the services rendered to the corporation.

Issue: May a bylaw authorizing payments to corporate officers based on corporate earnings be declared invalid because payments bear no relation to the services rendered by the corporation?

Rule: Although a bylaw authorizing payments to corporate officers may be declared invalid if the payments bear no relation to the services rendered to the corporation, since the question of reasonable compensation for officers is primarily one for the shareholders, there must be a valid ground for disapproving the payments in light of all equitable factors.

Weinberger v. UOP, Inc. (1983) Ha, He, SSB

Facts: Signal, Inc. controlled a majority UOP's stock and over half of UOP's board were its employees. Relying in part on a study conducted by directors common to Signal and UOP that was not disclosed to UOP, Signal proposed a merger. It was approved by a majority of the non-Signal directors and non-Signal minority shareholders of UOP. Some minority shareholders sought to rescind the cash-out merger on grounds of unfairness.

Issue: May minority shareholders of a subsidiary rescind a merger with its parent approved by a majority of the minority shareholders?

Rule: Failure of the fairness test in a parent-subsidiary merger, whether it is the test of fair dealing, such as the withholding of material information by a director common to both corporations, or the fair price test, may be sufficient grounds to rescind the transaction.

Miller v. Miller (1974) Ha

Facts: A shareholder brought suit to hold directors (Ds) liable for usurping a corporate opportunity by forming their own companies in areas related to the corporation's business. Ds disclosed the business activities of their new companies fully to the original corporation, used no corporate assets establishing the new companies, and their activities supplied the original corporation with a captive market that

helped make it the most successful U.S. company in its line of business.
Issue: May corporate directors be liable for usurping a corporate opportunity if they acted in good faith and fully disclosed their actions to the corporation?
Rule: Corporate directors are not liable for usurping a corporate opportunity unless the complaining party can prove that the business opportunity was also a corporate opportunity ("line of business test") and equitable considerations indicate that there was a violation of the fiduciary duty of good faith and fair dealing.

Speed v. Transamerica Corp. (1956) Ha
Facts: A corporation (D) owning 80 percent of another corporation's stock and in control of its board of directors breached a fiduciary duty to minority shareholders (P) by failing to disclose information. P claimed to be entitled to receive the value of losses equivalent to the value of the stock from the time of the breach.
Issue: Are directors who breach a fiduciary duty to minority shareholders liable for decreases in the value of the stock from the time of their breach?
Rule: Directors who breach a fiduciary duty to minority shareholders are liable for decreases in the value of the stock from the time of their breach.

Debaun v. First Western Bank and Trust Co. (1975) Ha
Facts: A shareholder sold a controlling block of shares in a corporation without investigating the buyer's questionable financial dealings in the past. The buyer subsequently looted the corporation.
Issue: Must a shareholder selling a controlling block of shares who has received indications that a purchaser intends to exercise the control acquired by him to loot the corporation reasonably investigate the buyer?
Rule: A controlling shareholder must make a reasonable investigation of a buyer if he has received indications that would cause a reasonable person to suspect that the buyer intends to use his control to loot the corporation.

Kidwell ex rel. Penfold v. Meikle (1979) He
Facts: Minority shareholders sought to impose Rule 10b–5 liability for a breach of fiduciary duty in the purchase of stock of another corporation.
Issue: May Rule 10b–5 liability be imposed for a breach of fiduciary duty that is also subject to common-law liability?
Rule: If shareholders are deceived in the transfer of stock, Rule 10b–5 liability may be imposed even if the breach is also subject to common-law liability.

Guth v. Loft, Inc. (1939) He
Facts: While securing a contract for the purchase of another corporation's products, a corporate president personally obtained a substantial stock interest in the other corporation.
Issue: May a corporate officer personally take advantage of a business opportunity in his corporation's line of business in which the corporation would have a reasonable interest or expectancy?
Rule: An opportunity presented to a corporation within its line of business may not be taken by an officer for his personal gain, and if the interest of the corporation is betrayed, it may claim for itself all profits gained through the transaction.

Southeast Consultants, Inc. v. McCrary Engineering Corp. (1980) He
Facts: The president of P corporation, together with a number of employees, left P to form his own corporation. P sought to bar the employees from working on a project that they had begun work on while still members of P.
Issue: May employees be liable for usurping a corporate opportunity?
Rule: Restrictions to taking advantage of corporate opportunities are applicable to directors and officers, but not ordinary employees.

Doleman v. Meiji Mutual Life Ins. Co. (1984) He
Facts: A corporation (D) purchased a block of controlling shares in another corporation for considerably more than its market price. D later offered to purchase the remaining shares from minority shareholders at a much lower rate. Minority shareholders (P) claimed D was liable for excluding them from the premium price offered to the controlling block owners.

Issue: Does a fiduciary duty between the purchaser of a control block and minority shareholders require that the premium offered for the control block be extended to the minority shares?
Rule: Purchasers of a control block are not required to pay to minority shareholders the same premium as was offered for the control-block.

Treco, Inc. v. Land of Lincoln Savings & Loan (1984) He
Facts: Fearing a takeover and liquidation, directors (D) amended their corporation's bylaws to require that further amendments be approved by two-thirds of the shareholders and removals of directors be approved by three-quarters of the shareholders. The lower court found that the amendments were approved by the directors in part, although not primarily, out of self-preservation.
Issue: Does the business judgement rule shield directors from liability when their actions are partially self-motivated?
Rule: Directors are protected from liability through the business judgement rule so long as their decisions are not primarily motivated out of self-interest.

Simon v. Socony-Vacuum Oil Co. (1944) He
Facts: Minority shareholders asserted an action to hold directors liable for corporate damages resulting from decisions of the directors to engage the corporation in activities that violated the Sherman Anti-Trust Act.
Issue: Are directors personally liable to a corporation for damages resulting from corporate participation in unlawful activity?
Rule: Directors are not personally liable for corporate damages resulting from their decisions if they did not knowingly exceed their authority and did not have reason to believe that the activity was unlawful.

Wilderman v. Wilderman (1974) He
Facts: The president and 50 percent shareholder of a corporation (D) set his own compensation without the approval of the other member of the board and 50 percent shareholder (P).
Issue: May a corporate president set his own compensation without authorization from the board of directors?

Duty of Loyalty

Rule: A corporate president may not set his compensation without authorization from the board and must prove the reasonableness of all compensation received.

Chelrob v. Barrett (1944) JB, V

Facts: Long Island Lighting (D) owned Queens Gas & Electric and Nassau & Suffolk Lighting and elected their respective directors. A majority of the directors of Queens and Nassau were also Long Island directors. Nassau purchased a large quantity of gas from Queens, at a price fixed by both boards of directors. A Queens shareholder claimed the price was unfair.

Issue 1: Is a corporation that exercises control over another corporation through election of its board of directors liable for consequential damages resulting from a transaction between the controlling corporation and the corporation it controls?

Rule 1: Power of control carries with it a duty to faithfully promote corporate interests. A controlling corporation is liable for consequential damages resulting from a transaction with the corporation it controls.

Issue 2: May a director in a position of divided loyalty who acted in good faith be personally liable for resulting damages to a corporation under the control of another?

Rule 2: Interested directors may not be held liable if they made their decisions in good faith and relied on competent personnel.

Remillard Brick Co. v. Remillard-Dandini Co. (1952) JB, SSB

Facts: After disclosing their interest to minority shareholders and directors, majority directors and shareholders of a corporation (D) entered a contract through which they stood to personally profit.

Issue: Do directors dispense with a conflict of interest by informing minority shareholders and directors of their interest?

Rule: Directors do not dispense with their fiduciary duty by informing minority shareholders and directors of a personal interest, and will be accountable for any unfairness to minority shareholders through interested transactions.

Puma v. Mariott (1971) JB

Facts: Shareholders brought a derivative action to set aside a transaction in which a corporation acquired all the stock of corpora-

tions principally owned by family members of four directors. The acquisition was authorized by unanimous resolution of disinterested directors, and there was no showing of influence by interested directors.
Issue: Does the business judgement rule apply to transactions in which interested members of the board do not participate in the corporation's decision?
Rule: The business judgement rule applies to transactions in which interested board members do not participate so long as there is no showing of dominance of disinterested directors by interested directors.

Ewen v. Peoria & E. Ry. Co. (1948) JB
Facts: Minority shareholders (P) of a corporation controlled by another corporation objected to the terms of an agreement between the two corporations.
Issue: Must a corporation set the terms of a transaction with another corporation under its control as if each had exerted bargaining power against the other?
Rule: A corporation must set the terms of a transaction with another corporation under its control as if each had exerted bargaining power against the other.

Wright v. Heizers Corp. (1977) JB
Facts: A corporation (D) provided financing to International Digisonics Corporation (IDC) and controlled a substantial part of its stock and three of its four board members. D demanded a pledge of all the stock of one of IDC's subsidiaries as security for a loan. A shareholder of IDC brought a derivative suit, alleging that the pledge of stock was used by D as protection against the outcome of other litigation.
Issue: Must a corporation controlling a majority of another corporation's board arrange transactions consistently with its duty of loyalty?
Rule: A corporation controlling a majority of another corporation's board must arrange transactions consistently with its duty to preserve and protect the controlled corporation.

268 Duty of Loyalty

Allaun v. Consolidated Oil Co. (1929) JB
Facts: A shareholder brought a derivative suit to enjoin the sale of all of a corporation's assets, alleging that the price was inadequate and the sale presented a conflict of interest for majority shareholders who were all creditors of the corporation and were to receive payment for overdue debts through the sale.
Issue: Are majority shareholders who are also overdue creditors of a corporation prohibited from voting in favor of a sale of a corporation's assets that would result in the payment of the debts?
Rule: Majority shareholders are not prohibited from voting in favor of sale of all of a corporation's assets that would result in payment of debts to them so long as the price is fair.

Weissman v. A. Weissman, Inc. (1953) JB
Facts: With his own money, a corporate officer purchased a mortgage owed to his corporation. The corporation objected when the officer subsequently sought to foreclose on the mortgage.
Issue: May a corporate officer personally buy up a claim against his company?
Rule: An officer may not personally buy up a claim against his company if, had the company bought the claim, the acquisition would have been advantageous to the corporation.

Bennett v. Propp (1962) JB
Facts: Acting without authorization, a chairman and principal executive (D) bought a large quantity of his corporation's stock with corporate funds after receiving a letter that indicated another corporation intended to purchase enough shares for a takeover.
Issue: May a director use corporate funds to maintain his control over a corporation?
Rule: A director breaches his fiduciary duty by using corporate funds to maintain personal control over a corporation unless there is an immediate threat of a takeover.

Herald Co. v. Seawell (1972) JB
Facts: A newspaper (D) formed a stock trust to avoid a potential takeover bid by a corporation (P) owning many regional newspapers. P claimed that the obstruction constituted an improper diversion of corporate assets.

Issue: Are non-profitable actions of directors designed to obstruct a takeover attempt of a newspaper valid?
Rule: Non-profitable actions designed to obstruct a takeover attempt of a semi-public corporation like a newspaper are valid if based on a desire to keep the paper responsive to public needs.

Schreiber v. Bryan (1978) JB

Facts: A minority shareholder (P) in a subsidiary alleged the usurpation of a corporate opportunity after the subsidiary's board, under control of the parent, decided to form an affiliated corporation that allegedly would compete with the subsidiary.
Issue: Must a parent corporation show that it has not usurped a corporate opportunity of a subsidiary?
Rule: A parent will be liable for usurping a corporate opportunity of a subsidiary unless it can show that dealings with a subsidiary are intrinsically fair.

Tryon v. Smith (1951) JB

Facts: A minority shareholder alleged that a majority shareholder had breached a fiduciary duty by failing to inform her of the price a third party offered for his stock.
Issue: Must majority shareholders inform minority shareholders of a price offered to purchase majority stock?
Rule: Majority shareholders have no duty to inform minority shareholders of the price offered for majority stock.

Shlensky v. South Parkway Building Corp. (1960) SSB

Facts: Minority shareholders brought suit against a corporation to set aside a transaction that was approved by a majority of directors with personal interests.
Issue: Must directors charged with violating a fiduciary duty establish the fairness of their transactions to the corporation?
Rule: Directors charged with violating a fiduciary duty who have not received approval from a majority of disinterested directors must establish the fairness of their transaction.

Fliegler v. Lawrence (1976) SSB

Facts: A shareholder brought a derivative suit to set aside a transaction involving interested directors that was approved by a majority of shareholders who also had personal interests in the transaction.

Issue: Does approval by interested shareholders of a transaction involving interested directors require that complaining shareholders establish the unfairness of the transaction to show a breach of fiduciary duty?

Rule: Approval by interested shareholders of a transaction involving interested directors will not shift the burden of establishing a breach of fiduciary duty to complaining shareholders.

Ruetz v. Topping (1970) SSB

Facts: Shareholders brought suit challenging the reasonableness of compensation received by corporate directors.

Issue: Is compensation received by corporate directors justified if it is shown to be reasonable through accounting information?

Rule: The reasonableness of compensation is not subject to determination by any precise rule, but must be determined according to the facts and circumstances of each case, including the director's qualifications, the difficulties and responsibilities of the position, the size and complexities of the business, and the general economic conditions.

Trans World Airlines, Inc. v. Summa Corp. (1977) SSB

Facts: A parent corporation did not permit its subsidiary to negotiate for the purchase of needed aircraft and forced the subsidiary to wait while it arranged for financing. Minority shareholders of the subsidiary sought to recover damages incurred because of the delay.

Issue: May a parent corporation restrict the activities of a subsidiary to the detriment of its shareholders?

Rule: A parent may not restrict the activities of a subsidiary to the detriment of minority shareholders and will be liable for resulting damages.

Santa Fe Industries, Inc. v. Green (S.Ct. 1977) SSB

Facts: Santa Fe (D) merged with Kirby Lumber, of which it was the majority shareholder, to buy out the minority shareholders. After a

complete audit and full disclosure, the minority shareholders (P) were offered $150 per share. P claims that the merger took place without prior notice to minority stockholders and that the purpose of the merger was to appropriate the difference between the offered price of $150 per share and the $772 per share based on the fair market value, of Kirby's physical assets, as valued by P. P brought the action in federal court alleging a violation of Rule 10b–5, in that D employed a "device, scheme or artifice to defraud" in the securities transaction.
Issue: Is a breach of fiduciary duty, without any deception, misrepresentation, or nondisclosure, a violation of § 10(b) and Rule 10b–5?
Rule: (White, J.) A claim of fraud and fiduciary breach only constitutes a cause of action under § 10(b) or Rule 10b–5 if the conduct alleged can be fairly viewed as "manipulative or deceptive" within the meaning of the statute.
Concurrence: (Stevens, J.) The facts alleged in the complaint do not constitute "fraud" within the meaning of Rule 10b–5.

Goldberg v. Meridor (1977) SSB

Facts: Minority shareholders (P) of Universal Gas & Oil Company (UGO) alleged that the officers of UGO issued shares to UGO's parent for inadequate consideration, failed to disclose the fraudulent nature of the transaction to the minority shareholders, and put out several press releases falsely stating that the deal was beneficial to UGO.
Issue: Can nondisclosure and misrepresentations by officers of a corporation regarding the sale of securities to its parent be the basis of a Rule 10b–5 claim by the corporation's minority shareholders?
Rule: If the facts concerning the sale of shares to a parent that were not disclosed or were misleadingly disclosed to the shareholders by the officers of a corporation breaching their fiduciary duty were material and reliance can be shown, perhaps in the form of missed opportunities to enjoin the action, then those who were misled may claim a violation of Rule 10b–5.

Stewart v. Lehigh Valley R.R. Co. (1875) V

Facts: D, defending a breach of contract action, asserted that the contract was void because at the time of its execution one of D's

directors also served as a director of the original contracting company.
Issue: Is a contract rendered unenforceable because it would present a conflict of interest for a director?
Rule: Contracts that present a conflict of interest for a director are not void by definition, but can be voided within a reasonable time at the option of the corporation.

Robotham v. Prudential Ins. Co. of America (1903) V
Facts: Prudential (D) and Fidelity attempted to act on a plan that would allow each to gain majority control over the other's stock. Half of Prudential's fourteen directors were directors in Fidelity.
Issue: Does the presence of directors on both sides of a transaction give stockholders the right to enjoin the action?
Rule: The presence of directors on both sides of a transaction does not give stockholders the right to an injunction, but does give them the right to subject the transaction to the scrutiny of the court.

Abeles v. Adams Engineering Co., Inc. (1961) V
Facts: A director of a corporation also owned a firm that received a sizable commission for securing a loan for the corporation.
Issue: May a contract be enforceable between a director and his corporation?
Rule: A contract between a corporation and one of its directors is not enforceable unless the director can establish that the contract is fair and reasonable.

Everett v. Phillips (1942) V
Facts: D and members of his family were directors of the Empire Power Corporation and owners of the vast majority of its stock. D also controlled a majority of stock in the Long Island Lighting Company. Empire Power loaned large sums of money to Long Island Lighting and extended the period of repayment when the loans were not repaid.
Issue: May a director be held liable for losses resulting from loans made by his corporation to another company in which he maintains a majority interest?
Rule: Directors can be charged with no wrong without proof that they willfully failed to protect the interests of their corporation in order to better serve their personal interests.

Johnston v. Greene (1956) V

Facts: A corporate president received an opportunity to personally invest in stock and patents because of his reputation as a well-known financier, but presented the opportunity to the corporation. Through the president's influence, the board decided to acquire the stock but not the patents. The president later arranged for the purchase of the patents by a group of corporations and individuals, including himself.
Issue: Does a president breach a fiduciary duty if he does not cause his corporation to take advantage of a business opportunity presented to him as an individual?
Rule: A president does not breach his fiduciary duty if his corporation fails to take advantage of a business opportunity that is presented to him as an individual and has no direct relation to the business of his corporation.

Lewis v. Fuqua (1985) V

Facts: Directors (D) personally purchased stock after rejecting an opportunity to acquire the stock for their corporation.
Issue: May a director be found guilty of usurping a corporate business opportunity by taking personal advantage of a business opportunity after turning down the opportunity on behalf of their corporation?
Rule: Directors are guilty of usurping a corporate business opportunity if they divert a corporate opportunity for their own personal gain.

Garner v. Wolfinbarger (1970) V

Facts: A shareholder brought suit against a corporate official. D attempted to invoke the attorney-client privilege to object to questioning about legal advice received by his corporation.
Issue: Does the attorney-client privilege absolutely protect against disclosure of communications between management and counsel to shareholders?
Rule: The availability of the attorney-client privilege to management is subject to the shareholders' right to show why it should not be invoked in the particular instance.

Wagenseller v. Scottsdale Memorial Hospital (1985) V
Facts: P, an at-will employee, claimed her refusal to participate in a skit involving the "mooning" of an audience while on a group outing with her supervisor was a proximate cause of her subsequent termination.
Issue: Is an employer liable for termination of an at-will employee under grounds contrary to public policy?
Rule: An employee is entitled to a jury trial if she can make a *prima facie* showing that her termination was based on a refusal to perform some act contrary to public policy. The question of causation must be established as a matter of fact.

Jones v. Williams (1897) V
Facts: P entered a contract through which he purchased one-sixth of a newspaper's stock and took a salaried position that gave him control over its management. The contract was negotiated by a 90 percent shareholder who effectively ran the corporation and was ratified by all stockholders. P brought suit to enjoin interference with his contract after the board of directors later attempted to influence the paper's editorial policy.
Issue: May a contract be enforced through specific performance if it compels an employer to retain a manager in his service?
Rule: A contract for control over a corporation's management may be enforced in equity if the manager cannot be adequately compensated through damages because of the difficulty of anticipating the effect of successful management over the corporation's pecuniary value and the value of the prestige to be gained by the manager.

Duane Jones Co. v. Burke (1954) V
Facts: After business problems arose, a group of directors and employees (D) threatened that there would be mass resignations and customers would leave the firm unless the president and majority shareholder (P) sold them his stock.
Issue: Does an employee violate his duty of loyalty by taking self-serving actions to the detriment of his corporation if he gains no advantage until after he is terminated?
Rule: An employee may be held liable for any self-serving action taken counter to his duty of loyalty while employed, whether he

receives the advantages of his action before or after termination from the corporation.

Rogers v. Hill (1933) V
Facts: A shareholder (P) sought to declare a corporate bylaw that paid the president and vice-president a certain percentage of net profits invalid. P claimed that the amounts paid were unreasonably large.
Issue: May a measure of compensation set by corporate bylaws be declared invalid because it rewards officers beyond a reasonable amount?
Rule: Payments under a bylaw may become so large as to warrant judicial investigation to determine whether and to what extent payments constitute waste of corporate money.

Home Interiors & Gifts, Inc. v. Commissioner of Internal Revenue (1980) V
Facts: The IRS (D) claimed that the salaries earned by executives of a corporation (P) exceeded reasonable compensation and could not be deducted in calculating net income.
Issue: May extraordinarily high executive salaries be considered reasonable compensation?
Rule: Abnormally high executive salaries may be classified as reasonable compensation if there are no grounds for concluding that the compensation represented an arrangement for the executives to draw off more than their fair share of the profits of the business.

276   Duty of Loyalty

Pogostin v. Rice (1984) V

Facts: A corporate board of directors approved an executive compensation plan based on the price of the corporation's stock. A shareholder claimed that the plan resulted in excessive payments to executives, unrelated to their productivity for the company.

Issue: May a corporate executive compensation plan be based upon the market price of the corporation's stock?

Rule: A board of directors has the right to compensate their officers and their judgement is considered conclusive, except in cases of actual fraud.

Berkwitz v. Humphrey (1958) V

Facts: A shareholder challenged a compensation plan that awarded employees "units" during their time with the corporation that were translated into pension benefits upon retirement based on the current price of the corporation's stock.

Issue: Is a plan valid that compensates retiring employees based on the corporation's current stock market price?

Rule: A plan that compensates retiring employees based on the current market value of the corporation's stock is invalid because it fails to bear a reasonable relation to the value of the services rendered by the employee, due to the influence of unrelated factors on the market price of the stock.

Ostlind v. Ostlind Valve Co. (1946) V

Facts: Williamson, a corporate director and shareholder, refrained from participating in a decision by the board to sell all the corporate assets to another corporation owned by him. Another shareholder (P) brought suit after Williamson, as a shareholder, voted in favor of ratifying the transaction.

Issue: Does a personal interest of a shareholder disqualify him from voting to ratify a corporate transaction?

Rule: Each shareholder represents himself and his own interests solely and is not precluded from voting because of conflicting personal interests.

Chapter 9

DUTY OF CARE AND DUTY TO ACT LAWFULLY

I. DUTY OF CARE

A. General Standards

To fulfill their duty of care, and avoid the possibility of personal liability, directors must meet the following two requirements:

1. Care of Ordinarily Prudent Person; and
   Directors must act with the care an ordinarily prudent person in a like position would exercise under similar circumstances.

2. Reasonable Belief of Best Interest
   In a manner the director reasonably believes to be in the best interests of the corporation.

B. Reliance

In making their decisions, directors may rely on information from officers, committees of the board, accountants, and lawyers, they reasonably believe to be competent.

C. Affirmative Duties

A director may not be liable for failing to detect wrongdoing, but he must act after receiving indications that would alert a reasonable person in his position. See *Graham v. Allis-Chalmers Mfg.*

D. Duty of Care and the Business Judgement Rule

The business judgement rule protects directors from personal liability in the making of business decisions. The following criteria must be met for the rule to be operative:

1. Not "Interested"
   Directors may not have a personal pecuniary stake in the decision.

2. Reasonably Informed
   Directors must be informed to the extent they reasonably believe appropriate under the circumstances. Directors seldom breach the duty of care so long as they have followed a reasonable process, in terms of preparation, before making their decision. See *Francis v. United Jersey Bank*.

3. Rational Belief
   They must rationally believe the business judgement is in the best interests of the corporation.

   a. Objective and Subjective
      The rational belief has both objective and subjective components.

      i. Subjective
         The director must believe his decision is in the corporation's best interest.

      ii. Objective
          The director's belief must be reasonable under an objective standard based on a person in his position.

   b. Wide Latitude
      Courts have typically afforded directors wide latitude in evaluating the "rationality" of their decisions. Breaches often require gross negligence or recklessness. See *Smith v. Van Gorkum*.

E. Causation
   Directors may not be personally liable for losses resulting from a breach of their duty of care if full attentiveness by the directors would not have prevented the loss.

II. DUTY TO ACT LAWFULLY

A director violates a duty to the corporation if he knowingly causes his corporation to disobey the law. The business judgement rule provides no protection against allegations of illegal acts. See *Miller v. American Telegraph and Telephone*.

CASE CLIPS

Bates v. Dresser (1920) CE
Facts: A small bank suffered losses over a three year period, and the president (D) in charge of operations received indications of embezzlement but did not attempt to discover the nature of the losses.
Issue: May a corporate president and director be liable for failure to discover ongoing embezzlement from a bank?
Rule: Unlike directors, a president may be liable for failing to discover ongoing embezzlement from a bank if he fails to take affirmative steps after receiving indications of peculation.

Kamin v. American Express Co. (1976) CE
Facts: Shareholders brought suit, alleging that a board of directors should be liable for losses resulting from the tax consequences of a board decision to distribute dividends.
Issue: May a board of directors be liable for corporate losses resulting from a business decision?
Rule: Alleged errors in business judgement by a board of directors do not state a cognizable cause of action.

Francis v. United Jersey Bank (1981) CE, CCM, He, SSB
Facts: P sought to recover losses from a corporate director who was unfamiliar with the basics of the corporation's affairs and finances after other directors siphoned off large sums of corporate funds.
Issue: May a director be held liable for losses resulting from a failure to be informed about corporate activity?

Rule: A director may be liable for losses resulting from a failure to be informed about the corporations activities if her negligence was a proximate cause of the loss.

Smith v. Van Gorkom (1985) CE, CCM, Ha, He, SSB, V

Facts: A corporate chairman and chief executive officer (D) convened a special meeting of the board of directors to gain approval for a proposal to sell one million shares of stock. The deal had been personally negotiated by the chairman without the knowledge of the other board members. The directors, without seeing any documentation, approved the sale after a two hour meeting.

Issue: Does the failure of a board of directors to seek information reasonably available breach their fiduciary duty to shareholders?

Rule: The failure of a board of directors to inform themselves of material information reasonably available may be gross negligence, for which they are liable to shareholders.

Miller v. American Telegraph and Telephone (1974) CE, CCM, JB, SSB

Facts: Stockholders brought an action against a board of directors for violating a federal law that prohibited corporations from making contributions to political parties.

Issue: May stockholders bring an action for an alleged breach of the directors' duty to exercise diligence in managing the corporation if the alleged breach involves illegal activity?

Rule: Stockholders may bring an action against directors for an alleged breach of their duty to manage the corporation if the breach involves illegal acts.

Shlensky v. Wrigley (1968) CCM, Ha

Facts: P claimed that the refusal of directors of a professional baseball team to equip their stadium with lighting was a poor business decision that constituted mismanagement of corporate assets.

Issue: May a shareholder bring a valid cause of action against a board of directors for mismanagement of corporate assets based solely on poor business judgement?

Rule: A shareholder complaint for director mismanagement based solely on poor business judgement does not state a valid cause of action.

Graham v. Allis-Chalmers Mfg. (1963) CCM, SSB, V

Facts: Shareholders sought to recover damages from directors based on corporate losses resulting from the violation of antitrust laws by non-director employees.
Issue: Are corporate directors liable for losses resulting from a failure to prevent employees from undertaking illegal activity?
Rule: Directors are entitled to rely on the integrity of subordinates and are not liable for losses resulting from a failure to prevent employees from undertaking illegal activity unless they have reason to suspect the same.

Litwin v. Allen (1940) Ha

Facts: Minority shareholders brought suit against directors of a corporation for losses resulting from a bond transaction containing an option clause that permitted benefits to accrue to the other party while losses would be borne by the bank.
Issue: May directors be personally liable for losses from a transaction in which they acted honestly but without prudence?
Rule: Directors are liable for corporate losses if they fail to exercise the degree of care that an ordinarily prudent man would use in a situation of like magnitude and importance, based on the facts as known to him at the time.

Gall v. Exxon Corp. (1976) Ha

Facts: A shareholder sought to hold corporate directors liable for financial losses and loss of goodwill from allegedly illegal payments made by the corporation to Italian political parties.
Issue: May a shareholder bring an action against corporate officers for alleged corporate losses resulting from their decisions?
Rule: Absent allegations of fraud, collusion, self-interest, or gross negligence in business decisions, a court should not interfere with the judgement of corporate officers at the instigation of a single shareholder.

Zapata Corp. v. Maldonado (1981) Ha   *derivative demand*
Facts: A shareholder initiated a derivative suit against corporate officers and directors. Four years later, an independent committee authorized by the board of directors recommended dismissing the action on behalf of the corporation.
Issue: May a board committee dismiss litigation initiated by a stockholder?
Rule: A board committee may dismiss derivative litigation if it meets the burden of proving independence, good faith, and reasonableness and, additionally, the court agrees with dismissal of the derivative suit in its own independent judgement.

Aronson v. Lewis (1984) Ha
Facts: A shareholder brought suit for an alleged breach of fiduciary duty by directors. The corporation (D) moved for summary judgement on the ground that the shareholder did not demand that the board of directors bring the suit before initiating his action.
Issue: May a stockholder's demand upon a board of directors be excused as futile prior to the filing of a derivative suit?
Rule: A stockholder's prior demand upon a board of directors may be excused as futile where facts are alleged with particularity that create a reasonable doubt that the directors' action was entitled to protection of the business judgement rule.

Hanson Trust PLC v. ML SCM Acquisition Inc. (1986) SSB
Facts: Corporate directors (D) approved an anti-takeover measure presented by management during a three hour board meeting. In making their decision, they relied on oral advice from financial advisors and legal counsel, but did question or investigate the information presented.
Issue: May directors be liable for failure to use reasonable diligence in gathering and considering information?
Rule: A board of directors may be liable to shareholders for losses resulting through its failure to use due diligence in the gathering and considering of material information.

Chapter 10

PROXY REGULATION

I. Shareholder Informational Rights

A. Shareholder Inspection of Records

1. Common Law Rule
   Shareholders could inspect corporate records to protect their interest if they could prove proper purpose and good faith.

2. Modern Rule
   Most states have statutes that limit the common law right of inspection. Jurisdictions differ on the extent to which they preserve the common-law rule of proper purpose, if at all.

3. Proper Purposes
   The following are generally valid grounds for inspection:

   a. Proper Management;
      To determine if the corporation is being properly managed.

   b. Condition; and
      To determine the condition of the corporation.

   c. Share Value.
      To determine the value of the petitioner's shares.

4. Improper Purposes
   Non-economic reasons are generally inadequate grounds for inspection.

a. Political or Social Reasons
To pursue a political or social agenda.

b. Personal Goals
To pursue personal goals unrelated to investment in the corporation.

B. Reporting to Shareholders

Corporations must provide shareholders with information according to laws promulgated by the Securities and Exchange Commission and stock exchange rules.

1. SEC Requirements Generally (Mnemonic: **Don't Rob Sears**)

    a. **Disclosure**
    The SEC has set forth disclosure requirements for securities registered with national exchanges and for securities of corporations with more than five million dollars in assets and more than five hundred shareholders.

    b. **Reporting**
    To trade on an exchange, companies must file a registration application, which includes certified financial statements, with the exchange and the SEC. Periodic reports must be filed to update financial and legal information, and certain reports must be sent to requesting shareholders.

    c. **Solicitation**
    Proxy solicitations must disclose all material facts for matters on which shareholders are required to vote. If control of corporate management is involved, the rules require disclosure of the names and interests of all participants in the proxy contest.

3. Stock Exchange Rules (Mnemonic: **R**ich **C**orporate **M**oguls)
   Corporations must also comply with rules issued by the stock exchanges, such as the following set forth by the New York Stock Exchange.
   a. **R**umors
      If rumors or unusual market activity indicate that information on a company's future plans has leaked out, the company has an obligation to make a public announcement to confirm or deny the rumors.

   b. **C**orporate Activity
      There must be immediate public disclosure as soon as discussions are begun with individuals outside of the corporation in preparation for mergers and acquisitions, stock splits, calls for redemption, or other similar actions.

   c. **M**aterial News Developments
      A listed company must release information that is reasonably expected to materially affect its market for securities to the public in a timely fashion.

II. PROXY RULES

Most shareholder decision-making in publicly held corporations is accomplished through proxy voting (the process in which the shareholder directs someone to cast his vote). Section 14(a) of the Securities and Exchange Act of 1934 subjects proxy voting and proxy solicitation (the process in which shareholders submit their proxies for voting) to SEC rules.

A. Coverage
SEC regulations apply to almost all solicitations and proxies of registered securities, except when less than ten persons are involved.

1. Proxies
   Under 14a–1(d), the definition of proxy for purposes of regulation includes any proxy, consent or authorization of a registered security.

2. Solicitation
All solicitations of proxies in registered securities are subject to SEC rules. Under Rule 14(a)–1(j), the SEC regulation of solicitation includes:

a. Requests for proxies;

b. Requests to revoke or not execute proxies; and

c. Communications reasonably calculated to result in the procurement, withholding, or revocation of a proxy.

B. Remedies

The SEC may seek injunctions against threatened or actual violations of the Securities Exchange Act of 1934, and imprisonment and personal fines may be imposed for willful violations.

C. Transactional Disclosure (Mnemonic: **Three Feather Pillows**)

The Proxy Rules require full disclosure for transactions that the shareholders are being asked to approve such as mergers, certificate statements, or election of directors.

1. **T**ype of Transaction (Rule 14a–3)
A person being solicited for proxies must be provided with a written proxy statement detailing the information to be disclosed for the specific type of transaction.

2. **F**alse Facts (Rule 14a–9)
No solicitation is permitted to contain any false or misleading facts and may not omit a material fact. In *TSC Industries, Inc. v. Northway, Inc*, the Supreme Court held "an omitted fact is material if there is a substantial likelihood that a reasonable shareholder would consider it important in deciding how to vote."

288   Proxy Regulation

   3. **P**rior Filing (Rule 14a–6)
      Preliminary copies of proxy materials must be filed with the SEC.

D. Periodic Disclosure (Mnemonic: **Fine Cuban Cigars**)
   Certain forms of annual disclosure are required.

   1. **F**inancial Update (Rule 14a–3)
      The proxy statement for the annual meeting at which directors are elected must include audited balance sheets for the two most recent years, audited income tax sheets for the three previous years, and other information.

   2. **C**ompensation (Item 7 of Schedule 14A)
      The proxy statement for the annual shareholders meeting must disclose the compensation of the five most highly paid executives and of the officers as a whole.

   3. **C**onflict of Interest (Item 8 of Schedule 14A)
      Conflicts of interests among directors, officers, and five percent beneficial owners must be disclosed to shareholders.

E. Attempted Takeovers
   Insurgents in a proxy fight are required to file certain types of information.

III. PRIVATE ACTIONS UNDER THE PROXY RULES

A. Right to Bring Action
   The Supreme Court recognized a shareholder's right to bring a direct or derivative action for violation of the Proxy Rules in *J.I. Case Co. v. Borak*.

B. Causation
   To set aside a transaction in which approval was gained through a misleading proxy solicitation, a shareholder must only prove the proxy statement's materiality to establish causality. He need not show that the misleading statement itself was responsible for the injury. See *Mills v. Electric Auto-Lite*.

IV. COMMUNICATIONS BY SHAREHOLDERS

With few exceptions, shareholders may present proposals to other shareholders at the expense of the corporation.

A. Significantly Related
   Proposals must be "significantly related" to the corporation's business, but relationship is not limited to the shareholder's economic investment and may include social or ethical questions. See *Lovenheim v. Iroquois Brands, Ltd.*

B. Ordinary Business
   Corporations may refuse to send proposals relating to ordinary business decisions, which are decided by the officers and not the shareholders.

CASE CLIPS

State ex rel. Pillsbury v. Honeywell, Inc.
(1971) CE, CCM, Ha, He, SSB

Facts: A stockholder asserted an action to inspect corporate records with the objective of ending the corporation's involvement in the manufacture of war munitions used in the Vietnam War.

Issue: Does a shareholder have a right to inspect corporate records for social or political reasons?

Rule: A shareholder may inspect corporate records only if his motive is germane to his economic interest as a shareholder.

Credit Bureau Reports, Inc. v. Credit Bureau of St. Paul, Inc.
(1972) CE

Facts: Shareholders brought suit to inspect a corporation's shareholder list in order to solicit proxies in opposition to management.

Issue: May shareholders inspect a corporation's shareholder list to solicit proxies in opposition to management?

Proxy Regulation

Rule: Since the desire to solicit proxies is a purpose reasonably related to a shareholder's interest as a shareholder, they may inspect corporate records for such purpose.

Mills v. Electric Auto-Lite Co. (S.Ct. 1970) CE, CCM, SSB, V

Facts: Shareholders brought a derivative suit against a corporation to set aside a merger accomplished through allegedly misleading proxy solicitations. The shareholders claimed that they were not required to prove a causal connection between the injury they suffered and the misleading proxy solicitations.

Issue: In claiming an injury from misleading information on a proxy solicitation, must shareholders prove that the injury resulted from reliance on misleading materials?

Rule: (Harlan, J.) A shareholder has made a sufficient showing of causal relationship between an injury and a misleading proxy solicitation information if he proves that proxy solicitation itself, rather than the particular defect, was an essential link in the accomplishment of the transaction.

Lovenheim v. Iroquois Brands, Ltd. (1985) CE, SSB

Facts: A shareholder brought suit to require that a corporation include information with other proxy materials about a proposal he intended to introduce at an upcoming shareholder's meeting on cruelty to animals in the production of one of the company's products. Sales of the product amounted to less than five percent of the corporation's total assets.

Issue: Must corporate management permit a shareholder to include information with other proxy materials in regard to a proposal about an area that accounts for less than five percent of its operations?

Rule: The test for deciding matters "significantly related" to a corporation's business is not limited to economics, and management may be obligated to distribute a shareholder's information that contains significant social and ethical implications with other proxy materials.

Rosenfeld v. Fairchild Engine & Airplane Corp. (1955) CE, CCM, He, JB, V

Facts: A stockholder sought to compel the return of corporate funds paid to reimburse both sides after a proxy contest. Payment to losing

side was authorized by the new board and payment to the prevailing group was ratified by the shareholders.
Issue 1: May a new board, after successfully ousting management in a proxy fight, authorize corporate funds to reimburse the old board for its expenses from the proxy fight?
Rule 1: Since management is entitled to incur reasonable expenses in the waging of a proxy fight over policy, a new board may authorize payments to reimburse the old board for reasonable expenses from a proxy fight.
Issue 2: May shareholders ratify payments to a new board for proxy expenses incurred in gaining control of the corporation?
Rule 2: Shareholders may ratify payments to a new board for the reimbursement of proxy expenses incurred in gaining control of the corporation.

J.I. Case Co. v. Borak (S.Ct. 1964) CCM, Ha, He, JB, SSB, V

Facts: Directors of J.I. Case Co.(D) released a proxy statement with allegedly false information to get shareholder approval of a merger being discussed at the time. The merger being subsequently executed with narrow approval by the shareholders, Borak (P) brought suit claiming a violation of § 14 of the Securities Exchange Act of 1934. D said the act gave no private right of action.
Issue: Does § 27 of the Securities Exchange Act of 1934 authorize a federal cause of action for rescission or damages to a corporate stockholder with respect to a consummated merger which was authorized pursuant to the use of a proxy statement alleged to contain false and misleading statements violative of § 14(a) of the Act?
Rule: (Clark, J.) Private parties have a right under § 27 to bring suit for violation of § 14(a) of the Securities Exchange Act of 1934.

Studebaker Corp. v. Gittlin (1966) CCM, Ha

Facts: A shareholder requested access to a corporation's list of shareholders, after obtaining authorizations from forty-two other shareholders, as part of an endeavor to make changes in its board of directors. When the corporation refused his request, the shareholder asserted an action to obtain the list. The corporation alleged that the shareholder failed to comply with requirements for the filing of proxy

materials under 14(a) of the Securities and Exchange Act in obtaining the authorizations of the other shareholders.
Issue: Must a stockholder comply with 14(a) of the Securities and Exchange Act before obtaining the authorizations of other stockholders to inspect a corporation's shareholder list?
Rule: A stockholder must comply with 14(a) of the Securities and Exchange Act before obtaining the authorization of other stockholders to inspect a shareholders list if the inspection is part of a continuous plan intended to end in proxy solicitation.

Rosen v. Alleghany Corp. (1955) CCM
Facts: At no cost to their corporation, officers (D) made statements orally and in newspapers that shareholders (P) claimed amounted to proxy solicitation. P sought to have their own proxy material mailed to shareholders by the corporation.
Issue: May shareholders compel a corporation to mail their proxy information at a corporation's expense if the corporation has engaged in proxy solicitation through public statements?
Rule: When a corporation has engaged in proxy solicitation at no expense to its shareholders, complaining shareholders have no right to compel the corporation to provide them a means of access to shareholders by mail.

Securities and Exchange Commission v. Transamerica Corporation (1947) CCM, V
Facts: A shareholder submitted four proposals to a corporation to be included with other proxy materials sent to other shareholders before their annual meeting. The corporation refused to include the proposals.
Issue: Must a corporation include a shareholder's proposals with other proxy materials?
Rule: A corporation must include in proxy materials a shareholder's proposals on subjects for which shareholders have the right to act under the state's corporation law.

Medical Committee for Human Rights v. SEC (1970) CCM, JB, SSB, V
Facts: A shareholder (P) sought to include a proposal with proxy materials calling for an end to a corporation's production of napalm.

The opposition was primarily based on concern for human life, but the proposal also included information detailing how the production of napalm was harmful for the corporation's business. The corporation (D), without explanation, refused to include the proposal.

Issue: Must corporate management include with its proxy materials a shareholder proposal has not been shown to be an improper subject for action by security holders?

Rule: Under § 14 of the Securities and Exchange Act of 1934, corporate management must include shareholder proposals with proxy materials, unless management proves that the proposal is not a proper subject for action because it is motivated by general political and moral concerns or is related to the conduct of ordinary business operations.

TSC Industries, Inc. v. Northway, Inc.
(S.Ct. 1976) CCM, Ha, JB, SSB

Facts: National bought control of TSC by acquiring thirty-four percent of TSC's voting securities from Charles E. Schmidt and his family. National then placed five of its own nominees on TSC's board and issued a joint proxy statement from itself and TSC recommending approval of a proposal to liquidate and sell all of TSC's assets to National. Northway, a TSC shareholder, brought suit claiming that the proxy statement was incomplete and materially misleading with regards to the degree of National's control over TSC in violation of § 14(a) of the Securities Exchange Act and Rules 14a–3 and 14a–9 promulgated thereunder.

Issue: When is an omitted fact from a proxy statement considered material under § 14(a) of the Securities Exchange Act of 1934?

Rule: (Marshall, J.) For the purposes of § 14(a) of the Securities Exchange Act and Rule 14a–9 promulgated thereunder, an omitted fact from a proxy statement is material if there is a substantial likelihood that a reasonable shareholder would consider it important in deciding how to vote, or, put another way, that a reasonable investor would have viewed the omitted fact as having significantly altered the "total mix" of information made available.

Rauchman v. Mobil Corporation (1984) Ha

Facts: Suliman S. Olayan, a Saudi Arabian citizen, was appointed to

294   Proxy Regulation

Mobil's board of directors. Irvin Rauchman, a shareholder, submitted a proposed amendment to Mobil's bylaws for inclusion in Mobil's proxy statement for the company's 1982 annual meeting that would have prevented a citizen of an OPEC country from sitting on Mobil's board of directors. Mobil refused to include the proposal in its statement.
Issue 1: Is there an implied private cause of action under § 14(a) of the Securities Exchange Act and Rule 14a–8 promulgated thereunder?
Rule 1: An implied private cause of action exists under § 14(a) of the Securities Exchange Act when it is premised upon an alleged violation of Rule 14a–8.
Issue 2: Can a company legitimately exclude from its proxy statement a proposal for an amendment to its bylaws to ban citizens from OPEC nations from sitting on its board of directors?
Rule 2: Rule 14a–8(c)(8) allows a company to exclude a proposal from its proxy statement if it relates to election to the company's board of directors.

Levin v. Metro-Goldwyn-Mayer, Inc. (1967) JB
Facts: A shareholder brought suit to hold management accountable for proxy solicitation expenses. The expenses were disclosed in a proxy statement.
Issue: May management commit a corporation to pay for services in the production of proxy solicitation?
Rule: Management may spend corporate funds on proxy solicitation so long as no illegal or unfair methods are employed and their actions are not overreaching or unreasonable.

SEC v. Medical Committee for Human Rights (1972) JB
Facts: Following a court order, a corporation included a shareholder proposal in proxy materials and the proposal was supported by less than 3 percent of the voting shareholders. The shareholders intended to include the proposal in future proxy materials.
Issue: May a corporation exclude a shareholder proposal from proxy materials for three years if the proposal drew support from less than 3 percent of the shareholders when last put to a vote?
Rule: Under Rule 14a–8(c)(4)(i), a corporation may exclude a proposal receiving support from less than 3 percent of the voting

shareholders from proxy materials for the following three years.

Long Island Lighting Company v. Barbash (1985) SSB
Facts: A local political candidate waged a campaign in which he urged public ownership of a private utilities corporation. He acquired shares in the corporation to demand a special shareholders meeting to put the issue to a vote. Before the vote was taken, a newspaper advertisement was taken out by a third party in favor of converting the corporation to public ownership. The corporation alleged that the advertisement was an unfiled solicitation of proxies that violated federal proxy rules.
Issue: Can public communications indirectly addressed to shareholders violate federal proxy rules?
Rule: A public communication "reasonably calculated" to influence shareholders' votes, viewed in the totality of the circumstances, may be a violation of Regulation 14(a) of the Securities and Exchange Act.

Securities and Exchange Commission v. May (1955) V
Facts: In attempting to solicit proxies to take over management of a corporation, shareholders included a series of questions that implied the current management had acted dishonestly. The SEC moved to enjoin the solicitation of proxies.
Issue: Does federal proxy regulation prohibit shareholders from soliciting proxies through statements that contain misleading implications?
Rule: Rule 14–A prohibits shareholders from employing "grossly misleading" statements in the solicitation of proxies.

Chapter 11

SHAREHOLDERS' SUITS

I. INTRODUCTION

A. Direct Suits Against the Wrongdoers

   1. If shareholders allege a contractual or statutory breach, they may chose to bring their cause of action directly against the wrongdoers.

   2. Examples:

      a. Management's refusal to permit inspection of corporate books; and

      b. An insider's failure to disclose material information when purchasing their shares.

   3. If the misconduct affects the rights of a number of stockholders, the suit may be brought as a class action.

B. Secondary Actions on Behalf of the Corporation

   1. If shareholders claim that management's wrongdoing has directly injured the corporation, a suit may be brought on the corporation's behalf (a derivative action). The shareholders' injury is derived from misconduct that has reduced the value of the corporation's assets and injured all shareholders according to their proportionate interest.

   2. Examples:

      a. Charges that the directors or officers have breached their fiduciary duties by taking excessive salaries; and

  b. Management has improperly declined to enforce a corporate cause of action against outsiders.

 3. Reasons for Bringing a Derivative Action

  a. Those in control of a corporation who breach their fiduciary duties to it will obviously not institute a cause of action to obtain relief against themselves.

  b. The majority shareholders will impede any attempt to elect new management.

  c. It is unfeasible to elect new management or effect changes for various reasons especially in large corporations, because of the gap between ownership and control.

  d. It is an important remedial and deterrent device to police and prevent management abuses and protect minority shareholders and others concerned with the welfare of the corporation.

C. Strike Suits

 1. Originally small stockholders desiring to abuse the derivative suit were able to institute actions for their personal gain (a private settlement) rather than correction of managerial misconduct. The complaining shareholder was willing to accept a fraction of the damage to the corporation because this personal recovery would be in excess of the benefit to the corporation were it to recover. Additionally, defendants were willing to pay either to avoid the nuisance of the suit or to escape the potential liability of a larger judgment.

 2. The opportunity to bring strike suits has been diminished by the requirement of prior demand on the board.

D. Mechanics of the Derivative Suit

1. The shareholder plaintiff must:

   a. Have been a shareholder at the time the damage occurred (the *contemporaneous ownership rule*);

   b. Presently hold stock in the corporation; and

   c. Have exhausted internal remedies. Thus, a prior demand on the board that it undertake the suit is required, and in some jurisdictions prior demand on the shareholder body is also required.

2. If the corporation refuses to sue in its own benefit, it is a defendant in the derivative suit.

3. Federal Rules of Civil Procedure 23.1 — *Derivative Actions by Shareholders* is the federal rule governing derivative suits.

4. All payments made in connection with the derivative action must be received by the corporation.

II. EXHAUSTION OF INTERNAL REMEDIES

A. Demand on Board

A shareholder, prior to instituting a derivative suit, must make a written demand on the board requesting that the board bring suit or take an alternative corrective action. Only after the board has rejected the demand may the plaintiff institute the action.

B. Demand on Shareholders

Jurisdictions are mixed as to the requirement of shareholder demand. While some states require it, others such as California (California General Corporate Code § 800) and New York (N.Y. Business Corporate Law § 626) do not.

C. Effects of Demand Excuse

Generally, if demand on the board is excused, a suit may proceed without any prior judicial review of its merits. However, the board may still appoint an independent committee to investigate the case and recommend further action.

D. Circumstances When Demand Is Excused

Demand on the board is excused where it would be futile. If, for example, the board is alleged to have participated in the misconduct, it is doubtful that it will approve an action against it; thus, demand would be futile and therefore excused.

E. Determining Demand Futility

1. Delaware View

    a. A plaintiff has the burden of proving a reasonable doubt about whether:

        i. the board was disinterested and independent; or

        ii. the decision was protected under the business judgment rule.

    b. According to the Delaware view, a shareholder will successfully prove futility if for example:

        i. Each member was hand-picked by the controlling shareholder, and a desire to safeguard their position on the board prompted the approval of the board's decision.

        ii. The decision is not protected under the business judgment rule because it is outside the parameters of reasonable business decision. See *Aronson v. Lewis*.

c. Demand will rarely be excused if the Delaware view is applied (see *Grobow v. Perot*). This is because:

   i. The facts must be pled with extreme specificity.

   ii. Charges of board misconduct are insufficient to categorize demand as futile.

   iii. The plaintiff will generally be unable to obtain discovery to substantiate the allegations.

   iv. Demand will not be excused unless there is a particularized showing that the board was not independent or acted irrationally.

2. New York View
New York applies a less stringent standard for excusing demand than Delaware. Demand will be excused if the board is charged with breach of the duty of due care. In addition, less specifity in the pleading is required.

F. Ramifications of Demand Refusal

1. The plaintiff will usually be barred from continuing the suit if the suit is against a third party who is not a corporate insider.

2. If, however, the suit is against a corporate insider, the board's decision not to continue with the suit will usually be respected (protected under the business judgment rule), unless there are allegations that the board:

   a. Participated or personally benefitted from the wrongdoing; or;

   b. The wrongdoer controlled or dominated the directors who rejected the shareholders' demand.

3. Because the criteria required for demand excuse and the continuance of an action after board rejection are similar, some urge that demand should be required in all cases. See ALI *Principles of Corporate Governance.*

G. The Independent Committee

1. Appointment of Committee
   After the plaintiff has submitted his demand on the board, it will usually respond by appointing a special independent committee, consisting of disinterested directors. The committee's role is to investigate the allegations and recommend the proper course of action for the corporation.

2. Insuring Independence
   To guarantee the committee's independence, membership is limited to those directors who have no financial stake in the transaction that the committee is investigating. Usually, the committee obtains the advice of independent counsel.

3. The Committee's Recommendation
   The committee will usually recommend that the plaintiff's suit be dismissed. This recommendation may be based on a conclusion that the allegations are without substantive merit. Alternatively, the committee may conclude that the burden to the corporation if it proceeds with the action will outweigh any potential recovery.

4. Overcoming the Committee's Recommendation
   There are conflicting standards for overcoming the committee's recommendation.

   a. New York View
      A court will reject the committee's recommendation only if the plaintiff proves that the members were not independent or did not adhere to procedure. However, if the court is convinced that the committee members were disinterested and adhered to procedure, the court will not review the

substantive merits of the committee's conclusion that the case be dismissed.

b. Delaware View
In certain instances, Delaware will allow its courts to review the substantive merits of the committee's conclusion that a case be dismissed. *Zapata Corp. v. Maldonado*, applied a two-step test to determine whether it should comply with the committee's recommendation of dismissal.

III. QUALIFICATIONS OF PLAINTIFF SHAREHOLDER

A. Requirement of Shareholder

A plaintiff instituting a derivative suit must be a stockholder in the corporation; thus, bondholders are excluded from instituting a derivative suit. Usually, preferred shareholders or convertible bond holders may bring a derivative suit.

B. Contemporaneous Ownership Rule

Under the contemporaneous ownership rule, the plaintiff must have owned his shares at the time the alleged misdeed or transaction occurred. An exception to this rule is that a plaintiff can bring a derivative suit to rectify a wrong occurring prior to his ownership, but continuing after his purchase.

C. Suit in the Corporation's Own Name

If the derivative suit is really one instituted by the shareholders, the contemporaneous ownership rule will not be avoided by bringing the action in the corporation's own name. (See *Bangor Punta Operations, Inc. v. Bangor & Aroostook R.R.*)

D. Continuing Ownership Rule

It is not sufficient for the shareholder instituting a derivative action to own the shares at the time the misdeed or transaction occurred;

he must continue to own the shares until the court renders a judgment.

IV. SECURITY FOR EXPENSES

A. A security-for expense statute insures that the plaintiff bringing suit has the financial stability to reimburse the corporation should his suit fail. Some form of security-for-expenses statute has been enacted in about a third of the states. These statutes were enacted in response to strike suitors with minor financial interests in the corporation.

C. In addition to requiring the posting of security, statutes that are applicable to only certain types of plaintiffs (i.e., only those with small shareholdings) create a potential substantive liability for the litigation expenses incurred by the corporation. In certain instances, this liability may include the litigation expenses of the officers and board members because of the indemnity obligation. Some statutes impose this liability only on those required to post security; thus, other plaintiffs cannot be made liable for litigation expenses even if they lose on the merits and it is clear that the suit was brought without reasonable cause.

C. Avoiding the Security-For-Expense Statute

A shareholder bringing a derivative suit may avoid the security-for-expense statute if:

1. The action is based on violation of a federal statute (i.e., 10b–5);

2. It is instituted in a state without a security statute;

3. Other shareholders intervene in the action so that their holdings are added to the plaintiffs' to constitute the necessary amount; or

4. The plaintiff obtains a stay of an order to post security so as to inspect the corporation's stock book in order to urge the other shareholders to join the suit. Because granting the plaintiff access to the corporation's shareholder list may result in added expense or negative publicity, the corporation may drop its demand for security. This method may be difficult for the plaintiff, especially against widely held corporations.

V. SETTLEMENT OF DERIVATIVE SUITS

A. To assure that any settlement is in the best interest of the corporation and its shareholders, most jurisdictions require prior court approval of any settlement.

B. To decide whether to approve the settlement, the court will examine whether the net financial benefit to the corporation under the settlement will outweigh the potential net benefit if the case were tried.

C. In federal courts and in most states, stockholders must be given prior notice of any settlement and the opportunity to intervene in the action (i.e., to oppose the settlement).

D. Pro Rata Recovery

Sometimes, a court will order some or all of the recovery to be allocated to the shareholders in proportion to their shareholdings. This occurs when either:

1. Wrongdoers are in control;

2. Most of the shares are held by those who in some way aided and abetted the wrongdoing;

3. The majority of the shares are now owned by people who do not have standing to bring suit or;

4. The prior shareholders cannot bring suit even though they have suffered an uncompensated injury.

VI. PLAINTIFF'S LITIGATION EXPENSES

A. Plaintiffs will usually recover reasonable litigation expenses, which are paid out of the amount recovered on behalf of the corporation.

B. Methods of Fee Calculation

1. Lodestar Method
   The key element is the reasonable value of the time used by the attorney (the actual number of hours is multiplied by a reasonable hourly fee). Because of the contingency aspect of a derivative action, a court will usually adjust the award upward.

2. Salvage Value Approach
   The court calculates the fee by awarding a percentage of the recovery.

3. Occasionally some courts will use the lodestar method for fee computation but will set a maximum percentage of recovery.

VII. CORPORATE COUNSEL

A. Attorney-Client Privilege

The corporation holds the attorney-client privilege independently of the shareholders; thus, corporate counsel may refuse to disclose advise given to the corporation. However, if the plaintiff shows good cause why the privilege should be suspended, the court will suspend it.

B. Mutual Representation

Usually corporate counsel may not represent the corporation and the defendants in the action. Because the attorney normally has a prior relationship with the defendants, he will represent the defendants, and the corporation will obtain independent counsel.

VIII. INDEMNIFICATION AND DIRECTORS & OFFICERS INSURANCE

A. Indemnification

   1. A corporation is required to indemnify an officer or director in most jurisdictions when:

      a. He is completely vindicated of the charges; or

      b. The corporation has previously obligated itself to indemnify by charter, law or contract.

   2. In other instances the corporation may choose to indemnify the director or officer.

B. In suits not brought by the corporation or derivatively (third party suits), the corporation may indemnify the director or officer if:

   1. They acted in good faith;

   2. They were pursuing what they believed to be the best interests of the corporation; or

   3. They believed that their conduct was lawful.

C. If the suit is brought on behalf of the corporation, the corporation may not indemnify the director or officer for any judgment or settlement recovered. However, the corporation may indemnify the director or officer for litigation expenses if the defendant is not found liable on the underlying claim.

D. Independent members of the board of directors or independent legal counsel decide whether the officers or directors are entitled to indemnification.

E. Usually the corporation may advance money for litigation expenses if the officer or director promises to repay the advances.

F. Most jurisdictions permit the defendant to petition the court to order indemnification, even if the corporation is prohibited or unwilling to make the payment voluntarily.

G. Directors and Officers Insurance

1. Usually, a directors and officers policy will exclude claims involving dishonest conduct, illegal compensation, self dealing, etc.

2. The policy will usually cover expenses that the corporation could not indemnify.

CASE CLIPS

Eisenberg v. Flying Tiger Line, Inc. (1971) CE, CCM, He, SSB
Facts: P, a resident of New York, brought suit against D on behalf of himself and all other shareholders of the corporation seeking to enjoin a reorganization and merger plan. P, a Delaware corporation with its principal place of business in California, removed the action from state court to a federal district court. In federal court P sought a court order requiring D to post security for the corporations costs. After the motion was granted, P refused to comply claiming his suit was personal and not derivative within the meaning of § 627 (the applicable state statute).
Issue: Is a suit brought by a shareholder on behalf of himself and other shareholders to block the execution of a reorganization and merger plan considered a shareholders' derivative suit?
Rule: A suit brought by a shareholder on behalf of himself and others to enjoin a proposed merger or reorganization plan is not derivative but rather a type of class suit (personal suit) in which the shareholder is enforcing a common right of all the shareholders.

Keenan v. Eshleman (1938) CE, CCM, He
Facts: Keenan and Brewer controlled Consolidated through a voting trust, and were majority shareholders, officers, and directors of Sanitary Corporation for which they received a salary. As directors of

Sanitary, they hired Consolidated to manage its affairs and paid it a monthly fee. The minority shareholders of Sanitary subsequently sued the majority shareholders of Sanitary who approved the fee to Consolidated, claiming double compensation.

Issue: In a shareholder's derivative suit is recovery limited to those shareholders who did not approve the corporation's action that prompted the cause of action?

Rule: Generally, because a shareholders derivative suit is brought on behalf of the corporation, equitable principles demand that the entire recoverable amount be paid to the corporation.

Perlman v. Feldmann (1955) CE

Facts: During a time of steel shortage, president, director and dominant shareholder (D) of a steel corporation sold his controlling interest to a group of steel users, who promptly elected their own board of directors. Minority shareholders (P) alleged that consideration paid for the stock included a corporate asset that D held in trust for the corporation: the ability to control the allocation of a corporate product in a time of short supply.

Issue: Is recovery limited to individual or minority shareholders in a shareholders' derivative suit?

Rule: Recovery can be limited to individual or minority shareholders if: (1) P is the only shareholder injured, (2) no creditors of the corporation would be hurt or (3) those participating in the wrong control the corporation and could misuse the recovery if the corporation would recover.

Bangor Punta Operations, Inc. v. Bangor & Aroostook R.R. (S.Ct. 1974) CE, He, SSB

Facts: Amoskeag brought suit on behalf of Bangor & Aroostook R.R. (BAR) against Bangor Punta Operations for mismanagement, misappropriation, and waste during the time Bangor & Aroostook Corp. and Bangor Punta controlled BAR.

Issue: Can a corporation recover for injuries that a subsidiary of a corporation sustained prior to that corporation's ownership of the subsidiary?

Rule: (Powell, J.) Shareholders of a plaintiff corporation must either sustain injury or receive less than full value for the court to recover for injuries sustained prior to ownership.

Dissent: (Marshall, J.) Present shareholders are entitled to recovery if any of them are able to bring suit as individuals. The directors of the corporation are under a fiduciary obligation to use due care to ensure that the corporation seek redress where a majority shareholder has drained the corporate resources for his own benefit to the detriment of minority shareholders.

Barr v. Wackman (1975) CE, CCM, JB

Facts: P brought a derivative action alleging self-dealing by the directors of Talcott in approving an unfair tender offer for Talcott. P brought the action without first demanding that the board either rescind the acceptance or bring suit on behalf of the corporation.

Issue: In a shareholders' derivative action, are allegations of board misconduct a sufficient excuse for failing to demand that the board of directors either rescind the agreement or bring suit on behalf of the corporation?

Rule: Demand will generally be excused where the wrongdoers control or comprise a majority of the directors; however, allegations of directorial fraud or self-interest are not in every case a prerequisite for excusing a derivative shareholder from making a demand upon the board. These determinations are decided on a case-by-case basis.

In re BankAmerica Securities Litigation (1986) CE

Facts: None provided.
Issue: None provided.
Rule: The substantive law of a state determines whether demand is required or excused. However, federal law should determine whether the demand or excuse has been pled properly, so as to meet the requirements of the Federal Rules of Civil Procedure.

Auerbach v. Bennett (1979) CE, He, JB

Facts: An internal investigation conducted by General Telephone & Electric (GTE) concluded that the corporation or its subsidiaries had made questionable payments to public officials or political parties in foreign countries and the United States. In certain instances, some of the directors had been personally involved. P brought a shareholders' derivative suit on behalf of GTE against the directors, Arthur Anderson & Co. (GTE's outside auditors), and the corporation, seeking to hold these Ds liable for the amount paid in bribes and kickbacks. A special litigation committee composed of three disinterested directors appointed by the board, concluded that it was not in the best interests of the corporation to proceed with the action.

Issue 1: Is a substantive decision of a special committee consisting of disinterested directors protected by the business judgment doctrine?

Rule 1: A substantive decision of a special committee is protected under the business judgment doctrine if the directors' decision was made in good faith. Permitting judicial inquiry into such issues would emasculate the business judgment doctrine as applied to the actions and determinations of a special committee.

Issue 2: Does the business judgment doctrine bar judicial inquiry into the "independence" of the members of a special committee, or the appropriateness of the procedural methods implemented by that committee?

Rule 2: The business judgment rule does not bar judicial inquiry to verify the "independence" of the disinterested members of a special committee. Additionally, because courts are well equipped by experience and practice in making procedural decisions, it may inquire into the appropriateness of the procedural methods implemented by that committee.

Zapata Corp. v. Maldonado (1981) CE, CCM, He, SSB, V

Facts: A shareholder initiated a derivative suit against corporate officers and directors. Four years later, an independent committee consisting of two disinterested directors recommended dismissing the action.

Issue: May a board committee dismiss litigation initiated by a derivative stockholder?

Rule: A board committee may dismiss derivative litigation if it meets a two-step test. The committee must first prove that it acted independently and in good faith, and then the court must agree with the dismissal of the derivative suit in its own independent business judgment.

Alford v. Shaw (1987) CE, CCM

Facts: In response to minority shareholders' charges of mismanagement, the board of directors of All American Assurance Company (AAA) appointed a special committee to determine whether it was in the best interest if AAA and its shareholders to initiate legal action against those implicated in any wrongdoing discovered. Before the committee completed the investigation, Ps filed a derivative action against the controlling shareholders and most of the directors. Upon completion of the investigation, the committee recommended that the majority of the P's claims be dismissed with prejudice, and two claims be settled.

Issue: Absent fraud or other instances of bad faith actions, is court approval required for the disposition of a shareholders' derivative suit?

Rule: Court approval is required for disposition of all shareholder derivative suits, even where the directors are not charged with fraud or self-dealing, or where the plaintiff and the board agree to discontinue, dismiss, compromise, or settle the lawsuit.

Grobow v. Perot (1988) CE

Facts: In a shareholders' derivative suit Ps alleged that the directors of General Motors (D) purchased Perot's shares at a premium to silence Perot's criticism of GM's executives and directors. This transaction was subsequently criticized by shareholders and other commentators.

Issue: Are allegations that fail to raise reasonable doubt either as to director independence or due care, protected under the business judgment rule, thus requiring demand on the board?

Rule: In the absence of more detailed charges, a court will view the decision of a board as being protected under the business judgment rule, thus demand is inexcusable. Allegations that either (1) all the relevant facts were not considered, (2) consultations with investment bankers, accountants, or lawyers were not sought, or (3) it failed to comply with proper procedures, would likely be specific enough.

Mayer v. Adams
(1958) CE, CCM, JB, SSB, V

Facts: In a shareholders' derivative action P claimed that in certain dealings between Phillips Petroleum and Ada Oil, the board of directors of Phillips engaged in fraudulent and improper conduct. P did not bring demand first to the shareholders.

Issue: If the ground of the derivative suit is fraud, is demand for stockholder action necessary?

Rule: Since shareholders cannot ratify corporate fraud, if the grounds of the derivative suit is fraud, prior demand on the shareholders is not required.

Note: The court was not called upon to enumerate the various circumstances in which demand on stockholders is excused and thus did not. The court cited cases involving irregularity or lack of authority in directorate action, as examples in which demand on the stockholder should be excused.

Bosch v. Meeker Cooperative Light & Power Ass'n (1960) CE

Facts: P sought to recover his litigation expenses, which stemmed from a derivative suit that he brought in which it was determined that a purported election of directors and a proposed amendment to the corporate bylaws were illegal.

Issue: Are plaintiffs who successfully bring a shareholders' derivative suit entitled to recover counsel fees stemming from that action, if there is no actual monetary benefit to the corporation?

Rule: Even though there is no direct pecuniary benefit to the corporation, the action did result in substantial benefit to the corporation, and thus, plaintiffs are entitled to recover counsel fees.

Haberman v. Tobin (1980) CE

Facts: P brought a shareholders' derivative suit against Allegheny Corporation and D. P's suit was dismissed when he ignored a lower court judge's order to post a security bond (in accordance with § 627 of the New York Business Corporation Law). P claimed that since he acquired shares in Alleghany worth over $50,000, he was exempt from posting the security bond.

Issue: Does a plaintiff in a derivative action who acquires the requisite outstanding stock after the action is commenced, but ignores court orders mandating the posting of a security bond, meet the requirements of § 627?

Rule: A shareholder who acquires the minimum ownership percentage of outstanding stock after a derivative action has been instituted, but ignores numerous court orders mandating the posting of a security bond, does not meet the requirements of § 627.

Dissent: Since the statute is silent as to when the criteria for stock ownership must be met to avoid posting security, a plaintiff upon the purchase of the requisite stock even after the action is instituted meets the requirements of § 627.

Tomash v. Midwest Technical Development Corp. (1968) CE
Facts: P, a director of Midwest (D), was found in violation of the Investment Company Act of 1940 resulting from his investments in companies that D also invested in. P resigned from the board and sought reimbursement for his litigation expenses defending the action brought by the SEC.
Issue: Is a director or officer charged with negligence and misconduct in the discharge of his duties and who is not vindicated of all the charges, entitled to indemnification as a matter of right for defense expenses stemming from that cause of action?
Rule: A director is not entitled to indemnification as a matter of right for defense expenses stemming from a cause of action in which he is charged with negligence and misconduct in the discharge of his duties and is only partially vindicated.

Clarke v. Greenberg (1947) CE, He
Facts: Ds brought a derivative action against the officers and directors of Associated Gas & Electric Co. alleging that they mismanaged the company's affairs. Before trial D settled the action without notice to the other shareholders and without court approval. D received $9,000 in exchange for his stock which had a market value of $51.
Issue: May a shareholder who brings and subsequently settles a shareholders' derivative suit keep the money recovered from the defendants for his own benefit?
Rule: A shareholder who brings a derivative suit is under a fiduciary duty to the corporation and other shareholders, thus any amount recovered belongs to the corporation.

Lewis v. Newman (1973) CE
Facts: A shareholders' derivative suit was brought on behalf of Howard Stores. In the suit it was alleged that Ds who controlled Howard caused the corporation to purchase stock from a former employee above market value, thus causing Howard to lose $750,000. Some of the shareholders moved to settle the suit and the court

ordered a hearing. The settlement proposed that Ds pay the corporation $45,000 and that the purchase price of the stock be reduced by $65,000.
Issue: What role should the court assume in the settlement of a shareholders' derivative suit?
Rule: A court will not determine the merits of the action; rather, it will determine whether the proposed settlement is fair, reasonable, and adequate.

Desimone v. Industrial Bio-Test Laboratories (1979) CE
Facts: Not provided.
Issue: Under what circumstances will a court approve a settlement of a class action?
Rule: A proposed settlement will receive court approval if it is fair, reasonable, and adequate. This conclusion is reached if it has been proved that (1) the settlement is not collusive, (2) the proponents are experienced counsel, (3) there has been sufficient discovery to enable counsel to act intelligently, (4) the number of objections is small. The court must also conclude that the settlement is reasonable in light of the plaintiff's chance of success.

Wolf v. Barkes (1965) CE, Ha, JB
Facts: P brought a shareholders' derivative suit against Curtis Publishing Corp. and some of its directors and officers. P alleged that Ds engaged in misconduct to obtain authorization for a Restricted Stock Option Plan. When the corporation and its officers reached a settlement out of court, P sought an injunction to restrain them from settling because his derivative suit was still pending.
Issue: Does F.R.C.P. § 23(c) require notice to all stockholders, and court approval of a proposed settlement of a pending shareholders' derivative suit?
Rule: Under § 23(c) a corporation may settle a pending derivative suit with individual defendants without giving notice or seeking court approval, since that suit is not compromised by the corporation doing so.

Garner v. Wolfinbarger (1970) CE, JB
Facts: A shareholder brought suit against a corporate official. D attempted to invoke the attorney-client privilege to prevent questioning about legal advice received by his corporation.
Issue: Does the attorney-client privilege protect communications between management and counsel from shareholders?
Rule: The availability of the attorney-client privilege to management is subject to the stockholders' right to show why it should not be invoked in the particular instance.

Aronson v. Lewis (1984) CCM, He, SSB
Facts: Lewis (P) brought a shareholders' derivative suit charging that an employment agreement between Meyers Parking System and Fink (a co-defendant) amounted to waste of the corporate assets. P alleged that demand on the board was excused.
Issue: Under what circumstances is demand upon a board of directors excused?
Rule: A court will excuse demand only after the pleaded facts prove that reasonable doubt exists as to whether (1) the directors are disinterested and independent (2) and the challenged transaction was the product of a valid exercise of business judgment.

Courtland Manor, Inc. v. Leeds (1975) CCM
Facts: Ds planned to construct a nursing home that corporation would operate, while a limited partnership would actually construct and own the facility. The corporation was formed and nine investors including P contributed $70,000 in exchange for stock in the corporation valued at $1,000 per share. All nine investors including D were named as directors. A lease was agreed between the partnership and the corporation and soon afterwards the corporation experienced financial difficulties and eventually fell into disarray, resulting in P acquiring control of the corporation at a fraction of its original cost. P subsequently brought suit alleging that the lease agreement was unfair to the corporation and excessively favorable to the partnership.
Issue: Are subsequent shareholders who have not suffered any loss entitled to recover for prior wrongs to that corporation?
Rule: Shareholders who purchased all or a majority of the shares of a corporation at a fair price, and have suffered no injury from any

wrongs occurring prior to the purchase are not entitled to recover for those wrongs. Allowing such recovery would constitute a windfall and enable the recovery of funds to which they had no claim, and encourage speculative litigation.

Goldie v. Yaker (1967) CCM

Facts: Shareholders of Intermountain Development Corp. (P) brought suit alleging that excessive valuation was placed on land sold by Ds (the incorporators of Intermountain). At the time of the sale, Ds were the only shareholders.

Issue: May plaintiffs who were not shareholders at the time the transaction of which they complain bring a derivative action?

Rule: To maintain a shareholders' derivative suit plaintiffs must have been stockholders at the time of the transaction of which they complain. There is disagreement however, as to whether this rule is applicable when as a part of the transaction fraud was contemplated upon the future shareholders.

Otis & Co. v. Pennsylvania R.R. (1946) CCM

Facts: D was named as a co-defendant in a derivative action in which some of the board of directors and officers were also named. P alleges that the certain members of the board breached their duty to Pennsylvania R.R. when they failed to "shop around for the best price on a new bond issue" and entered into a contract for the sale of bonds with Kuhn, Loeb & Co.

Issue: May a corporation that is joined as a party defendant in a shareholders derivative suit in which the officers and directors of a corporation are charged with breach of duty raise affirmative defenses?

Rule: Except for cases in where fraud of the directors or management is the essence of the derivative suit, a corporation should have the right to answer and raise affirmative defenses.

Cannon v. Acoustics Corp. (1975) CCM, Ha, SSB

Facts: Ps brought a shareholders' derivative suit on behalf of Acoustics Corp. and its wholly owned subsidiary (Perlite) against four officer-directors of the corporations. Both of the corporations and the individual defendants were represented by the same counsel.

Issue: May a single lawyer or law firm both the individual and corporate defendants in a derivative action?
Rule: Since the interest of the corporate client is paramount and should not be influenced by any interest of the individual defendant clients in a derivative suit, a corporate client should be represented by independent counsel from the outset even though counsel believes in good faith that no conflict of interest exists. The defendant corporation maintains the right to select the new independent counsel.

Armstrong v. Frostie Co. (1971) CCM
Facts: P brought a derivative suit charging D with wrongfully canceling his franchise. According to P, the recession of the franchise forced him to sell his stock before the trial to avoid personal bankruptcy. He also claimed that the purchaser of the stock fraudulently conspired with D and others, and convinced him to settle on terms advantageous to D.
Issue: May a former stockholder bring a direct suit charging the defendant with conduct that was injurious to the corporation even if the cause of action is normally considered derivative?
Rule: Injury to a corporation must be asserted by the corporation or derivatively by a stockholder for its benefit. A former shareholder is barred from bringing a derivative suit even where the defendant's conduct causes the sale of his shares.

✯ Cohen v. Beneficial Indus. Loan Corp. (S.Ct. 1949) Ha, JB, V
Facts: P brought a derivative suit charging D, its managers, and directors with mismanagement and fraud. After D rejected P's demand that it institute proceedings, P filed this action. A New Jersey statute held P liable for all expenses and attorney's fees of the defense if his suit failed, and D moved to have D post a security bond.
Issue: Does a state statute that imposes liability for defense expenses and requires the posting of a security bond violate the Fourteenth Amendment?
Rule: (Jackson, J.) A state has the power to enact a statute that holds a plaintiff in a derivative suit responsible for the litigation expenses of the defense and requires the posting of a security bond.

Surowitz v. Hilton Hotels Corp. (S.Ct. 1966) CE, Ha

Facts: P, a Polish immigrant with a limited English vocabulary and no formal education, brought a shareholders' derivative suit in which she charged D, and its directors and officers, with violations of the Securities Act of 1933, the Securities Exchange Act of 1934, and the Delaware General Corporation Law. An oral examination of P conducted by D's counsel showed that she did not understand the intricacies of the complaint, and that she had relied on her son-in-law's explanation of the suit and pertinent facts to verify the complaint.

Issue: In a complaint where a unsophisticated litigant alleges serious charges of fraud, is a summary dismissal required if the P's verification of the complaint is based on counsel's assurance that either the statements in the complaint are true or that he believed them to be true?

Rule: (Black, J.) A court will not summarily dismiss a complaint where a unsophisticated litigant alleges serious charges of fraud, if the charges are shown to be based on a reasonable belief growing out of careful examination even if the verification was based on counsel's assurances.

Schiff v. Metzner (1964) Ha

Facts: After the Supreme Court found that du Pont's ownership of General Motors was a violation of § 7 of the Clayton Act, four derivative suits were brought by shareholders of GM. The cases were subsequently consolidated, and an injunction was issued restraining all stockholders of GM from prosecuting any derivative action except for the consolidated suit. When P brought a derivative action several years later, it was stayed by the judge assigned to the consolidated case.

Issue: Should a judge stay the proceedings of a shareholders' derivative suit in the interest of economy of time and effort for itself, counsel, and litigants?

Rule: No type of case is more appropriate for judicial concern for the economy of time and effort for itself, counsel, and litigants than shareholders' derivative suits.

Ross v. Bernhard (S.Ct. 1970) Ha, He, JB, V

Facts: P brought a shareholders' derivative suit which charged that the board of directors was controlled by the corporation in violation of the Investment Company Act of 1940 and had breached other fiduciary duties. P demanded against a jury trial on the corporation's claims.

Issue: Is the right to a jury trial in a shareholders' derivative suit guaranteed by the Seventh Amendment?

Rule: (White, J.) The Seventh Amendment guarantees that parties in a shareholders' derivative suit are afforded the same right to a jury trial that historically belonged to the corporation and to those against whom the corporation pressed its legal claims.

Dissent: (Stewart, J.) The Seventh Amendment's guarantee of the right to a jury trial is limited to those actions which were tried before a jury when the Amendment was adopted. Since a derivative suit is an equitable claim, it is not protected by the Seventh Amendment.

Glenn v. Hoteltron Systems (1989) Ha

Facts: P and D were equal partners and directors of Ketek Electric Corp. P brought an individual and derivative action charging that D diverted the assets of Ketek for his own use. The trial court ruled in P's favor and ordered D to pay damages to Ketek. P appealed the ruling claiming that a payment to Ketek would enable D to share in the judgment and thus, D should be required to pay the individual shareholders.

Issue: Should a shareholder who improperly diverts corporate assets pay the individual shareholders (excluding himself) rather than the corporation?

Rule: In a shareholders' derivative suit the recovery is gained because the corporation has suffered a loss; thus, one who improperly diverts corporate assets should repay those assets to the corporation rather than the other shareholders.

Cowin v. Bresler (1984) He

Facts: A minority shareholder in Bresler & Reiner (B & R), a publicly held corporation, brought suit against D in his individual capacity. In his suit, P alleged that D (a director and majority shareholder of B & R) engaged in fraudulent deeds and misconduct

with the intent to deliberately deflate the stock price of B & R, thus enabling him to convert it to a private corporation.
Issue: Are suits seeking money damages for improper management of a corporation required to be brought as derivative actions?
Rule: In the absence of a special injury to an individual shareholder, claims of corporate mismanagement must be brought derivatively, because these claims belong to the corporation and not to its shareholders. Since the shareholder's damage is not independent of that inflicted upon the corporation and the other shareholders, the restitution that the corporation receives will compensate each shareholder in proportion to his equity ownership.

Jepsen v. Petersen (1943) He
Facts: P, a minority shareholder in Black Hills Amusement Company, brought a derivative suit on the corporation's behalf charging the directors with mismanagement. The alleged misdeed took place prior to P's acquisition of stock.
Issue: May a stockholder bring a derivative suit charging the officers or directors of a corporation with misconduct the if wrongdoing took place prior to the acquisition of stock?
Rule: A derivative suit may not be brought by a present stockholder in a corporation who did not hold stock in that corporation at the time of the mismanagement, unless the mismanagement or its effects continue and are injurious to him, or it affects him specially and peculiarly in some other manner.

Wolgin v. Simon (1984) He
Facts: P brought a derivative action alleging that the board of directors of Wetterau Inc. breached its fiduciary duty by wasting corporate assets while trying to defeat a takeover bid. P made a demand for suit, which was rejected by the directors. However, a demand for suit was never brought upon the other shareholders.
Issue 1: Is it necessary for a shareholder to make a demand for suit on the other shareholders prior to the institution of a derivative suit?
Rule 1: In the absence of *ultra vires*, fraudulent, or illegal acts (which cannot be ratified by shareholders), a demand for suit on the other shareholders must be made prior to the institution of a derivative suit.
Issue 2: Is an allegation that fails to show conclusively why the shareholders of a corporation would have refused a demand for suit

upon the shareholders a sufficient excuse for lack of shareholder demand?
Rule 2: One cannot simply allege, as a legal conclusion, that relief was not demanded because it would have been futile to do so. Rather, the plaintiff must state with particularity the facts showing why he failed to seek redress from the stockholders.

Jones v. Niagara Frontier Transportation Authority (1983) He
Facts: P, brought a derivative action *pro se* on behalf of Walter L. Jones Development Corporation, of which he was the sole stockholder and chief executive officer. In the suit, P contended that Development Corp. was denied a contract due to racial discrimination.
Issue: May a corporation proceed in an action *pro se*?
Rule: It is an established rule that a corporation, which is an artificial entity that can only act through agents, cannot proceed *pro se*. Since of necessity, a natural person must represent the corporation in court, we have insisted that that person be an attorney licensed to practice law before our courts.

Kinser v. Coffee [sic] (1982) He
Facts: Claiming oppressive conduct by other shareholders because they were not reelected as directors, minority shareholders (P) sought to dissolve their corporation.
Issue: Does failure to reelect directors constitute oppressive conduct mandating the dissolution of a corporation?
Rule: A single act in breach of a fiduciary duty does not constitute oppressive conduct mandating the dissolution of a corporation unless there has been a disproportionate loss to the minority, or those in control can no longer be trusted to manage the corporation fairly in the interests of the shareholders.

Giuricich v. Emtrol Corp. (1982) He
Facts: A 50 percent shareholder brought suit for the appointment of a custodian to break a deadlock within a close corporation that had indefinitely prevented the election of successor directors.
Issue: May a court appoint a custodian when a shareholder deadlock has prevented the election of successor directors?

322 Shareholders' Suits

Rule: Unlike a director deadlock situation, a shareholder deadlock situation does not require a showing of irreparable injury to the corporation, and a court may appoint an impartial custodian to resolve a deadlock that permits control of a corporation to remain indefinitely in the hands of a self-perpetuating board of directors.

Parklane Hosiery Co., Inc. v. Shore (S.Ct. 1979) He
Facts: Shore (P) brought a shareholders' derivative suit for damages caused by a materially false and misleading proxy statement. Before this action came to trial in state court, the SEC filed suit against the same Ds in federal district court, alleging the same violations. D later sought to relitigate the same issue in state court. P moved for partial summary judgment on the issues that had been resolved in the first suit.
Issue: Can one who was not a party to a prior judgment assert that judgment offensively to collaterally estop a party from relitigating issues resolved in the earlier suit?
Rule: (Stewart, J.) A litigant who was not a party to a prior judgment may use that judgment offensively to prevent a party from relitigating issues resolved in an earlier suit.

Lewis v. Anderson (1982) He
Facts: P filed a shareholders' derivative suit against Disney (D), charging that a stock option plan adopted without shareholder approval authorizing employee stock options at lower prices breached its fiduciary duty to D's stockholders. A special litigation committee was appointed to investigate P's charges and decide whether it was in D's best interest to pursue the action. The board recommended that the board of directors seek shareholder ratification of the option plan. The shareholders subsequently ratified the plan and the special litigation committee then decided that further prosecution of the action was unwarranted. After P concluded that he could not prove that the special litigation committee had not acted in good faith, he moved to dismiss his action and petitioned the court to award him the attorney fees and expenses.
Issue: May a plaintiff recover litigation expenses if his action has conferred a substantial benefit upon a class represented by the defendant?

Rule: The substantial benefit doctrine permits a plaintiff to recover attorneys' fees if his action has conferred a substantial benefit upon a class represented by the defendant.

Shapiro v. American Home Assurance Co. (1984) He
Facts: P, as president of Giant Stores, entered into a directors and officers insurance contract in which he misrepresented his knowledge concerning potential claims against Giant. P was subsequently convicted of securities fraud. D refused to honor the insurance policy, claiming that the falsity of P's statement invalidated the insurance contract from the start.
Issue: Does an insurance policy indemnifying all directors and officers become completely invalid because of one officer or director's misrepresentation on the application?
Rule: An insurance company may refuse to honor a policy indemnifying all directors and officers, even if only one officer or director misrepresented fact on the application. The coverage may be denied whether or not other officers and directors had knowledge of the misrepresentation.

Knapp v. Bankers Securities Corp. (1956) JB
Facts: P brought a shareholders' derivative action to compel the declaration of dividends. D moved a court order requiring P to post a security bond for D's litigation expenses stemming from P's action.
Issue: Is a suit instituted by a shareholder seeking the declaration of dividends considered a shareholders' derivative suit or a personal cause of action?
Rule: Because only the stockholders will benefit from cause of action seeking the declaration of dividends, it is a personal action.

Shaw v. Empire Savings & Loan Ass'n (1960) JB
Facts: P claimed that the conduct of Oschin, the majority shareholder of Empire Savings & Loan Ass'n, depreciated the value of his shares. In addition, P claimed that Oschin was issued shares for less than the book value of the stock.
Issue: May a stockholder bring an action as an individual where, under the facts alleged, the only remedy is in the form of a shareholders' derivative suit?

324   Shareholders' Suits

Rule: A shareholder may bring an individual cause of action, even if it appears that the damage is the result of the violation of some special duty owed the shareholder, and the corporation may also have a cause of action.

In re REA Express, Inc. (1976) JB

Facts: REA Express Inc. was incorporated in 1928 by the nation's railroads to provide transport service for small packages to the public. Approximately eighty-six railroads held all of REA's stock from the time of its formation until 1968. During this period the share-holding railroads contracted with REA to provide transport services to it. In 1969 nearly all the shareholders divested themselves of their REA stock. REA alleged that from the beginning it was the victim of an antitrust conspiracy.

Issue: Can subsequent shareholders recover for damages occurring prior to their ownership?

Rule: Subsequent shareholders are barred from bringing suit for damages occurring prior to their ownership. Allowing them to recover would enable new shareholders to obtain a windfall recovery of a large part of the purchase price.

Pollitz v. Gould (1911) JB

Facts: P brought a shareholders' derivative action on behalf of Wabash Railroad Company to set aside as fraudulent a transfer of stock having a par value of several million dollars.

Issue: May a stockholder bring a shareholders' derivative suit for the purpose of avoiding an improper transaction executed at the expense of the corporation even if the transaction occurred prior to his acquisition of the stock?

Rule: In the absence of special circumstances, a shareholders' derivative suit may be brought by a stockholder acquiring the stock subsequent to the transaction which is challenged.

In re Kauffman Mutual Fund Actions (1973) JB

Facts: P, a shareholder in several mutual funds, brought a shareholders' derivative without making a prior demand on the directors.

Issue: Are unsubstantiated allegations of minority control of a board sufficient to excuse the demand on the directors requirement?

Rule: Demand on the directors will only be excused if allegations of minority domination of the majority are supported by conclusive facts linking the minority board and the wrongdoing.

Levitt v. Johnson (1964) JB

Facts: P, a minority shareholder in a mutual fund brought suit claiming that charging improper and excessive fees violated the Investment Company Act of 1940. Demand on the directors was properly excused. Because the fund had more than 48,000 shareholders, P claimed that demand on the shareholders would impose upon him an unconscionable financial burden.
Issue: Is demand on shareholders excused in a derivative action if notification of all the shareholders in a corporation would involve an unfair burden and expense?
Rule: Although prior demand on shareholders is usually required, it will be excused if notification would impose an unfair burden upon the shareholding plaintiff and the suit is otherwise meritorious.

Shaffer v. Heitner (S.Ct. 1977) JB

Facts: P brought a shareholders' derivative suit in Delaware, the state in which Greyhound was incorporated, alleging that the corporation and its officers and directors were the cause of Greyhound's loss in an antitrust action in Oregon. Jurisdiction was based on sequestration of Greyhound's stock, which pursuant to Delaware state law, was deemed to be located in Delaware.
Issue: Absent other contacts of a defendant with a state, will sequestration of property deemed to be located in the state provide a state court with a basis for quasi-in-rem jurisdiction?
Rule: (Marshall, J.) Property that is not itself the subject matter of the litigation does not alone provide a basis for jurisdiction. The exercise of jurisdiction over the interests of persons is consistent with the Due Process Clause only where the "minimum contacts" standard of *International Shoe* is met.

Perrine v. Pennroad (1946) JB

Facts: P brought a shareholders derivative suit claiming that the Pennsylvania Railroad Co. had promoted and financed a separate

investment company Pennroad Corp. (P) for the benefit of Pennsylvania Railroad Co.
Issue: Are the directors called upon to exercise honest business discretion in the settlement of business disputes?
Rule: In the settlement of disputes in which corporations are interested, the directors of the corporation (who are its duly accredited managers) are called upon to exercise honest business discretion. They are not responsible for mere honest mistakes, and accordingly the court will not interfere with such actions.

Shlensky v. Dorsey (1978) JB, SSB
Facts: P instituted a shareholders derivative suit claiming that D illegally expended corporate funds. After the parties entered into a settlement agreement which received court approval the case was dismissed. Subsequent to the dismissal, P reinstated the suit claiming that the settlement was fraudulently obtained, void, and should be revoked.
Issue: In determining the fairness of a settlement of a shareholders' derivative suit, is the principal element the extent of the benefit conferred to the corporation?
Rule: The extent of the benefit conferred to the corporation is the principal element considered in determining the fairness of a settlement of a shareholders' derivative action.

Merritt-Chapman & Scott Corp. v. Wolfson (1974) JB, Ha
Facts: Wolfson along with others (Ps) participated in a plan to cause D to secretly purchase hundreds of thousands of shares of its own common stock which led to charges of criminal violations of federal securities regulations. Ps sought indemnification for their legal defense relating to the charges.
Issue: Are corporate agents, who are criminally charged for their conduct relating to a corporate activity, entitled to indemnification for their legal expenses?
Rule: Corporate agents, who are criminally charged for their conduct relating to a corporate activity, are entitled to indemnification for their legal expenses only on those charges of which they are vindicated.

Kaplan v. Wyatt (1984) SSB

Facts: P brought a derivative suit against D (the chief executive officer) alleging self-dealing and excessive compensation. The corporation appointed a special litigation committee of two persons, one of whom had dealings with the corporation. The committee concluded that the suit had no merit and that it was not in the best interests of the corporation to proceed with the litigation.
Issue: Is a corporation required to appoint a special litigation committee to investigate and recommend whether the action should proceed?
Rule: A corporation must appoint a special litigation committee whose responsibility is to recommend whether the corporation should proceed with the cause of action.

In re E.C. Warner Co. (1950) SSB

Facts: A.E. Wilson was president, treasurer, and director of E.C. Warner. He was sued in three similar derivative actions. After all three actions were dismissed in Wilson's favor, the corporation petitioned for voluntary dissolution. In the ensuing proceedings, Wilson's attorney filed claims for reimbursement of his legal fees.
Issue: Is a director who prevails in a shareholders' derivative suit entitled to reimbursement by the corporation?
Rule: A director who prevails in a shareholders' derivative suit is entitled to reimbursement by the corporation.

Gordon v. Elliman (1954) V

Facts: P brought a shareholders' derivative suit to compel payment of a dividend. The trial court stayed the proceedings under § 61–b of the General Corporation Law which required the posting of security for costs in actions instituted or maintained in the right of any corporation.
Issue: Is a suit compelling the declaration of a dividend a derivative or an individual cause of action?
Rule: A suit compelling the declaration of a dividend is a derivative cause of action.

Marco v. Dulles (1959) V

Facts: P brought a shareholders derivative suit against the former directors of Blue Ridge Corporation and others charging wrongful diversion of corporate assets. At the time the misdeeds took place D was a director of Blue Ridge and also a senior partner in the law firm of Sullivan & Cromwell (the law firm representing the Ds and Blue Ridge).

Issue: May an attorney represent a client in an action brought by a former client in which he is a co-defendant?

Rule: An attorney may represent a client in an action brought by a former client in which he is a co-defendant.

Alleghany v. Kirby (1964) V

Facts: D failed to produce subpoenaed documents before negotiating a settlement in a self-dealing case brought against him.

Issue: May a settlement agreement between a corporation and a self-dealing director be set aside because the director failed to submit evidence which would have strengthened the corporation's case prior to the settlement?

Rule: A corporate director's failure to submit evidence which would have strengthened the corporation's case prior to the settlement is insufficient to set aside the settlement.

Mills v. Electric Auto-Lite Co. (S.Ct. 1970) V

Facts: P brought a shareholders' derivative suit demanding the right to inspect the list of shareholders of the corporation to solicit opposition to management.

Issue: May a shareholder recover litigation fees stemming from a successful shareholders' derivative suit if there is no monetary award to the corporation?

Rule: (Harlan, J.) Even if the corporation does not receive a monetary award, a shareholder may recover the litigation fees stemming from that action.

Bird v. Penn Central Co. (1972) V

Facts: P issued two different insurance policies, one covering Penn Central Co. (D) and the other covering the directors and officers of D. One application was completed for both policies and P claims that it contained a false answer.

Issue: Does a false statement on a directors and officers insurance policy make the policy voidable by the insurer?

Rule: A false statement, which amounts to a material misrepresentation, renders a policy voidable by the insurer.

Chapter 12

STRUCTURAL CHANGES

I. MERGERS

A. Merger and Consolidation Defined

   1. Merger
      One corporation acquires another corporation whereby the owners of the acquired corporation that ceases to exist become owners of the larger corporation that continues to exist.

   2. Consolidation
      Two corporations join together and form a new corporation whereby the owners of the old corporations that cease to exist become owners of the new corporation.

B. Mergers and Related Transactions

   1. Statutory Merger

      a. Method
         Articles of merger are filed with the SEC and securities of the acquired, disappearing corporation are exchanged for securities of the surviving corporation. By operation of law the survivor obtains all the rights, privileges, franchises, and assets of the acquired corporation and assumes all of their liabilities.

      b. Approval
         Usually the approval of the board and shareholders of both corporations are required. However, there are exceptions:

         1. Short-Form Mergers
            If the acquiring corporation already owns 90% or more of the target's stock, the merger can occur without the approval of the shareholders or board of either corpora-

tions under most statutes, including Delaware and the RMBCA.

2. Small Scale (Whale-Minnow) Mergers
If the outstanding shares of the acquiring corporation do not increase by more than 20% to effectuate the merger, the approval of the shareholders of that corporation is not required under most major corporate statutes. (Many statutes allow for cash-out acquisitions rather than stock mergers in this situation.)

c. Tax Consequences
Statutory Mergers qualify as a *Type A* reorganization, a merger-type tax free transaction in the Internal Revenue Code, if the shareholders of the acquired corporation are left with a "continuity of interest" in the surviving corporation, that is, most of the compensation they receive is in the form of the survivor's stock. If property other than stock is permissibly issued as compensation under a Type A reorganization, tax must be paid on this property or "boot."

2. Cash-for-Assets Combination

a. Method
The acquirer purchases all or substantially all of the acquiree's assets with cash that is then distributed upon dissolution proportionately to the shareholders in a liquidating distribution. The acquirer receives all of the aquiree's business, but will not assume its liabilities, subject to the law of fraudulent transfers, the bulk sales provisions of the UCC, and possible use of the *de facto* merger doctrine (see below).

b. Approval
The board and a majority of the shareholder votes that could be cast of the selling corporation must approve the sale. The board, but not the shareholders, of the acquiring corporation must approve the purchase.

332   Structural Changes

   c. Tax Consequences
   After a cash-for-assets exchange, the target must pay a corporate-level tax, as it would in any other sale. If the target then dissolves and pays the cash to its shareholders in a liquidating distribution, the shareholders must pay a personal tax on the cash. This is effectively a double taxation scheme and is, therefore, in terms of tax consequences, not a favorable transaction to the owners of an acquired corporation.

3. Cash-for-Stock

   a. Method
   The acquirer buys the stock of the target from individual shareholders in exchange for cash or debt and can then either dissolve the target, keep it as a subsidiary, or merge the acquired corporation into itself (a *back-end* merger), paying the remaining holders of stock cash, debt, or its own stock (see Tender Offer, below). The acquirer obtains all of the acquired corporation's assets and assumes it liabilities.

   b. Approval
   Board approval of the acquiree corporation is not required; each shareholder individually decides whether to sell their shares.

   c. Tax Consequences
   After a cash-for-stock exchange, the former owners of the target's stock must pay a personal tax on the gain they have made on their shares from the time they were purchased. This one tax is usually less than the two taxes paid in a cash-for-assets transaction combined, making this, in terms of tax consequences, a more favorable type of transaction for the shareholder of the target.

4. Stock-for-Assets Exchange

a. Method
In exchange for stock, the acquiree transfers all or substantially all of its assets to the acquirer. The acquired corporation then usually, but need not, dissolve and distributes the acquirer's stock to its shareholders.

b. Approval
The acquirer's board must approve this transaction, but unlike a statutory merger, its shareholders do not, provided there is sufficient authorized but unissued shares to complete the transaction. The acquiree's board and shareholders must approve this sale of assets.

c. Tax Consequences
Stock-for-Assets exchanges qualify as a *Type C* reorganization, a tax free merger-type transaction in the Internal Revenue Code, if one corporation acquires substantially all of another corporation's assets in exchange for the its voting stock. The compensation given to the acquiree must consist of at least 80 percent voting stock, and any other cash or property included will be taxed.

5. Stock-for-Stock Exchange (Stock Swap)

a. Method
The acquirer trades its own stock for stock in the acquiree individually with each shareholder.

b. Approval
The approval of the acquirer's board but not its shareholders is required. The approval of the board or a majority of shareholders of the acquiree is not required since each shareholder decides whether or not to tender his shares. Some states, however, allow the board and a majority of the shareholders to approve a "plan of exchange," whereby each

acquiree shareholder is required to tender his shares, having the same effects of a statutory merger.

c. Tax Consequences
Stock-for-Stock exchanges qualify as a *Type B* reorganization, a tax free merger-type transaction in the Internal Revenue Code, if one corporation acquires at least 80% of the voting stock and 80% of any other class of stock of another corporation in exchange for solely its own stock.

6. Triangular or Subsidiary Merger

   a. Forward Triangular Merger

      i. Method
         The acquirer creates a subsidiary that acquires a target corporation through a merger using the parent's stock, its only assets. The shareholders of the acquired corporation are left with shares of the parent as in a stock-for-stock exchange. Here, however, all minority interests in the target are automatically eliminated.

      ii. Approval
          Approval of the board but not the shareholders of the acquirer-parent is required. Approval of both the board and shareholders of the acquirer-subsidiary is required, but the parent, represented by the board, is the only shareholder. As in any other merger the approval of both the board and shareholder of the acquiree is required.

   b. Reverse Triangular Merger

      i. Method
         The acquirer creates a subsidiary as in the forward triangular merger, but in this procedure the subsidiary merges into a target. The target survives as a subsidiary of the acquirer maintaining its own assets and liabilities. In addition, unlike a forward triangular merger, any

contract rights or tax advantages held by the target remain in existence. All the shareholders of the target are automatically eliminated.

  ii. Approval
  As with the forward triangular merger, approvals of all boards involved and a majority of the shareholders of the original subsidiary and the target are required.

II. SHAREHOLDER PROTECTION: APPRAISAL RIGHTS

A. Appraisal Rights Defined

1. Dissenting shareholders of a merging corporation are usually afforded rights that allow them to receive a judicially determined "fair value" for their shares and be "cashed out" of the merger.

2. Appraisal rights are usually conditioned on the right to vote and the nature of the transaction.

3. Unlike the RMBCA, some states deny appraisal rights to shareholders of a publicly traded corporation.

4. Unless the transaction is illegal, deception has been used, or the transaction is unfair due to self-dealing by corporate insiders, the appraisal remedy is the exclusive remedy for dissenting shareholders when it is available.

B. Procedure

1. The appraisal process typically follows a certain pattern:

  a. Notice by the corporation to its shareholders of their appraisal rights at the time it announces a merger;

b. Notice by the shareholders that they want to exercise their appraisal rights before the corporate vote is taken on the merger;

c. Shareholders who wish to use the appraisal remedy must vote against the merger when the vote is taken;

d. After the merger has been approved by vote, shareholders who wish to use the appraisal remedy must then demand payment of the fair value of their shares and deposit their stock with the corporation giving up any rights they had as shareholders;

e. The corporation must then make an offer to, and in some states pay, shareholders the fair value of their shares; and

f. If there is any disagreement over the value of the shares, either party can petition a court to determine the "fair value."

2. Valuation of Shares

a. The court usually appoints an appraiser to determine the "fair value" of the shares without reference to the current transaction (i.e., the possible increase in share value due to the merger).

b. Many courts use the *Delaware block* approach to determine the "fair value" of a stock in an appraisal proceeding. The Delaware block method calls for a judicial determination of the Market value, the earnings value, and the net asset value of the stock, followed by the assignment of a percentage weight to each of the elements of value. The judge is left to his own discretion; he is not constrained to follow the valuations submitted by either side.

C. Kinds of Transactions and Appraisal Rights

1. Mergers
   Most states offer dissenting shareholders of either corporation involved in a merger the appraisal remedy to protect their interests.

   a. Short-Form Merger
      Shareholders of the subsidiary usually are given appraisal rights, even if without voting rights. Shareholders of the parent are usually not afforded appraisal rights.

   b. Whale-Minnow Merger
      Shareholders of the acquiring corporation are not given appraisal rights even though they have voting rights. Shareholders of the acquiree usually have appraisal rights.

2. Sale of Assets
   Most states offer dissenting shareholders of a corporation selling "substantially all" of its assets the appraisal remedy to protect their interests, with some exceptions:

   a. Delaware does not give shareholders in an asset sale this protection; and

   b. Under some statutes, such as the RMBCA, shareholders of a corporation that is to go through a dissolution and a liquidating distribution in a short time following the sale of assets will not be afforded the appraisal remedy.

3. Triangular Mergers
   In most triangular mergers, forward and reverse, shareholders of the acquiring corporation do not get appraisal rights, while shareholders of the target do. One common exception is that shareholders of a target in a reverse triangular merger that trades its own stock for the stock of the acquiring corporation, instead of statutorily merging the subsidiary into itself, do not get appraisal rights.

D. The De Facto *Merger* Doctrine

1. In order to protect stockholders or creditors, courts in some states treat transactions that are not mergers by definition but by effect as mergers, with merger procedural requirements, such as voting and appraisal rights.

2. What is Covered?

    a. In states that apply the *de facto* merger doctrine, it is usually a sale of assets or a stock takeover that is considered under it. Courts have traditionally been concerned with a few situations, applying the doctrine when:

        i. A corporation dissolves and goes through a liquidating distribution after a sale of its assets;

        ii. A corporation liquidates or merges into the acquiring corporation after a stock-for-stock exchange; or

        iii. An acquiring corporation uses its own stock, rather than cash or debt, as consideration.

    b. In the case of triangular mergers, it has been held that if the parent and the subsidiary still exist as separate entities after the merger, then the parent is not a party to the merger, the merger is not a *de facto* merger with the parent, and the parent's shareholders do not have any appraisal rights.

3. Many states, including Delaware, reject the *de facto* merger doctrine.

4. Many states that reject the *de facto* merger doctrine still protect those with tort claims against an acquired corporation when the transferring of liabilities has not been stipulated in contract by treating the acquisition as a merger.

E. Other Protection: Judicial Review of Substantive Fairness

Shareholders can sometimes have a court review the substantive fairness of a transaction if:

1. There is self-dealing, insiders control both sides of a transaction, either in the form of a two-step acquisition or a parent-subsidiary merger. In this case, those in favor of the transactions must show its fairness; or

2. The transaction was made at arms length. In this situation, however, those making the claim bear the burden of proof. This remedy might be unavailable if shareholders have appraisal rights.

III. FREEZEOUTS

A. Freezeout Defined

A *freezeout* is any transaction whereby the controlling owners eliminate the equity ownership of minority shareholders.

B. Techniques

1. Sale of Assets or Stock
   Controlling shareholders of a corporation or a second corporation run by them can buy substantially all the assets or the stock of the corporation with cash to freezeout the minority.

2. Short-Form Merger
   If one corporation owns 90 percent or more of another corporation it can, in most states, acquire the smaller corporation by paying off the minority shareholders in cash rather than stock in itself.

3. Reverse Stock Split
   Many states grant corporations the right to eliminate shareholders of a fractional amount of shares with cash. Therefore, a

corporation can effect a reverse stock split and then buy out, freezeout, shareholders with fractional shares.

C. Situations where freezeouts generally take place include the second step in a two-step acquisition, the merger of long-term affiliates, and when a corporation "goes private."

D. Remedies

   1. Federal Law
   Rule 10b–5 is pertinent if insiders have withheld or misrepresented material facts, and Rule 13e–3 requires extensive disclosure in any going–private transaction.

   2. State Law
   Courts generally seek to determine whether the transaction is basically fair, including its price, procedure, and what has been disclosed. Many courts also look at whether the transaction serves a valid business purpose. (However, it is unlikely that a court will use the business purpose when evaluating a going–private transaction.)

E. Squeezeouts

Freezeouts, generally legal transactions, are distinguished from squeezeouts. *Squeezeouts*, most often arising in the context of close corporations, are when controlling shareholders illegally attempt to coerce minority shareholders to give up their stock.

IV. RECAPITALIZATIONS

A. Recapitalization Defined

Recapitalization occurs when those in control of a corporation, usually common stockholders themselves, attempt to cancel an arrearage in preferred dividends, benefiting holders of common stock at the expense of preferred shareholders.

B. Methods

Recapitalization can be effected through amending the articles of incorporation or merging with a corporation that does not provide for the payment of accrued preferred dividends.

C. Preferred Shareholder Protection

1. In most states, preferred shareholders vote and must approve as a separate class both amendments to the articles of incorporation and mergers. In some states, however, such as Delaware, preferred shareholders do not have the right to vote, particularly in the case of mergers.

2. Dissenting shareholders are protected by the right to demand an appraisal, and the corporation must pay the fair value of their shares, which certainly includes unpaid dividend arrearage. Therefore, mergers that are in effect recapitalizations are permitted and will not be blocked by the courts.

V. TENDER OFFERS AND TAKEOVERS

A. Tender Offer

There is no statutory definition of what constitutes a tender offer. In general, a tender offer is a public offer to shareholders of a corporation for their stock in exchange for cash or securities at a price above the market.

1. To determine whether an offer is a tender offer for the purposes of securities regulations, courts have followed the recommendation of the SEC and consider the following eight criteria, which are relevant but are not to be used as a litmus test:

    a. Active and widespread solicitation of public shareholders for the shares of an issuer;

    b. Solicitation made for a substantial percentage of the issuer's stock;

342 Structural Changes

      c. Offer to purchase made at a premium over the prevailing market price;

      d. Terms of the offer are firm rather than negotiable;

      e. Offer contingent on the tender of a fixed number of shares, often subject to a fixed maximum number to be purchased;

      f. Offer open only for a limited period of time;

      g. Offeree subjected to pressure to sell his stock; and

      h. Public announcements of a purchasing program concerning the target company precede or accompany rapid accumulation of large amounts of the target company's securities.

  2. Regardless of the amount of stock purchased, privately negotiated purchases and open–market purchases usually will not constitute tender offers

B. Hostile Takeover
A hostile takeover is the acquisition of a publicly held corporation (*target*), usually through a cash tender offer, by a buyer (*bidder* or *raider*) against the wishes of the management of the corporation.

C. Federal Regulation: The Williams Act
The Williams Act is a set of 1968 amendments to the Securities Exchange Act of 1934 meant to maintain a neutral balance between bidders and the shareholder and management of the target by providing shareholders and management with information about bidders and reducing pressure to make a decision.

  1. Disclosure by 5 Percent Owner
Any person or group who directly or indirectly acquires over 5 percent of any class of stock in a publicly held corporation must file, or already owns over 5 percent and purchases more stock must refile, what is known as a "Schedule 13D" statement, which discloses, among other things, the investor's purpose and source of funds. § 13(d)(1) of the Securities Exchange Act of 1934.

2. Regulation of Tender Offers

   a. Disclosure
      Any bidder making a tender offer for over 5 percent of a corporations stock must disclose, among other things, his identity, source of funds, and purpose by filing a "Schedule 14D" statement. § 14(d) of the Securities Exchange Act of 1934.

   b. Rules for Tender Offers

      i. A tender offer must be held open for at least twenty days.

      ii. Any shareholder who tenders to a bidder has the right to withdraw his tendered shares during the first fifteen days, or after sixty days if the shares have not been purchased.

      iii. If shareholders tender more shares than the bidder has offered to buy, the bidder must buy on a pro rata basis from among the shares deposited during the first ten days or a longer period as designated by the bidder.

      iv. If a bidder increases the price of his offer, the higher price must be paid to all tendering stockholders, including those who already tendered at the lower price, and the offer must be kept open for at least ten more days. See § 14(d) of the Securities Exchange Act of 1934 and Rules 14d and 14e.

   c. Antifraud Provision
      Section 14(e) of the Securities Exchange Act of 1934 prohibits misstatements and omissions of material facts and any "fraudulent, deceptive, or manipulative act" in connection with a tender offer.

i. Without misrepresentation or nondisclosure (and most likely intent in private suits), § 14(e) can not be violated, regardless of the fairness of the deal.

ii. Except in cases of omissions, plaintiffs will normally have to show reliance on the alleged misrepresentation.

iii. Standing and Relief under § 14(e)

(1) A target can seek injunctive relief against a bidder.

(2) A bidder can seek injunctive relief against the target's management or other bidder.

(3) Tendering shareholders can seek injunctive relief or damages if they relied on false and misleading information.

(4) Non-tendering shareholders can seek both injunctive and damages if they have been harmed by a violation of §14(e).

d. Hart-Scott-Rodino Act
The Hart-Scott-Rodino Antitrust Improvements Act of 1976 applies to acquisitions where one party has sales or assets of more than $100 million and the other party has sales or assets of more than $10 million, requires notification by the bidder to the government, and imposes a waiting period.

D. State Regulation
Many states (presently, about a dozen) have statutes regulating takeover bids.

1. Most of these statutes require a public announcement and a specific filing with a designated state official before an offer to purchase a certain amount of stock is made.

2. Some state statutes allow a state officer to bring a hearing to review tender offers. State statutes that also empower the state

official to suspend the share-acquisition when he determines that the offer is unfair or inequitable have been found unconstitutional under the Commerce Clause or Supremacy Clause.

3. Some state statutes regulate the terms of the bid through methods similar to the federal pro rata and best price rules, shareholder voting rules, or proscriptions against back-end mergers.

E. Corporate Defenses

1. Shark Repellants
   Shark repellants are the common name for strategies used to guard against hostile takeovers. Some common shark repellants are:

   a. Structuring the board election system in such a way as to make it difficult or impossible for a hostile bidder to immediately gain control of the board. One example would be the staggering of the elections so that only a minority of the members are elected each year;

   b. Requiring more than a majority of the shareholder's approval for a merger or sale of assets. Some forms of this type of tactic are called *fair price provisions*;

   c. Creating a class of stock only to be sold to those loyal to management;

   d. Prohibiting greenmail in the corporation's charter to discourage raiders who only seek greenmail. *Greenmail* is the payment to a raider by the target for the repurchase of the acquired shares at a higher price than the raider paid for them usually in exchange for his agreement not to engage in any more takeover attempts for a certain time period (a *standstill* agreement); and

e. Creating a *poison pill* plan that makes the target less attractive by triggering certain events upon the acquisition of a certain percentage of stock. Poison pill plans usually do not require the approval of the shareholders. Examples of poison pills include *call* and *put* plans that respectively allow shareholders to buy cheap stock and sell their shares at a pre–determined price thereby weakening the raider's position or lowering the firm's value.

2. Defenses Against Takeovers in Progress
Once a hostile takeover is in progress, to protect itself the target can:

   a. Find a friendly bidder (*white knight*), and perhaps grant him a lock–up, which is an option to acquire certain assets that is triggered by designated events. A primary lock–up provision allows a white knight to acquire the corporation's best business (*crown jewels*) if the friendly bid is defeated or defeat becomes inevitable;

   b. Pay the raider greenmail in exchange for a standstill agreement;

   c. Increase its debt through defensive acquisitions or go through a corporate restructure to make itself less attractive;

   d. Sell less than a majority of stock (usually 25 % or less) to a friendly party that will not tender to the raider (*a white squire*). This defense is most common in Delaware where any owner of over 15 % of a corporation's stock can, by triggering the state's anti–takeover statute, block a back–end merger or asset sale;

   e. Repurchase shares from the public and increase insiders' stake or execute an exclusionary repurchase, which is a repurchase wherein the target refuses to buy the bidder's shares; and

f. Target the bidder, attempting to swallow the bidder before the bidder swallows the target (the *pac man* defense).

3. The Legality of Corporate Defenses

   a. Federal Law
   Unless he can show that the management has deceived the shareholders of the target, a violation of § 14(e) of the Securities Exchange Act of 1934, a disgruntled bidder will probably be unsuccessful in seeking relief based on federal law.

   b. State Law — The Business Judgment Rule
   In Delaware, as well as other states, a target and its management will usually be afforded the protection of the business judgment rule. According to the business judgment rule, a court will not substitute its views for the board's if the latter's decision can be attributed to any "rational business purpose." A boards' action must be reasonable in relation to the threat posed to the corporate enterprise and done in the proper exercise of sound business judgement, namely, the decision was made in good faith, on an informed basis, and in the honest belief that the action taken was in the best interests of the company.

      i. State courts have generally allowed greenmail defenses, exclusionary repurchases, and poison pill plans that do not effectively prevent all takeovers.

      ii. State Courts are likely to strike down lock-up provisions, especially crown jewel options, that, instead of creating, prematurely end a bidding contest.

CASE CLIPS

Katz v. Bregman (1981) CE

Facts: D, chief executive officer of Plant Industries, Inc., led the board of directors in an attempt to sell substantially all of the assets of Plant to Vulcan Industrial Packaging, Ltd., while receiving higher offers from Universal Drum Reconditioning Company. P, a shareholder of Plant common stock, brought suit to enjoin the sale to Vulcan on behalf of himself and the other owners of Plant common stock.

Issue: Under Delaware law, does the sale of substantially all the assets of a corporation require the approval of its shareholders?

Rule: Under Delaware law, the sale of substantially all the assets of a corporation by its board of directors other than in the regular course of business requires the approval of at least a majority of its shareholders.

Piemonte v. New Boston Garden Corp. (1979) CE, CCM

Facts: Ps were dissenting stockholders in Boston Garden Arena Corporation, a Massachusetts corporation whose stockholders voted on July 19, 1973 to merge with the D entitling each plaintiff to demand an appraisal and payment of the "fair value" of their stock in the resulting or surviving corporation.

Issue: What is the procedure used in making a judicial determination of the "fair value" of dissenting shareholder's stock when a majority has voted to sell or merge their corporation?

Rule: The Delaware courts have adopted a general approach to the appraisal of a stock's "fair value," known as the "Delaware block approach," that calls for a judicial determination of the market value, the earnings value, and the net asset value of the stock, followed by the assignment of a percentage weight to each of the elements of value. The judge's decision is left to his own discretion; he is not constrained to follow the valuations submitted by either side.

Hariton v. Arco Electronics, Inc. (1963) CE, CCM, JB, SSB

Facts: D and Loral Electronics Corporation negotiated an amalgamation of the companies whereby D agreed to transfer all its assets to Loral in exchange for 283,000 newly issued shares of Loral. D would then distribute the shares to its stockholders as part of a complete liquidation, after first obtaining approval of the plan and voluntary dissolution by a shareholder vote. At the Arco meeting all the stockholders voting (about 80 percent) approved the plan. P, stockholder who did not vote, sued to enjoin the consummation of the plan on the grounds that it was illegal.

Issue: Is a stock-for-assets reorganization plan, accomplished through § 271 of the Delaware General Corporation Law, legal when it also includes a mandatory plan of dissolution and distribution, that has the same effect as a merger?

Rule: The sale of assets effected under § 271 of the Delaware General Corporation Law in consideration of shares of stock of the purchasing corporation is legal when the agreement of sale also embodies a plan to dissolve the selling corporation and distribute the shares to the stockholders of the seller, so as to accomplish the same result as would be accomplished by a merger of the seller into the purchaser.

Farris v. Glen Alden Corp. (1958) CE, Ha, JB,SSB, V

Facts: D was a mining corporation. List Industries was a general holding company with interests in motion picture theaters, textile and real estate companies, oil and gas operations, warehouses and aluminum piston manufacturing. D and List entered into a reorganization plan whereby D increased its outstanding shares from 2,500,000 to 7,500,000 and gave the increase to List in exchange for List's assets, including over $8 million in cash, and liabilities, including a $5 million dollar note used to acquire a 38.5 percent interest in D. Upon the approval of a majority of D shareholders, a new corporation, List Alden, would emerge, with directors of both original corporations in charge. P, a shareholder of D, claimed that this sale of assets was in effect a merger, accruing to him the rights and remedies of a dissenting shareholder.

Issue: Must a stock-for-assets reorganization plan, which is in effect a merger, meet the statutory merger guidelines protecting dissenting shareholders?

Rule: According to state law, a reorganization plan under which the assets and liabilities of one corporation are exchanged for the stock of the other corporation, leaving the surviving corporation with a new name is a *de facto* merger or consolidation and must meet the state statutory merger requirements protecting the dissenting shareholders with appraisal rights.

Applestein v. United Bd. & Carton Corp. (1960) CE, CCM

Facts: Epstein, the sole owner of Interstate Container Corporation, entered into stock-for-stock exchange agreement with D. Epstein traded all the stock in Interstate for a 40 percent interest in D and the positions of president and a director, thus taking "effective control" of D. D failed to inform its shareholders in its proxy statement calling for the vote of their rights of dissent and appraisal.

Issue: Does a stock-for-stock transfer in which one corporation exchanges all its shares for an interest in another corporation grant the stockholders of either corporation appraisal rights for dissenting shareholders.

Rule: According to state law, if a stock-for-stock transfer is, in effect, a merger of one corporation into another, it is a *de facto* merger and the shareholders of each are entitled to be notified of their statutory rights of dissent and appraisal.

Terry v. Penn Central Corp. (1981) CE, SSB

Facts: Penn Central Corp. sought to acquire Colt Industries Inc. by merging Colt with PCC Holdings, a wholly owned subsidiary of Penn. Terry and Hunt, shareholders of Penn who objected to the transaction, were denied by the District Court the declaratory and injunctive relief to assert voting and dissenters' rights to which appellants asserted they were entitled.

Issue: In a triangular merger, is a merger with a wholly owned subsidiary considered a *de facto* merger with the parent, thus granting dissenters' rights to shareholders of the parent?

Rule: If a parent and its subsidiary still exist as separate entities after a corporation is merged into the subsidiary the parent is not a party to the merger, the merger is not a *de facto* merger with the parent, and the parent's shareholders do not have any dissent and appraisal rights.

Sterling v. Mayflower (1952) CE

Facts: Hilton Hotels Corporation wished to merge with its subsidiary Mayflower Hotel Corporation. After obtaining an objective valuation of the fair exchange rate of shares, minority stockholders of Mayflower sought to enjoin the merger on grounds that the terms were unfair to them.

Issue: In a proposed merger of a subsidiary into its parent, how should the relative value of the stock of the corporation be determined?
Rule: A merger effects an exchange of stock in a going concern for stock in another going concern; therefore, the liquidating value of the acquired corporation's shares should not be used in a merger. All relevant factors must be considered in arriving at a comparison value that is fair to all shareholders.

Weinberger v. UOP, Inc. (1983) CE
Facts: Signal, Inc. controlled a majority UOP's stock and over half of UOP's board were its directors or employees. Relying in part on a study conducted by directors common to Signal and UOP that was not disclosed to UOP, Signal proposed a merger. It was approved by a majority of the non-Signal directors and non-Signal minority shareholders of UOP. Some minority shareholders sought to rescind the cash-out merger on grounds of unfairness.
Issue: May minority shareholders of a subsidiary rescind a merger with its parent that has been approved by a majority of the minority shareholders?
Rule: Failure of the fairness test in a parent-subsidiary merger, whether it is the test of fair dealing, such as the withholding of material information by a director common to both corporations, or the fair price test, may be sufficient grounds to rescind the transaction.

Rabkin v. Philip A. Hunt Chemical (1985) CE, CCM
Facts: Olin, majority shareholder of Hunt, had an agreement to pay twenty-five dollars a share for the rest of the Hunt stock if bought within a year of its first purchase from Turner and Newall Industries. The directors of Olin, some controlling the Hunt board as well, were aware of the agreement and purposely waited until the agreement expired before making a cash-out acquisition of Hunt for twenty dollars. P, minority shareholders of Hunt, brought suit for unfair dealing.
Issue: Can a claim of unfair dealing, absent fraud, survive a motion to dismiss?
Rule: An action alleging unfair dealing does not turn solely on issues of deception, but also encompasses broader concerns respecting the

matter of procedural fairness, such as how the transaction was timed, initiated, structured, negotiated, disclosed to directors, and how the approvals of the directors and stockholders were obtained. Thus, in an allegation of unfair dealing, a non-fraudulent transaction price may be the preponderant consideration. However, averments containing specific acts of misrepresentation or other items of misconduct must be carefully examined.

Hanson Trust PLC v. SCM Corp. (1985) CE
Facts: Hanson made a tender offer of sixty dollars per share to SCM stockholders. Insiders at SCM and Merril Lynch, their "White Knight," made a counter proposal for a leveraged buy out at seventy dollars per share. After Hanson raised their offer to seventy-two dollars per share, SCM-Merrill raised their leveraged buyout offer to seventy-four dollars with a "crown jewel" irrevocable lock-up option to Merril for SCM's two most profitable businesses effective if any outside party acquired more than a third of SCM's outstanding stock. Faced with what it saw as a "poison pill," Hanson canceled its tender offer and proceeded to make five privately negotiated cash purchases and one open market purchase of SCM stock. SCM considered this a "*de facto* tender offer" in violation of § 14(d) of the Williams Act, and had the district court issue a preliminary injunction to stop Hanson's purchases. Hanson appealed the injunction.
Issue: What constitutes a tender offer within the meaning of § 14(d) of the Williams Act?
Rule: To decide whether a solicitation constitutes a "tender offer" within the meaning of § 14(d), one must determine whether, in light of all circumstances, the solicitation will lack information necessary for a careful appraisal if the pre-acquisition filing strictures are not followed.

Unocal Corp. v. Mesa Petroleum Co. (1985) CE, CCM, He
Facts: Mesa, a shareholder of Unocal, made a tender offer that the board of directors of Unocal considered both inadequate and coercive. The board made a selective stock exchange offer, excluding Mesa, to protect the corporation. The Court of Chancery granted Mesa a preliminary injunction enjoining Unocal's discriminatory self-tender, and Unocal appealed.

Issue: Can a corporation make a self-tender offer for its own shares that excludes from participation a stockholder making a hostile tender offer for the company's stock?
Rule: Directors of a corporation can make a selective stock exchange if it is reasonable in relation to a threat posed to the corporate enterprise and the board acted in the proper exercise of sound business judgment, namely, the decision was made in good faith, on an informed basis, and in the honest belief that the action taken was in the best interests of the company. According to the business judgment rule, a court will not substitute its views for the board's if the latter's decision can be attributed to any "rational business purpose."

Moran v. Household International, Inc. (1985) CE, He
Facts: In response to fears of possible takeover attempts using coercive acquisition techniques, the board of directors of Household initiated a Preferred Share Purchase Rights Plan. The Plan provided that Household common stockholders were entitled to the issuance of one Right per common share under either of two triggering conditions. The first triggering condition was the announcement of a tender offer for thirty percent of Household's shares, and the second was the acquisition of twenty percent of Household's shares by a single entity or group. If a Right was not exercised for preferred stock, and thereafter, a merger or consolidation occurs, the Rights holder could exercise each Right to purchase $200 of the common stock of the tender offeror for $100.
Issue: Is the Preferred Share Purchase Rights Plan a valid defensive mechanism against takeovers?
Rule: If a Preferred Share Purchase Rights Plan bears a reasonable relation to a threat posed to the corporate enterprise, such as coercive acquisition techniques, and the board acted in the proper exercise of sound business judgement, directors of a corporation that institute a Preferred Shares Purchaser Rights Plan will be afforded the benefit of the business judgment rule. (See above).

Revlon, Inc. v. MacAndrews & Forbes Holdings, Inc.
(1986) CE, CCM

Facts: The directors of Revlon instituted defensive tactics to protect the company from what it considered to be an unfavorable takeover attempt. The plan, consisting of a Rights plan and Exchange offer for Notes to shareholders and a lock-up option and a no-shop provision favorable to Forstmann, a friendlier bidder, continued after it became inevitable that Revlon was going to be sold.

Issue: In the face of an active bidding contest for corporate control, can directors enact defensive measures favoring certain bidders over others?

Rule: A board may have regard for various constituencies in discharging its responsibilities, provided there are rationally related benefits accruing to the stockholders. However, such concern for non-stockholder interests is inappropriate when an auction among active bidders is in progress, and the object no longer is to protect or maintain the corporate enterprise but to sell it to the highest bidder. Market forces must be allowed to operate freely to bring the target's shareholders the best price for their equity.

CTS Corporation v. Dynamics Corporation of America
(S.Ct. 1987) CE, CCM

Facts: The Control Share Acquisitions Chapter (Act) of the Indiana Business Corporation Law, which effectively conditions acquisition of control of a corporation on approval of a majority of the pre-existing disinterested shareholders, went into effect in 1986. When Dynamics (P) attempted to gain control of CTS (D), the board of directors of CTS, an Indiana corporation, elected to be governed by the provisions of the Act. P alleged that the Act is pre-empted by the Williams Act and violates the commerce clause.

Issue: Is a state statute that has the practical effect of conditioning the acquisition of control of an in-state corporation on the approval of a majority of the pre-existing disinterested shareholders pre-empted by the Williams Act and in violation of the commerce clause?

Rule: (Powell, J.) State legislation, such as the Control Share Acquisitions Chapter of the Indiana Business Corporation Law, that places shareholders on more equal footing with takeover bidders and protects shareholders equally against both in-state and out-of-state offerors by requiring shareholder approval of changes in control does

not pre-empt, but furthers, the purposes of the Williams Act and is not in violation of the commerce clause.
Dissent: (White, J.) A state law that permits a majority of the state's corporation stockholders to prevent individual investors, including out-of-state stockholders, from selling their stock to an out-of-state tender offeror and thereby frustrate any transfer of corporate control, is just the kind of state law that the commerce clause forbids.

Bove v. The Community Hotel Corp. of Newport, Rhode Island (1969) CE, CCM, Ha, SSB

Facts: Newport Hotel Corp. was organized by the board of directors of Community Hotel for the sole purpose of effecting a merger, whereby Newport would acquire the sole ownership of all the property and assets owned by Community Hotel. The merger plan was admittedly a scheme to achieve a recapitalization that would eliminate the parent's preferred stock and the dividends accumulated thereon without the unanimous vote of the preferred shareholders required for amending Community's articles of association. Under the relevant merger statute, only two-thirds vote of those stockholders were needed. P, preferred stockholders of D, sought to enjoin the merger.
Issue 1: Does a merger of a parent corporation into a wholly owned subsidiary, created for the sole purpose of achieving a recapitalization that will eliminate the parent's preferred stock and dividends accumulated thereon, qualify under the statute permitting any two or more corporations to merge into a single corporation?
Rule 1: Legislation concerning mergers does not make underlying purpose a standard for determining permissibility; mergers that are designed to further the mutual interests of two existing and nonaffiliated corporations and those executed solely to substantially change an existing corporation's capital structure are equally valid. A merger between a parent and a subsidiary corporation, even under circumstances where the merger device has been resorted to solely for the purpose of obviating the necessity for the unanimous vote that would otherwise be required in order to cancel the priorities of preferred shareholders is not prohibited by statute.
Issue 2: May the right of a holder of cumulative preferred stock to dividend arrearages and other preferences be canceled by a statutory merger?

Rule 2: Since dissenting stockholders are protected by the right to demand an appraisal and the corporation must pay the fair value of their shares, which certainly includes unpaid dividend arrearages, mergers that are in effect recapitalizations which cancel the rights of preferred shareholders to dividend arrearages are permitted.

Perlman v. Feldmann (1955) CCM

Facts: During a time of steel shortage, president, director and dominant shareholder (D) of a steel corporation sold his controlling interest to a group of steel users, who promptly elected their own board of directors. Minority shareholders (P) alleged that consideration paid for the stock included a corporate asset that D held in trust for the corporation: the ability to control the allocation of a corporate product in a time of short supply.

Issue: May corporate president and dominant stockholder be liable to minority shareholders for profits gained through the sale of his controlling interest?

Rule: If there is a possibility of individual gain by a fiduciary at the expense of his corporation, the fiduciary must establish the fairness of his dealings or is subject to liability.

Wellman v. Dickinson (1979) CCM

Facts: Sun Company, Inc., acquired roughly 34% of the stock of Becton, Dickinson & Company. This was accomplished through gaining 16% of the shares from Dickinson, and his daughter making some thirty telephone solicitations and forcing out the former CEO. Plaintiffs alleged a violation of § 14 of the Williams Act.

Issue: What constitutes a tender offer within the meaning of § 14 of the Williams Act?

Rule: An exact definition of tender offer has not been set forth by the Securities Exchange Commission, but they have listed eight characteristics of tender offers: (1) active and widespread solicitation of public shareholders for the shares of an issuer; (2) solicitation made for a substantial percentage of the issuer's stock; (3) offer to purchase made at a premium over the prevailing market price; (4) terms of the offer are firm rather than negotiable; (5) offer contingent on the tender of a fixed number of shares, often subject to a fixed maximum number purchased; (6) offer open only a limited period of time; (7) offeree subjected to pressure to sell his stock; and (8) public announcement of a purchasing program preceding or accompanying rapid accumulation of large amounts of the target company's securities. The absence of one particular factor does not mean that a purchase plan is not a tender offer. Depending upon the circumstances involved in a particular case, one or more of the above features may be more compelling and determinative than the others.

Brascan Ltd. v. Edper Equities Ltd. (1979) CCM

Facts: Edper, unsuccessful on its own, told Connacher, president of Gordon Securities Ltd., a Canadian brokerage house that also operated on the American Stock Exchange, it might purchase three million shares of Brascan at a premium if they were available. Over the course of two days, Gordon solicited holders of large blocks of Brascan shares. Edper acquired over six million shares of Brascan, half of which came from Gordon Securities or its customers.

Issue: Does an acquisition of a large number of shares slightly above market price in itself constitute a tender offer within the meaning of § 14(e) of the Williams Act?

Rule: The Williams Act is not meant to cover every purchase of a substantial percentage of an issuers stock. Absent any of the other relevant factors, such as active and widespread solicitation, a firm price, the offer being contingent on a fixed minimum number of shares, the offer being open for a fixed period of time, the offerees being subjected to pressure to sell, or public announcement of purchasing program, a purchase of a large block of a certain stock is not considered a tender offer subject to the provisions of the Williams Act.

Edgar v. MITE Corp. (S.CT. 1982) CCM, He

Facts: Mite initiated a cash tender offer for all outstanding shares of Chicago Rivet & Machine Co., a publicly held Illinois corporation, filing a Schedule 14D–1 with the Securities and Exchange Commission to comply with the Williams Act. At the same time, it sought a declaratory judgment on the unconstitutionality of the Illinois Business Act and preliminary and permanent injunctions to prohibit the Illinois Secretary of State from enforcing the Illinois Act. The Illinois Business Act allowed the Illinois Secretary of State discretionary power over its requisite registration for tender offers of Illinois target companies.

Issue 1: Does the Illinois Business Take-Over Act frustrate the objectives of the Williams Act making it unconstitutional under the supremacy clause?

Rule 1: (White, J.) The Illinois Business Act violates the supremacy clause because the provisions of the Illinois Act that favor the incumbent management (such as those that call for precommencement notification, introduce extended delay into the tender offer process, and allow the Secretary of State of Illinois to pass on his determination of the substantive fairness of a tender offer) upset the purpose of the Williams Act; namely, protection of the investor without favoring either management or the takeover bidder.

Issue 2: Does the Illinois Business Take-Over Act violate the commerce clause?

Rule 2: (White, J.) The commerce clause, which allows incidental regulation and prohibits direct regulation of interstate commerce by the states, is violated by the Illinois Business Act for two reasons: (1) The Act directly regulates and prevents, unless its terms are satisfied, interstate tender offers that in turn would generate interstate transactions; and (2) The Act imposes an excessive burden on interstate commerce considering the local interests the Act purports to further.

Concurrence: (Powell, J.) I agree with Justice Stevens that the Williams Act's neutrality policy does not necessarily imply congressional intent to prohibit state legislation designed to assure — at least in some circumstances — greater protection to interests that include, (but often are broader than), those of incumbent management.

Concurrence: (Stevens, J.) I am not persuaded that Congress' decision to follow a policy of neutrality in its own legislation is tantamount to a federal prohibition against state legislation designed to provide special protection for incumbent management.

Schreiber v. Burlington Northern, Inc. (S.Ct. 1985) CCM

Facts: Burlington originally made a hostile tender offer for El Paso Gas Co. proposing to purchase 25.1 million El Paso shares at twenty-four dollars per share and reserving the right to terminate the offer if any of several specified events occurred. Shareholders of El Paso responded favorably, but Burlington did not accept the tendered shares. After renegotiating with El Paso's management, Burlington announced the terms of a new and friendly takeover agreement. The rescission of the first tender offer caused a diminished payment to those shareholders who had tendered during the first offer. P filed suit on behalf of herself and similarly situated shareholders, alleging that Burlington, El Paso, and members of El Paso's board violated § 14(e) of the Securities Exchange Act of 1934.

Issue: Is misrepresentation or nondisclosure a necessary element of a violation of § 14(e) of the Securities Exchange Act of 1934?

Rule: (Burger, J.) The term "manipulative" as used in § 14(e) of the Securities Exchange Act's prohibition of "fraudulent, deceptive or manipulative acts or practices . . . in connection with any tender offer" requires misrepresentation or nondisclosure and "connotes conduct designed to deceive or defraud investors by controlling or artificially affecting the price of securities." Without misrepresentation or nondisclosure, § 14(e) cannot be violated.

Cheff v. Mathes (S.Ct. 1964) CCM

Facts: Directors of Holland Furnace Company, three of which had a significant interest in the corporation, feared a hostile takeover by Maremont, an active corporate financier who had bought an interest in Holland after his merger offer was turned down. Maremont had a reputation of acquiring and liquidating companies and had criticized Holland's unique distribution techniques, which the board considered vital to the company operation. After the board saw large numbers of employees consider leaving, they decided to buy Maremont shares, financing the purchase substantially with borrowed funds. Plaintiffs, shareholders, filed a derivative suit, claiming that Maremont posed no real threat, the employee unrest could have been caused by other factors, and that the real reason for the purchase was to perpetuate control.

Issue: What constitutes an improper use of corporate funds by the directors of a corporation to purchase shares of the company?

Rule: (Carey, J.) If the purchase of shares of a corporation by its board of directors using corporate funds was motivated by a sincere belief that buying out the dissident stockholders was necessary to maintain what the board believed to be proper business practices, the board will not be held liable for such decision, even though hindsight indicates the decision was not the wisest choice. On the other hand, if the board has acted solely or primarily to perpetuate themselves in office, the use of corporate funds for such purchases is improper.

In re Valuation of Common Stock of Libby, McNeill & Libby (1979) CCM

Facts: Nestlé, holding a majority of Libby shares, decided to make it a wholly owned subsidiary and offered to purchase publicly held shares for $8.125 per share. When it had acquired 90 percent, it proceeded to execute a short-form merger, whereby minority shareholders were required by statute to either accept compensation under the merger plan or the amount awarded in an appraisal proceeding. An appraiser determined a fair value of $6.04 per share for holders of 66,140 Libby shares. The Superior Court accepted the appraiser's component values but rejected his weighting, and set a value of $8.55 per share.
Issue: How should the "fair value" paid to dissenting shareholders for their stock be determined in an appraisal proceeding?
Rule: Under the Maine Business Corporation Act and the Model Business Corporations Act (§ 81), there is no definite rule for determining "fair value"; the proper result in each case will depend upon the particular circumstances of the corporation involved. The component elements in determining "fair value" are stock market price, investment value, and net asset value. All three components of "fair value" may not influence the result in every valuation proceeding (e.g., asset value is usually not heavily weighted unless the valuation is for liquidation purposes), yet all three should be considered.

B. & H. Warehouse, Inc. v. Atlas Van Lines (1974) CCM

Facts: Minority shareholders alleged that a corporation had converted their shares by requiring that stock be offered to the corporation at book value before it could be sold.
Issue: May a restriction be imposed on stockholders that requires offering shares to the corporation at book value before selling?
Rule: A requirement that shareholders offer their shares to the corporation at book value before selling may not be imposed on shareholders because it is a restriction broader than necessary to effectuate a valid corporate purpose.

Honigman v. Green Giant Co. (1961) CCM

Facts: A corporation's Class A common stock had voting rights and Class B did not. The board devised a plan that was to exchange Class B stock for one share of a new voting common stock that was to have one vote per share, and exchange Class A for a new "convertible common" that was to be entitled to one thousand votes per share. As a result of the plan, the voting power of the Class A stock would decrease from 100 percent to 9.3 percent, and the Class A share of the net worth of the company would increase from .01 percent to 9.3 percent. The recapitalization plan was approved by all of Class A stockholders and 92.3 percent of Class B stockholders.

Issue: May a recapitalization plan result in the issuance of premium shares to one class of stock?

Rule: A recapitalization plan may result in the issuance of premium shares to one class of stock so long as proposers of the plan can show fairness to all classes of stock and the corporation.

Jones v. H.F. Ahmanson & Co. (1969) CCM

Facts: A minority shareholder in a Savings and Loan Association brought suit against majority shareholders, alleging that they had breached their fiduciary duty to minority shareholders by creating a holding company that allowed only certain majority shareholders to exchange their shares.

Issue: May majority shareholders dispose of their stock without regard to its effect on minority shareholders?

Rule: Majority shareholders have a fiduciary responsibility to minority shareholders to use their power to control the corporation in an equitable manner.

Matteson v. Ziebarth (1952) CCM

Facts: A director eliminated another director who had blocked a transaction by organizing another corporation and merging the original corporation into it. The dissenting shareholder sought to set aside the merger agreement.

Issue: May a minority shareholder set aside a merger agreement on grounds of unfairness?

Rule: A minority shareholder may not set aside a merger agreement on grounds of unfairness unless he can prove actual fraud or unless the facts concerning the alleged unfairness were unknown to the shareholder when the corporate action was approved.

Coggins v. New England Patriots Football Club, Inc. (1986) CCM

Facts: The sole voting shareholder of a corporation organized a new corporation to execute a merger agreement to eliminate the public ownership of the old corporation. A shareholder of the old corporation sought to set aside the cash freezeout merger on grounds of unfairness.

Issue: May a shareholder set aside a merger through which a controlling shareholder and corporate director eliminate public ownership?

Rule: A shareholder may set aside a cash freezeout merger on grounds of unfairness, unless the corporate directors who benefit from the transfer of ownership can prove that the merger was accomplished for a legitimate business purpose and that, in the totality of circumstances, it was fair to the minority.

Tanzer Economic Associates v. Universal Food Specialties (1976) CCM

Facts: A shareholder sought to enjoin a short-form merger between two corporations in related fields that complied with statutory requirements. One corporation was a wholly owned subsidiary, and its parent controlled 90 percent of the stock of the other.

Issue: May a minority shareholder set aside a short-form merger accomplished for legitimate business purposes?

Rule: A minority shareholder may not set aside a short-form merger unless he can prove that there is no legitimate business purpose for the merger.

Yanow v. Teal Industries, Inc. (1979) CCM

Facts: A shareholder sought damages and to rescind a short-form merger, alleging that a corporate officer had caused unfair transactions to lower the value of the shareholder's stock before the merger. The shareholder dissented from the merger, but did not complete the appraisal remedy prescribed by statute.

Issue 1: Is a dissenting shareholder's recourse after a short-form merger limited to the share appraisal remedy prescribed by statute?

Rule 1: A shareholder's recourse after a short form merger is limited to payment of the value of his shares in accordance with statutory guidelines.
Issue 2: May a former shareholder assert an action against corporate officers for actions taken to lower the value of his stock before a short-term merger?
Rule 2: Since it represents a direct rather than derivative claim, a former shareholder may assert an action against corporate officers for actions taken to lower the value of his stock before a short-form merger.

Conagra, Inc. v. Cargill, Inc. (1986) CCM
Facts: A corporate board entered a merger agreement with another corporation, contingent on shareholder approval. Before the agreement was submitted to the shareholders, the directors received a better offer from a third corporation, canceled the shareholders' meeting, and accepted the new offer.
Issue: May corporate directors rescind a merger contract before it is approved by shareholders if a better contract is presented?
Rule: In accordance with their fiduciary duty to shareholders, corporate directors may rescind a merger agreement before it has received shareholder approval.

Smith v. Good Music Station, Inc. (1957) CCM
Facts: A director and 50 percent shareholder in a close corporation accepted an offer to sell all the assets of the corporation for cash and an agreement that would employ him and his wife as consultants for five years. The majority of the board approved the sale. Subsequently, a minority shareholder not present at the approval brought suit to enjoin the sale because of the personal consideration that passed to the director-shareholder.
Issue: Is a director absolutely disqualified from approving a sale of all corporate assets when part of the consideration for the agreement passes to him personally?
Rule: A director is not absolutely disqualified from approving a sale of all corporate assets when part of the consideration passes to him personally if the director is a substantial stockholder in the corporation.

PPG Industries, Inc. v. Guardian Industries Corp. (1979) CCM

Facts: PPG and Permaglass entered an agreement that granted rights to each other's patents. The agreement provided that the licenses granted to Permaglass were to be non-transferrable. Permaglass later merged into Guardian under applicable statutes. After Guardian began to utilize technology from the patent agreement, PPG asserted an action to enjoin the use.

Issue: After a statutory merger, does the surviving corporation acquire the rights to technology gained by the acquired corporation in a non-transferrable transfer agreement?

Rule: A surviving corporation does not acquire the rights to technology from an acquired corporation if the acquired corporation is not legally able to transfer the technology.

Roanoke Agency, Inc. v. Edgar (1984) He

Facts: A corporation asserted an action to compel a Secretary of State to approve amendments in the corporation's articles of incorporation that would allow non-voting shares to be issued.

Issue: May shareholders waive their right to vote cumulatively for directors by unanimous vote?

Rule: Under the legislative history of the state's constitutional amendments, shareholders may unanimously waive their right to vote cumulatively in the election of directors.

Krull v. Celotex Corp. (1985) He

Facts: After a merger, a successor corporation claimed that it was not liable for punitive damages that had been assessed to the predecessor corporation before the merger.

Issue: Is a successor corporation liable for punitive damages incurred by a predecessor corporation?

Rule: A successor corporation is liable for all debts and liabilities of a predecessor corporation.

Alpert v. 28 Williams St. Corp. (1984) He

Facts: A group of investors (D) acquired majority control of a corporation. Under their control, the board approved a merger with another corporation owned by the investors that included a stipulation for a cash buyout of minority shareholders (P). The minority shareholders claimed the two-step process breached a fiduciary duty.

Issue: May majority shareholders eliminate minority shareholders through a two step merger process?
Rule: Majority shareholders may eliminate minority shareholders through a two step merger process so long as the transaction is fair as a whole to minority shareholders and is justified by an independent corporate business purpose.

Kline v. Johns-Manville (1984) He
Facts: A corporation sold one of its many product lines to another corporation. An individual injured while the product line was still produced by the original corporation brought suit to hold the successor liable.
Issue: Is a successor liable for defective products of a predecessor if the successor has not acquired all the predecessor's assets?
Rule: A successor corporation is not liable for defective products of a predecessor corporation if the successor has purchased only one part of a predecessor's assets.

Landreth Timber Co. v. Landreth (S.Ct. 1985) He
Facts: D sold 100 percent of the stock of Landreth Timber, allegedly without adequately disclosing the consequences of a fire that had damaged the timber mill that was the principal asset of the corporation. P sued under Rule 10b–5 for rescission.
Issue: Is the sale of all the stock of a company a securities transaction subject to the antifraud provisions of the federal securities laws?
Rule: (Powell, J.) The sale of 100 percent of the stock in a corporation, although actually the sale of the business itself, is still considered the sale of securities subject to the antifraud provisions of the federal securities laws.

Gould v. Ruefenacht (S.Ct. 1983) He
Facts: Not provided.
Issue: Is the sale of 50 % of the stock of a closely-held corporation a securities transaction subject to the antifraud provisions of the federal securities laws?
Rule: (Powell, J.) The sale of an instrument bearing the label "stock" and possessing all the characteristics of traditional stock is

considered a security within the meaning of the federal securities laws, without judicial application of the sale of business rule.

Breed v. Barton (1981) He

Facts: Minority shareholders (P) filed notice to dissent from a proposed merger and brought appraisal proceedings to receive the fair value of their stock in cash. P, as individuals and derivatively, subsequently brought another suit, claiming fraud and an inadequate price offered for its stock by the corporation while under the influence of the successor corporation.

Issue: Does assertion of appraisal rights by shareholders who dissent from a corporate merger eliminate the possibility of bringing derivative or individual actions?

Rule: Dissenting shareholders who have their stock appraised in a judicial proceeding abandon alternative rights as shareholders and may not bring derivative or individual actions against a corporation.

Hernando Bank v. Huff (1985) He

Facts: Dissenting shareholders (P) rejected the amount offered for their stock after a merger and brought suit to receive a court-determined amount that equalled the value of controlling shares.

Issue: Is a minority share of stock valued as though it were a controlling share in the corporation?

Rule: A minority share is not valued as if it were a controlling share in a corporation, but is valued according to its market, asset, and investment value.

In re Wheeling-Pittsburgh Steel Corp. (1985) He

Facts: Wheeling-Pittsburgh Steel Corporation borrowed heavily for a modernization program and substantially weakened its financial position. After a restructuring proposal failed, Wheeling sought to reject its collective bargaining agreement with the United Steel Workers of America, the union representing its employees.

Issue: Can a corporation in bankruptcy reject its collective bargaining agreements?

Rule: A corporation can reject its collective bargaining agreements if it fulfills the nine prerequisites listed in § 1113 of Chapter 11 of the Bankruptcy Code.

Levin v. Mississippi River Fuel Corp. (1967) JB
Facts: A shareholder of Class B stock brought suit to allow members of his class of stock to vote separately on a proposed consolidation of his corporation with another.
Issue: Are holders of distinct classes of stock entitled to vote separately on proposed plans of consolidation?
Rule: Under state law, holders of distinct classes of stock in a corporation whose articles of consolidation require class voting are entitled to vote separately on motions for consolidation.

McNulty v. W. & J. Sloane (S.Ct. 1945) JB
Facts: A shareholder brought suit, claiming that an amendment of a corporation's articles of incorporation that eliminated dividends that had accumulated but had not been declared was invalid.
Issue: May a corporation eliminate cumulative dividends that have accrued but not been declared?
Rule: (Shientag, J.) A state legislature may authorize corporations to amend their articles of incorporation to reclassify stock and eliminate cumulative dividends that have accrued but not been declared.

Bowman v. Armour & Co. (1959) JB
Facts: Shareholders (P) alleged that an amendment to a corporation's articles of incorporation as part of recapitalization plan was invalid because it required them to exchange their stock for debenture bonds.
Issue: May articles of incorporation be amended to require a compulsory redemption of stock?
Rule: Articles of incorporation may not be amended to require a compulsory redemption of stock.

Langfelder v. Universal Laboratories, Inc. (1947) JB
Facts: A merger converted a corporation's preferred stock to a new form of preferred and common stock and eliminated the accumulated dividends of the former preferred stock. Minority shareholders of the corporation asserted an action to enforce a provision in the corporation's charter that authorized payments to shareholders if a reduction in the capital stock led to a reduction in the value of the preferred stock.

Issue: Are contract provisions in a corporate charter designed in favor of shareholders obliterated by a merger entailing a conversion of stock?
Rule: Any rights inherent in any class of stock may be obliterated by a merger, unless the terms of the merger are unfair to shareholders.

Barrett v. Denver Tramway Corp. (1944) JB
Facts: Holders of preferred stock claimed that a recapitalization plan that would divest them of rights to accrue dividends was unfair.
Issue: Is a recapitalization plan that divests holders of preferred stock of accumulated dividends valid?
Rule: Under Delaware law, a recapitalization plan is valid unless it can be shown that the plan resulted from actions of bad faith.

Dentel v. Fidelity Savings & Loan Assn. (1975) JB
Facts: The bylaws of a savings and loan provided that memberships were to be issued to savings account holders and borrowers who were to have voting powers as stockholders. The bylaws could be amended by a vote of three-fourths of the directors. Two businesses vied for control of the association, with one controlling the stock and the other maintaining control of non-stockholding members. A stockholder brought suit after the directors voted to amend the bylaws to eliminate the stockholder voting rights.
Issue: May corporate bylaws be amended by the board to eliminate the voting rights of shareholders?
Rule: An amendment of corporate bylaws that divests shareholders of voting rights is valid as long as, viewed in the totality of the circumstances, it is not unfair to shareholders.

Gimbel v. Signal Companies, Inc. (1974) JB
Facts: A corporation entered an agreement to sell a wholly-owned subsidiary constituting 26 percent of its assets. A minority shareholder brought suit, alleging that the sale required shareholder approval.
Issue: Does sale of a wholly-owned subsidiary require authorization of a majority of the outstanding stock?
Rule: Under Delaware law, shareholder approval is not required for sale of a wholly-owned subsidiary that does not constitute all or substantially all of a corporation's assets.

Raab v. Villager Industries, Inc. (1976) JB
Facts: Stockholders (P) submitted objections to a proposed merger and requests for a valuation of their stock. Other stockholders (P) demanded payment for their stock. Among those requesting valuation of stock and those demanding payment for stock were stockholders of joint tenancy where one party had signed the requests without purporting to act for the other.
Issue 1: Is a written objection to a merger and a request for valuation of stock signed by only one party in a joint tenancy valid?
Rule 1: A written objection to a merger and a request for valuation of stock signed by one party in a joint tenancy is valid because it provides sufficient pre-vote notice to the corporation of the possibility of votes against the merger.
Issue 2: Is a demand for payment for stock signed by one party in a joint ownership valid?
Rule 2: A demand for payment, as the last step in a final transaction between a corporation and a dissenting shareholder, requires the signature of all stockholders of record.

Gibbons v. Schenley Industries, Inc. (1975) JB
Facts: Minority shareholders objected to the value an appraiser assigned to their stock before a merger.
Issue: Is the value of a minority stockholder's shares before a merger determined solely by market value prior to any effects of the proposed merger?
Rule: Although market price prior to a proposed merger is central to the value of a minority stockholder's shares, the overall appraisal is also based on average corporate earnings over the previous five years.

Schulwolf v. Cerro Corp. (1976) JB
Facts: Shareholders sought to enjoin a proposed merger of their corporation with a related business, claiming that their shares after the merger, while bestowing certain voting rights, would not allow them to participate in increasing the corporation's future profits (i.e., residual equity).

Structural Changes

Issue: May dissenting shareholders enjoin a proposed merger that has a proper corporate purpose and affords them the opportunity to sell their shares at a fair price?
Rule: A proposed merger may not be enjoined if there is a proper corporate purpose and dissenting shareholders have the opportunity to sell their shares at a fair price.

Cole v. Schenley Industries, Inc. (1977) JB

Facts: A dissenting shareholder challenged a merger, alleging that the failure of proxy statements to adequately reveal the value of a share of stock and how much cash would be transferred in the merger violated § 14(a) of the Securities and Exchange Act of 1934
Issue: Do proxy statements that fail to adequately reveal the value of a share of stock violate § 14 of the Securities and Exchange Act of 1934?
Rule: Proxy statements that disclose essential facts pertaining to a merger, such as cash holdings, net proceeds from the sale of a subsidiary and liquid assets, and that do not misrepresent material facts, do not violate § 14 of the Securities and Exchange Act of 1934.

Singer v. Magnavox Co. (1977) JB

Facts: Minority shareholders alleged a breach of fiduciary duty because a merger was accomplished solely as a means of eliminating them from the corporation. Majority shareholders countered that there was no violation of fiduciary obligations because minority shareholders were offered full value for their shares.
Issue: May majority shareholders cause a merger for the sole purpose of eliminating minority shareholders on a cash-out basis?
Rule: Because of the fiduciary obligation owed to minority shareholders, majority shareholders may not cause a merger to be made for the sole purpose of eliminating minority shareholders, even if they are offered fair value for their stock.

Lynch v. Vickers Energy Corp. (1977) JB

Facts: A majority shareholder made an offer to purchase all of a corporation's outstanding stock at twelve dollars a share. The tender offer failed to disclose that a member of the corporation's management had estimated the net asset value significantly above the minimum amount disclosed in the offer and that majority shareholders had authorized open market purchases for bids up to fifteen dollars a share. After tendering her shares, a shareholder claimed that the failure to disclose these facts violated the majority's fiduciary duty.

Issue: Must a majority shareholder making a tender offer disclose all facts a reasonable shareholder would consider important in deciding whether to sell or retain stock?

Rule: A majority shareholder must disclose all facts a reasonable shareholder would consider reasonably important in deciding whether to sell or retain stock.

Gabhart v. Gabhart (1977) JB

Facts: A minority shareholder (P) in a close corporation did not attend a meeting at which the board decided to transfer the assets of the corporation to a new corporation in which P would no longer be a shareholder. The minority shareholder brought suit to enjoin the merger after it had received the approval by the stockholders of both companies but before the merger became effective.

Issue: Is a minority shareholder who would be squeezed out of a corporation through a proposed merger limited to means provided by statute for realization of his equity?

Rule: A minority shareholder who may be squeezed out of a corporation is not limited to statutory means for realization of his equity and may challenge the proposed merger as a *de facto* dissolution of the corporation.

Piper v. Chris-Craft Industries, Inc. (S.Ct. 1977) JB

Facts: Not provided

Issue: Does an unsuccessful tender offeror, in a contest for control of a corporation have an implied cause of action for fraud under § 14(e) of the Securities and Exchange Act of 1934?

Rule: (Brennan, J.) An unsuccessful tender offeror in a contest for control of a corporation does not have an implied cause of action for fraud under § 14(e) of the Securities and Exchange Act of 1934 and must rely on whatever remedy is created by state law.

Orzeck v. Englehart (1963) V

Facts: After a corporation gained control of another corporation by purchasing all its capital stock without complying with merger provisions under Delaware Corporation Law, a shareholder challenged the validity of the purchase.

Issue: May a corporation gain control over another corporation without complying with state merger provisions by purchasing all its stock?

Rule: Under Delaware Corporation Law, a corporation may gain control of another corporation without complying with statutory merger provisions by purchasing all its stock.

711 Kings Highway Corp. v. F.I.M.'s Marine Repair Serv., Inc. 74
A & P Trucking Co., United States v. 50
A. Jensen Farms Co. v. Cargill, Inc. 25
A.P. Smith Mfg. Co. v. Barlow 74
Abeles v. Adams Engineering Co., Inc. 272
Abercrombie v. Davies 125
Adams v. Jarvis 51
Adams v. Smith 259
Adelman v. Conotti Corp. 193
Aero Drapery of Ky., Inc. v. Engdahl 261
Affiliated Ute Citizens v. United States 236
Alco Products, Inc. v. White Motor International Corp. 182
Alford v. Frontier Enterprises, Inc. 93
Alford v. Shaw 310
Allaun v. Consolidated Oil Co. 268
Alleghany v. Kirby 328
Allen v. Biltmore Tissue Corp. 127
Allenberg Cotton Co. v. Pittman 90
Alpert v. 28 Williams St. Corp. 364
American Nat'l Bank & Trust Co. v. Haroco, Inc. 243
Applestein v. United Bd. & Carton Corp. 350
Application of Vogel 129
Arditi v. Dubitzky 137
Armstrong v. Frostie Co. 317
Arnold v. Browne 78
Aron v. Gillman 141
Aronson v. Lewis 283, 315
Asbury Hospital v. Cass County 94
Assn'n Preservation of Freedom of Choice, Inc. v. Shapiro 101
Auer v. Dressel 111
Auerbach v. Bennett 309
Automotriz Del Golfo De California S.A. De C.V. v. Resnick 77
B. & H. Warehouse, Inc. v. Atlas Van Lines 138, 360
Bailes v. Colonial Press, Inc. 178
Baldwin v. Canfield 114
Bangor Punta Operations v. Bangor & Aroostook R.R. 308
BankAmerica Securities Litigation, In re, ... 309
Barr v. Wackman 309
Barrett v. Denver Tramway Corp. 368
Bartle v. Home Owners Cooperative 81
Basic, Inc. v. Levinson 226
Bates v. Dresser 280
Beard v. Elster 254
Benintendi v. Kenton Hotel 126
Bennett v. Breuil Petroleum Corp. 203
Bennett v. Propp 268
Berger v. Columbia Broadcasting System, Inc. 92
Berkwitz v. Humphrey 276
Bernardin, Inc. v. Midland Oil Corp. 80

Berwald v. Mission Development Co.	172
Bing Crosby Minute Maid Corp v. Eaton	175
Bird v. Penn Central Co.	328
Black v. Harrison Home Co.	135
Blau v. Lehman	246
Blount v. Taft	137
Blue Chip Stamps v. Manor Drug Stores	227
Bodell v. General Gas & Electric Corp.	177
Bohannan v. Corporation Commission	112
Bosch v. Meeker Cooperative Light & Power Ass'n	312
Bove v. The Community Hotel Corp. of Newport, Rhode Island	355
Bowman v. Armour & Co.	367
Boyd v. Leasing Associates, Inc.	42
Brascan Ltd. v. Edper Equities Ltd.	357
Breed v. Barton	366
Brophy v. Cities Service Co.	246
Brown v. McLanahan	134
Brunswick Corp. v. Waxman	99
Burg v. Horn	260
C.R.A. Realty Corp. v. Crotty	241
Cady, Roberts & Co., In the Matter of	225
Cahall v. Lofland	190
Camp v. Genesco, Inc.	182
Campbell v. Loew's Inc.	111
Cannon v. Acoustics Corp.	316
Cantor v. Sunshine Greenery, Inc.	75
Caplan v. Lionel Corp.	257
Caplin v. Marine Midland Grace Trust Co. of New York	191
Carpenter v. United States	230
Carpenter, United States v.,	230
Carter v. Portland General Electric Co.	114
Case v. New York Central R.R.	259
Cauble v. Handler	50
CBI Industries, Inc. v. Horton	240
Charlestown Boot and Shoe Co. v. Dunsmore	111
Cheff v. Mathes	359
Chelrob v. Barrett	266
Chiarella v. United States	229
Clark v. Dodge	126
Clarke Memorial College v. Monaghan Land Co.	130
Clarke v. Greenberg	313
Clifton v. Tomb	75
Coggins v. New England Patriots Football Club, Inc.	362
Cohen v. Beneficial Indus. Loan Corp.	317
Cohen, Matter of v. Cocoline Products, Inc.	116
Cole v. Schenley Industries, Inc.	370
Collins v. Lewis	50
Comark, In re	48
Conagra, Inc. v. Cargill, Inc.	363

Case	Page
Continental Securities Co. v. Belmont	116
Costello v. Fazio	79, 200
Courtland Manor v. Leeds	315
Cowin v. Bresler	319
Cranson v. International Business Machines	86
Credit Bureau Reports, Inc. v. Credit Bureau of St. Paul, Inc.	289
Cristo Bros., Inc., Matter of,	137
CTS Corporation v. Dynamics Corporation of America	354
Cude v. Couch	45
Davis v. Sheerin	136
Debaun v. First Western Bank and Trust Co.	263
Delaney v. Fidelity Lease Ltd.	45
Dentel v. Fidelity Savings & Loan Assn.	368
Desimone v. Industrial Bio-Test Laboratories	314
DeWitt Truck Brokers, Inc. v. W. Ray Flemming Fruit Co.	87, 197
Diamond v. Oreamuno	232
Dirks v. SEC	229
Dodge v. Ford Motor Co.	102, 181
Doleman v. Meiji Mutual Life Ins. Co.	264
Don Swann Sales Corporation v. Echols	80
Donahue v. Rodd Electrotype Co.	125, 187
Drashner v. Sorenson	39
Dreifuerst v. Dreifuerst	39
Drive-In Development Corp., In re	135
Duane Jones Co. v. Burke	274
E.C. Warner Co., In re	327
E.K. Buck Retail Stores v. Harkert	130
Eastern Oklahoma Television Co., Inc. v. Ameco, Inc.	190
Edgar v. MITE Corp.	357
Edwards Company, Inc. v. Monogram Industries, Inc.	93
Eisenberg v. Flying Tiger Line, Inc.	307
Eliasberg v. Standard Oil Co.	260
Elkind v. Ligget & Myers, Inc.	239
Ellis v. Mihelis	52
Ernst & Ernst v. Hochfelder	228
Escott v. BarChris Construction Corp.	233
Essex Universal Corp. v. Yates	257
Everett v. Phillips	272
Ewen v. Peoria & E. Ry. Co.	267
Excelsior Water & Mining Co. v. Pierce	180
Farris v. Glen Alden Corp.	349
Feder v. Martin Marietta Corp.	242
Fenwick v. Unemployment Compensation Commission	42
Fett Roofing & Sheet Metal Co., Inc., In re	199
Financial Industrial Fund, Inc. v. McDonnell Douglas Corp.	234
First National Bank of Boston v. Bellotti	98
Flamm v. Eberstadt	247
Flanagan v. Jackson Wholesale Bldg. Supply	76
Fliegler v. Lawrence	270

Flynn v. Bass Bros. Enterprises, Inc.	235
Ford, People v.	101
Francis v. United Jersey Bank	280
Freeman v. Decio	241
Frick v. Howard	85
Fridrich v. Bradford	238
Frigidaire Sales Corp. v. Union Properties, Inc.	40
Frink v. Carman Distributing Co.	189
Fuller v. Krough	192
G. Loewus & Co. v. Highland Queen Packing Co.	200
Gabhart v. Gabhart	371
Gall v. Exxon Corp.	282
Galler v. Galler	126
Garner v. Wolfinbarger	273, 315
Gearing v. Kelly	127
Gelder Medical Group v. Webber	52
Gentry v. Credit Plan Corp. of Houston	78
Gerdes v. Reynolds	256
Gibbons v. Schenley Industries, Inc.	369
Gilligan, Will & Co. v. Securities and Exchange Commission	201
Gilman Paint & Varnish Co. v. Legum	53
Gimbel v. Signal Companies, Inc.	368
Giuricich v. Emtrol Corp.	131, 321
Glenn v. Hoteltron Systems	319
Globe Woolen Co v. Utica Gas & Elec. Co.	253
Goldberg v. Meridor	237, 271
Goldie v. Yaker	316
Goldwater v. Oltman	54
Goodman v. Ladd Estate Co.	73, 113
Goodnow v. American Writing Paper Co.	193
Goodwin v. Agassiz	225
Gordon v. Elliman	327
Gottfried v. Gottfried	186
Gould v. Ruefenacht	365
Graham v. Allis-Chalmers Mfg.	282
Gratz v. Claughton	231
Green v. Occidental Petroleum Corp.	245
Green v. Victor Talking Machine Co.	99
Grissum v. Reesman	41
Grobow v. Perot	311
Guth v. Loft, Inc.	264
Haberman v. Tobin	312
Hanson Trust PLC v. ML SCM Acquisition Inc.	283
Hanson Trust PLC v. SCM Corp.	352
Hariton v. Arco Electronics, Inc.	348
Hatt, Herbert G.	186
Hayes Oyster Co., State ex rel., v. Keypoint Oyster Co.	258
Heller v. Boylan	262
Herald Co. v. Seawell	268

Hernando Bank v. Huff	366
Hessler, Inc. v. Farrell	96
Hidell v. International Diversified Investments	189
Holzman v. de Escamilla	40
Home Interiors & Gifts, Inc. v. Comissioner of Internal Revenu	275
Hooper v. Mountain States Securities Corp.	190
Hospes v. Northwestern Mfg. & Car Co.	175
How & Associates, Inc. v. Boss	84
Huddleston v. Herman & Maclean	245
Humphrys v. Winous Co.	134
Hurley v. Ornsteen	135
Hyman v. Velsicol Corp.	202
Inter-Continental Corp. v. Moody	73
Irving Trust Co. v. Deutsch	260
J. F. Anderson Lumber Co. v. Meyers	82
J.I. Case Co. v. Borak	234, 291
Jackson v. Nicolai-Neppach Co.	141
Jamison Steel Corp., In re	139
Jammies Intern., Inc. v. Lazarus	242
Jepsen v. Petersen	320
Jercyn Dress Shop, In re	52
John Kelley/Talbot Mills v. Commissioner of Internal Revenue	187
Johnston v. Greene	273
Jones v. H.F. Ahmanson & Co.	244, 258, 361
Jones v. Harris	140
Jones v. Niagara Frontier Transportation Authority	321
Jones v. Williams	274
Kaiser-Frazer Corp. v. Otis & Co.	201
Kamin v. American Express Co.	199, 280
Kaplan v. Wyatt	327
Karfunkel v. USLIFE Corp.	183
Karrigan v. Unity Savings Assn.	261
Katz v. Bregman	347
Katzowitz v. Sidler	180
Kauffman Mutual Fund Actions, In re	324
Kaufmann v. Lawrence	183
Kayser-Roth Corporation, United States v.	89
Keenan v. Eshleman	307
Kelly v. Bell	96
Kemp & Beatley, Inc., Matter of	141
Kennerson v. Burbank Amusement Co.	131
Keough v. St. Paul Milk Co.	188
Kern County Land Co. v. Occidental Petroleum	231
Kidwell ex rel. Penfold v. Meikle	264
Kinser v. Coffee [sic]	136, 321
Klein v. Weiss	44
Kline v. Johns-Manville	365
Klinicki v. Lundgren	255
Knapp v. Bankers Securities Corp.	323

Kridelbaugh v. Aldrehn Theatres Co. 83
Kruger v. Gerth 136
Krull v. Celotex Corp. 364
Kulka v. Nemirovsky 82
Landreth Timber Co. v. Landreth 232, 365
Langfelder v. Universal Laboratories, Inc. 367
Larson v. Commissioner 53
Lee v. Jenkins Brothers 112
Lehrman v. Cohen 125
Lester, Ex rel. 43
Levin v. Metro-Goldwyn-Mayer, Inc. 294
Levin v. Mississippi River Fuel Corp. 367
Levitt v. Johnson 325
Lewis v. Anderson 322
Lewis v. Fuqua 273
Lewis v. H.P. Hood & Sons, Inc. 195
Lewis v. Newman 313
Lewis v. S.L. & E., Inc 253
Libby, McNeill & Libby, Valuation of Common Stock, In re 360
Liggett v. Lee 89
Lincoln Stores v. Grant 255
Ling and Co. v. Trinity Sav. and Loan Ass'n 134
Litwin v. Allen 282
Lloydona Peters Enterprises v. Dorius 113
Long Island Lighting Company v. Barbash 294
Louis K. Liggett Co. v. Lee 89
Lovenheim v. Iroquois Brands, Ltd. 290
Lynch v. Vickers Energy Corp. 370
Mackensworth v. American Trading Transportation Co. 90
Mader's Store for Men, Inc., In re 198
Maldonado v. Flynn 238
Maley v. Carroll 196
Marciano v. Nakash 261
Marco v. Dulles 328
Marsh v. Gentry 46
Martin v. Peyton 37
Martin v. Schuler 189
Matteson v. Ziebarth 361
Mayer v. Adams 311
Mazzuchelli v. Silverberg 43
McArthur v. Times Printing Co. 75
McCain, State ex rel. v. Construction Enterprises, Inc. 91
McNulty v. W. & J. Sloane 367
McQuade v. Stoneham 126
Medical Committee for Human Rights v. SEC 292
Meehan v. Shaughnessy 51
Meinhard v. Salmon 38
Meiselman v. Meiselman 133
Merrill Lynch, Pierce, Fenner & Smith, Inc. v. Livingston 239

Merritt-Chapman & Scott Corp. v. Wolfson	326
Michelson v. Duncan	254
Mickshaw v. Coca Cola Bottling Co.	134
Miller v. American Telegraph and Telephone	281
Miller v. Magline, Inc.	194
Miller v. Miller	262
Miller v. San Sebastian Gold Mines, Inc.	175
Mills v. Electric Auto-Lite Co.	290, 328
Minton v. Cavaney	78, 197
Mitchell v. Texas Gulf Sulfur Co.	236
Moe v. Harris	95
Mohr v. State Bank of Stanely	112
Moore v. Bay	196
Moran v. Household International, Inc.	353
Morris v. Standard Gas & Electric Co.	171
National Bisuit Co. v. Stroud	48
National Tile & Terrazzo Co., Inc., In re	195
Neimark v. Mel Kramer Sales, Inc.	173
Nelkin v. H.J.R. Realty Corp.	132
O'Rorke v. Geary	95
Ogallala Fertilizer Co. v. Salsbery	41
Old Dominion Copper Mining & Smelting Co. v. Bigelow	100, 174
Old Dominion Copper Mining & Smelting Co. v. Lewisohn	100, 174
Orser v. George	54
Orzeck v. Englehart	371
Osborne v. Locke Steel Chain Co.	259
Ostlind v. Ostlind Valve Co.	276
Otis & Co. v. Pennsylvania R.R.	316
Owens v. Palos Verdes Monaco	38
Page v. Page	46
Palmer v. Arden-Mayfair, Inc.	94
Parklane Hosiery Co., Inc. v. Shore	322
Pepper v. Litton	89
Perlman v. Feldmann	256, 308, 356
Perrine v. Pennroad	325
Piemonte v. New Boston Garden Corp.	348
Pillsbury, State ex rel. v. Honeywell, Inc.	115, 289
Pioneer Specialties, Inc. v. Nelson	131
Pipelife Corp. v. Bedford	179
Piper v. Chris-Craft Industries, Inc.	371
Pisani, United States v.	94
Pogostin v. Rice	276
Polk v. Good	204
Pollitz v. Gould	324
PPG Industries, Inc. v. Guardian Industries Corp.	364
Pringle v. Hunsicker	83
Providence and Worcester Co. v. Baker	176
Puma v. Mariott	266
Quaker Hill, Inc. v. Parr	85

Raab v. Villager Industries, Inc. ... 369
Rabkin v. Philip A. Hunt Chemical ... 351
Radom & Neidorff, Inc., In re ... 136
Rafe v. Hindin ... 129
Randall v. Bailey ... 171
Randall v. Loftsgaarden ... 237
Rapoport v. 55 Perry Co. ... 38
Ratner d/b/a The Stereo Corner v. Central Nat'l. Bank of Miami ... 91
Rauchman v. Mobil Corporation ... 293
REA Express, Inc., In re ... 324
Real Estate Capital Corp. v. Thunder Corp. ... 113
Reilly v. Segert ... 172
Reliance Electric Co. v. Emerson Electric Co. ... 240
Remillard Brick Co. v. Remillard-Dandini Co. ... 266
Revlon, Inc. v. MacAndrews & Forbes Holdings, Inc. ... 354
Richert v. Handly II ... 48
Richert v. Handly I ... 48
Riely, United States v. ... 194
Ringling Bros.-Barnum & Bailey Combined Shows v. Ringling ... 129
RKO-Stanley Warner Theatres, Inc. v. Graziano ... 74
Roach v. Mead ... 49
Roanoke Agency, Inc. v. Edgar ... 364
Robertson v. Levy ... 86
Robotham v. Prudential Ins. Co. of America ... 272
Roccograndi v. Unemployment Compensation Board of Review ... 88
Rogers v. Hill ... 275
Rosen v. Alleghany Corp. ... 292
Rosenfeld v. Fairchild Engine & Airplane Corp. ... 290
Ross Transport, Inc. v. Crothers ... 177
Ross v. Bernhard ... 319
Rouse v. Pollard ... 49
Ruetz v. Topping ... 270
Sabine Towing & Transportation Co. v. Merit Ventures, Inc. ... 92
Salgo v. Matthews ... 133
Santa Fe Industries, Inc. v. Green ... 228, 270
Schiff v. Metzner ... 318
Schnell v. Chris-Craft Industries, Inc. ... 114
Schreiber v. Bryan ... 269
Schreiber v. Burlington Northern, Inc. ... 358
Schulwolf v. Cerro Corp. ... 369
Schwartz v. Marien ... 193
Schwartz v. United Merchants & Manufacturers ... 118
Scientific Holding Co., LTD. v. Plessey ... 116
Scott v. Multi-Amp Corp. ... 254
SEC v. May ... 294
SEC v. Medical Committee for Human Rights ... 294
SEC v. Ralston Purina Co. ... 185, 232
SEC v. Texas Gulf Sulfur ... 226
SEC v. Transamerica Corporation ... 292

Security Finance Co., In re	139
Sedima, S.P.L.R. v. Imrex Co.	243
See v. Heppenheimer	178
Selig v. Wexler	139
Shaffer v. Heitner	325
Shapiro v. American Home Assurance Co.	323
Shaw v. Empire Savings & Loan Assn.	323
Sherman v. Fitch	118
Sherwood & Roberts-Oregon, Inc. v. Alexander	84, 95
Shlensky v. Dorsey	326
Shlensky v. South Parkway Building Corp.	269
Shlensky v. Wrigley	281
Simon v. Socony-Vacuum Oil Co.	265
Sinclair Oil Corp. v. Levien	172, 258
Singer v. Magnavox Co.	370
Slappey Drive Indus. Park v. United States	184
Smith v. Atlantic Properties, Inc.	128, 181
Smith v. Dixon	49
Smith v. Good Music Station, Inc.	363
Smith v. Gross	185
Smith v. Kelly	52
Smith v. Van Gorkom	281, 282
Snyder v. Memco Engineering & Mfg. Co., Inc.	195
Southeast Consultants, Inc. v. McCrary Engineering Corp.	264
Speed v. Transamerica Corp.	263
Spencer v. Anderson	191
Stanley J. How & Associates, Inc. v. Boss	84
Stark v. Flemming	88
State Teachers Retirement Board v. Flour Corp.	245
Sterling v. Mayflower	350
Steuer v. Phelps	54
Stewart Realty Co. v. Keller	84
Stewart v. Lehigh Valley R.R. Co.	118, 271
Stirling Homex Corp., In re	192
Stodd v. Goldberger	198
Stokes v. Continental Trust Co. of City of New York	176
Stone v. Eacho	81
Strong v. Fromm Laboratories, Inc.	132
Strong v. Repide	244
Studebaker Corp. v. Gittlin	291
Sulphur Export Corp. v. Carribean Clipper Lines, Inc.	80
Summers v. Dooley	38
Superintendent of Insurance v. Bankers Life & Casualty Co.	237
Surowitz v. Hilton Hotels Corp.	318
Swann v. Mitchell	47
Talbot v. James	253
Tankersley v. Albright	139
Tanzer Economic Associates v. Universal Food Specialties	362
Tarnowski v. Resop	25

Terry v. Penn Central Corp. 350
Teschner v. Chicago Title & Trust Co. 184
Theodora Holding Corp. v. Henderson 85
Thompson & Green Machinery Co. v. Music City Lumber Co. 79
Thos. Branch & Co. v. Riverside & Dan River Cotton Mills, Inc. 179
Tift v. Forage King Industries 82
Timberline Equipment Co., Inc. v. Davenport 76
Tomash v. Midwest Technical Development Corp. 313
Toro Co. v. Ballas Liquidating Co. 90
Touche Ross & Co. v. Redington 234
Trans World Airlines, Inc. v. Summa Corp. 270
Treco, Inc. v. Land of Lincoln Savings & Loan 265
Tri-State Developers, Inc. v. Moore 92
Triggs v. Triggs 140
Truckweld Equipment Co., Inc. v. Olson 78
Tryon v. Smith 269
TSC Industries, Inc. v. Northway, Inc. 292
Union Pacific Railroad Co. v. Trustees, Inc. 98
United Paperworkers Int'l Union v. Penntech Papers, Inc. 97
United States Trust Co. v. First Nat. City Bank 203
Unocal Corp. v. Mesa Petroleum Co. 352
Village of Brown Deer v. Milwaukee 117
Vogel v. Melish 140
Vohland v. Sweet 41
Volkman v. DP Associates 42
Wagenseller v. Scottsdale Memorial Hospital 274
Walkovsky v. Carlton 76, 198
Weil v. Beresth 138
Weinberger v. UOP, Inc. 262, 351
Weissman v. A. Weissman, Inc. 268
Wellman v. Dickinson 356
Westec Corp., In re 97
Whatley, Matter of 87
Wheeling Steel Corp. v. Glander 97
Wheeling-Pittsburgh Steel Corp., In re 366
Wilderman v. Wilderman 187, 265
Wilkes v. Springfield Nursing Home, Inc. 128
Wills v. Wills 47
Wilson v. McClenny 130
Wilzig v. Sisselman 46
Winston v. Federal Express Corporation 241
Wolf v. Barkes 314
Wolgin v. Simon 320
Wollman v. Littman 128
Wright v. Heizers Corp. 267
Wroblewski v. Brucker 44
Yanow v. Teal Industries, Inc. 362
Yeng Sue Chow v. Levi Strauss Co. 138
Yucca Mining & Petroleum Co. v. Howard C. Phillips Co. 112

Zahn v. Transamerica Corporation 183, 257
Zaist v. Olson 77
Zajac v. Harris 37
Zajac v. Harris (1967) CE 37
Zapata Corp. v. Maldonado 283, 310
Zetlin v. Hanson Holdings, Inc. 256
Zidell v. Zidell, Inc. 131
Zion v. Kurtz 133
Zubik v. Zubik 93

BLOND'S LAW GUIDES

Precisely What You Need to Know

Civil Procedure
Cound
Field
Rosenberg
Louisell

Contracts
Farnsworth
Dawson
Kessler
Fuller
Murphy

Criminal Procedure
Kamisar
Saltzburg
Weinreb/Crim.Process
Weinreb/Crim.Justice
Miller

Evidence
McCormick
Green
Weinstein
Kaplan
Cleary

Property
Dukeminier
Browder
Casner
Cribbet

Torts
Prosser
Epstein
Keeton
Franklin

Constitutional Law
Barrett
Brest
Ducat
Gunther
Lockhart
Rotunda
Stone

Criminal Law
Kadish
LaFave
Kaplan
Weinreb
Dix
Johnson
Inbau

Corporate Tax
Lind
Kahn
Wolfman
Surrey

Corporations
Cary
Choper
Hamilton
Henn
Jennings
Solomon
Vagts

Family Law
Areen
Foote
Krause
Wadlington

Administrative Law
Bonfield
Breyer
Gellhorn
Cass
Schwartz
Mashaw

International Law
Sweeney
Henkin

Income Tax
Klein
Andrews
Surrey
Kragen
Freeland
Graetz

(800) 366-7086